The Integrated Architecture Framework Explained

Jack van 't Wout · Maarten Waage ·
Herman Hartman · Max Stahlecker ·
Aaldert Hofman

The Integrated Architecture Framework Explained

Why, What, How

Springer

Jack van 't Wout
Capgemini Nederland BV
Papendorpseweg 100
3528 BJ Utrecht
Netherlands
jack.vant.wout@capgemini.com

Herman Hartman
Capgemini Nederland BV
Papendorpseweg 100
3528 BJ Utrecht
Netherlands
herman.hartman@capgemini.com

Aaldert Hofman
Capgemini Nederland BV
Papendorpseweg 100
3528 BJ Utrecht
Netherlands
aaldert.hofman@capgemini.com

Maarten Waage
Capgemini Nederland BV
Papendorpseweg 100
3528 BJ Utrecht
Netherlands
maarten.waage@capgemini.com

Max Stahlecker
Capgemini Nederland BV
Papendorpseweg 100
3528 BJ Utrecht
Netherlands
max.stahlecker@capgemini.com

ISBN 978-3-662-50607-3 ISBN 978-3-642-11518-9 (eBook)
DOI 10.1007/978-3-642-11518-9
Springer Heidelberg Dordrecht London New York

ACM Computing Classification (1998): J.1, I.6, H.1, H.4

Cover design: KünkelLopka, Heidelberg

Printed on acid-free paper

Springer is part of Springer Science + Business Media (www.springer.com)

Foreword

When I joined Capgemini back in 1996 I was amazed by investment that had been made in developing Enterprise Architecture, and at the root of this, the IAF methodology. Back in the mid 1990s the importance of architecture was dimly recognised but certainly it was not widely understood as a crucial element of successful enterprise wide IT implementation. A decade later with the huge growth in the role, the sophistication, and importance of Information Technology it has become recognized, and established for the value it brings.

With this recognition has come various forms of 'standardization' ranging from the work of the Open Group and its moves to establish TOGAF as a common framework, together with ITAC to certify architects, through to a wide variety of product vendor architects, even to some industry sectors establishing their own architectures. Has this diminished, or even may be removed the need for IAF?

Well it might have done if the world had stood still, but it hasn't. Simultaneously the range and complexity of technology has increased, the functionality has been extended to embrace new front office capabilities and most of all the externalization and globalization of business has added a whole new extra dimension. Standardization might have improved connections and interfaces, and in so doing produced 'systems' of apparently limitless extendibility, but it has done little to improve the necessary 'understanding'.

So here we are 13 years later, 13 years of consistent development of IAF, and yet looking ahead the requirement for even more development is clear. But looking back it's equally clear to see the value delivered and the foundation it has built in Enterprises in so many countries. The future will rest of the past, the legacy of IAF is one of enabling for the future and there are not many areas of technology where that remark can truthfully be made.

This book records an impressive journey, and points to an important future, and is written by those for whom Enterprise Architecture and IAF is a passion. Reading the book will help develop that same passion, as well as increasing the understanding of one of the most important aspects of any enterprises success in business today. I thank my colleagues for introducing the topic to me, and for helping me to appreciate its value to my everyday work.

Woking, UK Andy Mulholland

Preface

IAF Is Here to Stay!

IAF is here to stay! Even though I am very much in favor of open standards such as TOGAF and ArchiMate, I still say IAF is here to stay! No; the authors didn't pay me off to say this, although I wouldn't say no to a nice bottle of wine. However, I make this statement out of my own conviction. I'll explain why in a moment, but let's first start with some history.

When I got involved in the field of architecture in 1997, Capgemini was already working toward the creation of the Integrated Architecture Framework (IAF). Since then, the IAF has been evolving continuously. Fueled by daily experiences, discussions among architects, ample feedback from client engagements, the original framework has evolved into its current version.

In the past, Capgemini has been rather shy in communicating about the IAF. Rather than showing this diamond in the making to the outside world, they kept it quiet and continued polishing it. In my own past as a full-time Professor at the University of Nijmegen, I was involved in several architecture related research activities, such as the ArchiMate project. When I became aware of IAF's existence, I immediately challenged Capgemini to more widely publish their IAF. Meanwhile my curiosity was mounting. To me, IAF provided a welcome, practice based, complementary view to the results of the ArchiMate research project. So, when I joined Capgemini at the start of 2008, I was more than happy to attend a course on IAF. This strengthened my conviction that it was time for Capgemini to finally produce a book on IAF. There was more than enough reason to be proud about IAF as a tried and tested architecture framework, and make it available to a wider audience. Therefore, early 2008 I started a lobby to produce an IAF book, and late 2008 we were finally able to give the go ahead to the team of authors to do the really hard work and produce the book. I am really grateful to the author team for their commitment in finishing this book. It shall be no secret that 2009 has been a difficult year for our industry. Despite commercial pressures, the authors spent numerous hours in their spare-time to continue working on this great book on architecture.

So how about open standards? Large parts of TOGAF 9's content framework have already been based on IAF. Currently, The Open Group has two complementary standards for architecture: TOGAF, the method for doing architecture, and ArchiMate, the language for representing architectures. So is there a future for IAF amidst all of these standards? Well, in my opinion there certainly is. Standards evolve based on consensus. As a result, standards can only (and must) evolve slowly. At the same time, consultancy firms such as Capgemini will continue to gather their own experiences. This is where company specific frameworks such as the IAF can play a crucial role. They will allow for faster innovations, leading the direction in which future versions of the standards can evolve.

Therefore, I expect IAF in its next evolution step to become fully compliant to the TOGAF/ArchiMate tandem, while at the same time going beyond these standards based on the fast amount of – ever growing – experience embodied in the IAF. In the first decennium of this century the 'I' in IAF stood for integrated to signify the need to integrate different views and aspects when developing an architecture. In the next decennium I expect this first 'I' to stand for innovating, to signify the fact that the Innovating Architecture Framework will lead the way for future versions of the open standards. Therefore, I can say with conviction: IAF is here to stay!

I sincerely hope you enjoy reading this book, as much as I have enjoyed seeing the authors write it!

Nijmegen, Netherlands Prof. Dr. H.A. (Erik) Proper

Preface

This book captures and communicates the wealth of architecture experience Capgemini has gathered in developing, deploying, and using IAF since its documentation in 1993. It intends to guide the reader through the corners and crevasses of IAF. We aim to help the reader understand why we have done the things we did to develop IAF specifically, and the IT architecture profession in the IT industry more in general. We hope we have achieved our objectives and readers are welcome to provide us with feedback. This is because we are sure we are not there yet. The architecture profession in the IT industry still needs a significant amount of time to mature. Just imagine how long it took architects in the building industry to come to the point where they are now.

Utrecht, The Netherlands

Jack van 't Wout
Aaldert Hofman
Max Stahlecker
Herman Hartman
Maarten Waage

Objectives of the Book

This book has two main objectives. The first is to explain the background and mindset behind IAF. As IAF usage becomes more widespread over the globe, more and more people need to understand its background and mindset to fully benefit from it. The second objective is to capture the body of knowledge we have been assembling since 1993. It is not uncommon to see the same question pop up on newsgroups and forums several times throughout the years. This book not only intends to provide answers to the most common ones, but should also provide answers to all those questions regarding IAF you have had through time, but never dared to ask.

Intended Readers

We have written this book with the following readers in mind:

(Potential) Architects who want to thoroughly understand IAF so they can use it in their environment. This does not mean that one can read this book and benefit fully from IAF without additional training. Architecture is a trade one has to learn together with colleagues, in real life.

Others who want to understand architects that use IAF. IAF architects have one thing in common. They apply IAF in their work. This means they use specific terminology, especially amongst themselves. People who want to know more about IAF's terminology and mindset are also invited to read at least a few parts of this book (e.g. Chap. 2 or Chap. 4).

Engineers who work with IAF deliverables. Engineers are working together with architects to create effective solutions that meet certain business objectives. Thus they might be interested in getting a better understanding of the thinking behind these IAF deliverables. We recommend taking a look at the physical artifacts & views (covered in Chap. 3) and IAF's interplay with solution development (covered in Chap. 4).

Participants of the Capgemini's Architecture Learning Program. Together with the training experience and this book, architects should not only be able to get up to speed even quicker but also better prepared than in the past. They will have a document that they can fall back on when they enter an area of IAF they have not been in a while. Especially Chap. 3 helps to get a better understanding of IAF's artifacts and views.

Experienced IAF architects. Of course experience IAF architects interested in learning more about the history of IAF or in specific IAF artifacts and their usage are invited to use the book as an extended glossary.

Structure of the Book

Throughout this book 'we' stands for 'we, as IAF architects' and thus might not be limited to just the authors – we hope we captured the thoughts and opinions of many people who use IAF in their daily work. That's why the book was extensively reviewed with a focus on those ideas that make IAF what it is now.

Chapter 1: *IAF background, value and strategy* explains why IAF was initially developed, what it has delivered, its added value, and how Capgemini intends to go on with the framework.

Chapter 2: *IAF's architecture* provides insight into the mindset and mechanisms that are part of IAF.

Chapter 3: IAF's *aspect areas explained* gives an overview of the most common architecture artifacts and views of IAF and shows what the content of the main elements of the framework are.

Chapter 4: *IAF in perspective with other frameworks and methods* elaborates on the different ways IAF can be used in projects, in combination with other tools, methods and frameworks.

Chapter 5: *Applying IAF and using its outcomes* shows the best ways IAF can be used to professionalize the architecture function in an organization.

Chapter 6: *Real life case studies* exemplifies the use of IAF through the description of a number of real life case studies.

Chapter 7: *The making of IAF* explains the history of IAF.

Acknowledgements

The Authors are pleased to pass on the following acknowledgements:

IAF would not have existed without the ongoing support of the *Capgemini University*. Through the years they have been sponsor for the development of IAF and the deployment material related to IAF. They have enabled internal business models that provided the architecture community with the means to develop their trade through the IAF. Key players from the university have been Stephen Smith and Régis Chassé.

Another group of people in Capgemini that have sponsored IAF through time is *Global delivery*. Especially Mark Standeaven and Bart Groenewoud have helped us come to where we are today, by sponsoring IAF and the architecture community.

Of course we also need to acknowledge all of our colleagues that have helped develop IAF since 1993. We apologize up-front for the names we have forgotten. No offence is intended, it just is a fact that so many people have shared their experience through time. With this proviso, key contributors include:

- *From the USA*: Doug Houseman, Anne Lapkin, Meir Shargal, Hervé Bertacchi, Leigh McMullen, Mike Cantor, Bob Reinhold, Aaron Rorstrom and others;
- *From the UK*: Geoff Pickering, Mike Paulson, Andrew Macaulay, Kirk Downey, Stuart Curley, Taj Letocha, Colin Metcalfe, Gunnar Menzel, Ian Suttle, Andy Mulholland, Peter Truman, Stuart Crawford, Una Du Noyer and others;
- *From the Nordic countries*: Ivar Laberg, Mats Gejnevall, Stefan Olsson, Joakim Lindbom, Paul Carr and others;
- *From the Netherlands*: Stefan van der Zijden, Hans Baten, Dave van Gelder, Annet Harmsen, Mark Hoogenboom, Petra van Krugten, Jeroen Jedema, Arend Saaltink, Jaap Schekkerman, Raymond Slot, Sander Zwiebel, Bas van der Raadt, Daniel Eleniak, Peter Barbier, Frank van Ierland, Peter Kuppen, Erik Onderdelinden, Marco Muishout, Barry de Vries, Han van Loenhout, Paul Hillman, Arnold van Overeem, Pieter Hörchner, Ron Tolido, Jeroen Bartelse, Lucas Osse and others;
- *From France and Iberia*: Bernard Huc, Hyacinthe Choury, Jean-Christophe Salome, Jacques Richer, Philippe Andre, Patrice Duboe, Bjorn Gronquist, Jorge Villaverde Illana, Luis Gonzales, and others;
- *From Australia*: Peter Haviland, Mick Adams and others;
- *From India*: Nitin Kadam, Shrinath Rao, Inderjit Kalsi.

Finally we also want to thank the people that have directly contributed to the creation of this book. Erik Proper was our inspirator, without him this would not have become real life. Dave van Gelder, Colin Metcalfe, and Doug Houseman provided us with additional inspiration, especially in the areas around governance. Barry de Vries helped us out with ArchiMate specific topics. Dave van Gelder and Eric Onderdelinden provided specifics on TOGAF 8 and 9.

Contents

Chapter 1
IAF Background, Value and Strategy

1.1 What Is IAF? A Short Summary

IAF is Capgemini's architecture framework. It is a toolbox that contains processes, products, tools and techniques to create all types of architectures which are intended to shape businesses and the technology that supports it. Its development started in 1993. It continuously evolves as best practices are added to the framework. IAF has been used in thousands of engagements in most business sectors and many countries.

1.2 Reasons for Having IAF

To answer the question 'Why was IAF developed?' we need to understand why architecture has become such an important topic in the IT industry. In the 1980s life in the IT industry was relatively straightforward. There were centrally managed computer systems with 'dumb terminals' to do the work. Then departmental or mini computers started to show up. Short after that, personal computers and various integration aspects entered into the arena. The IT landscape became more and more complex. Part of the complexity was that we had to design solutions in terms of both software and hardware, whereas until then the mainframe always was implied, and only additional terminals, additional disk space, and additional processing power were to be considered. Thus we needed tools to manage this complexity. Architecture was the term that was coined to describe our activities to successfully manage the complexity. Architecture and Infrastructure seemed interchangeable notions – we still see some residues of that here and there – but the link with other aspects was obvious and needed a broader view.

Within Capgemini work began to formalize what we meant with architecture as part of a transformation program called Snowball that was intended to introduce client-server technology and iterative development into the organization.

Architecture was our approach used to explain how we defined which infrastructure was needed to support the business. The architecture development method

J. van 't Wout et al., *The Integrated Architecture Framework Explained*,
DOI 10.1007/978-3-642-11518-9_1,

(ADM)[1] became part of the training material in the transformation program. The ADM was originally developed in the UK and deployed worldwide. It demonstrated that architecture was a justifiable set of activities in the overall business transformation process. It provided us with standardized mechanisms and templates to communicate our architecture development work. The ADM as an infrastructure architecture method taught us how very beneficial it was to have a common language, approach and set of tools to do our work.

Another reason for having IAF was that projects were getting bigger and more complex. The requirement for transnational staffing of the projects also increased. It was hard to get the right architect in the right place, as they all did their architecture work their own way, except for the infrastructure architecture part, which was better aligned across the architects in this area. Within Capgemini we realized we needed to standardize more of the architecture activities that we performed.

An additional reason for having IAF was that it would provide us with a means to communicate what we did, and align ourselves with other professions that were working on the projects. IAF should not only help us structure our own work but also allow us to innovate the way we do architecture.

We knew we could not do it all at once, so we needed a 'framework' in which we could position the various architectural subjects to cover. We studied the available industry frameworks and architecture approaches and could not find anything that suited our requirements. Thus we decided to develop our own, and the Integrated Architecture Framework (IAF) was born.

1.3 The Value of IAF

For more than 16 years, since 1993, IAF has proven its value. The framework has been used in over 3000 projects worldwide, ranging from chip design to the creation of complete new lines of business for global players. It has been formally adopted by many organizations outside of Capgemini. Implicitly it has been adopted by even more organizations, as they requested us to create an IAF based architecture for them. In doing that we trained their staff to use IAF.

IAF has an elemental line of thought that has proven to be valuable and robust in many different types of projects. The core mechanisms that form IAF's basis are sacrosanct. Traceability of decisions, basing decisions on principles, and reducing complexity by separating concerns are three of these mechanisms that can be applied in any situation.

IAF has also proven to be flexible. It can be adopted by all the different types of projects in which architecture is required. It has been used standalone and in

[1] Despite having the same acronym this ADM is not related to the TOGAF ADM.

combination with other methods and approaches. This works so well because IAF was designed as a flexible toolkit, and not as a rigid cookbook. Of course this flexibility also has its drawbacks. Since IAF is not prescriptive, it is more difficult to initially understand and use because users have to select their own tools. They are not told what to do in a step by step fashion.

One of the core principles of the framework, a traceable link between the business and IT, has proven its value to our customers many times. They could understand and explain why specific investments were being made. It was relatively simple to understand the impact of change in a specific area because of that traceability. One was able to trace back which parts of the business would be impacted by a specific change in IT, for example in case of an upgrade of a server, package or database management system.

Another factor that demonstrates IAF's value is productivity. It is not uncommon to expect an IAF architect becoming productive within hours after on-boarding a new project. They understand the 'language' used, and can almost immediately start to contribute to the result. For example, a colleague from the UK once joined a Dutch project and indeed spotted a flaw in the network architecture within half an hour. Second opinions on architectures created in one country are sometimes executed by colleagues in another country to ensure quality. This could not be done effectively without our common IAF language.

IAF is also based on practical experience and knowledge. All Capgemini architects are encouraged to share their best practices. All version upgrades have been based on input from real life practitioners. IAF has always focused on describing what was needed to be done, as well as providing guidance on how it could be done. This makes it one of the most sophisticated, practically proven, and documented architecture frameworks in the IT industry.

Because of its focus on architecture content, IAF has proven to be a valuable tool in combination with TOGAF[2]. TOGAF 8 focuses on process, and advises to incorporate other frameworks for the content. This results in a good fit between TOGAF and IAF which led to the incorporation of IAF elements into the recently released TOGAF 9. How TOGAF (versions 8 and 9) and IAF fit together is explained in more detail in Chap. 4.

1.4 IAF Strategy

Capgemini promotes open standards. We participate in different open standards bodies like The Open Group. We believe that sharing knowledge and experience is the best way to improve the results of the IT industry. Does this mean that we have abandoned IAF, since it's not an open standard? We can

[2] An industry standard architecture framework of The Open Group.

answer this with a clear 'no'. There are a number of reasons why we intend to continue with IAF. The three most important ones are elaborated below.

The most important reason for continuing with IAF is the fact that many of our customers have adopted the framework. They want to protect that investment. They expect support from Capgemini, and we intend to deliver that support.

A second reason for continuing with IAF as a non open standard is the fact that Capgemini wants to continue to play a leading role in increasing the maturity of the architecture profession. To do that Capgemini needs a vehicle that can be used to improve and test architecture tools under their own control. As IAF is in our own control we intend to use it as an innovation platform that continuously provides input to open standards bodies like The Open Group.

Thirdly we want to protect our investment in what matters for us: our architects.

1.5 A Short Recap of IAF Versions

Our architecture innovation investment is demonstrated by its versions. Here they are:

Version 1 was developed in 1994 and expanded until 1998. Its main focus was to build the fundament of the framework. That was done by harvesting the best practices we had and expanding them where needed. We started from the infrastructure side and expanded into creating tools for client – server architectures as well as for security and governance.

Version 2 was developed in 1998 and used until 2000. Its main focus was to provide full support for information systems architecture, and laid foundations in other areas.

Version 3 was developed in 2000. It incorporated best practices from Ernst & Young, which had recently been acquired. Version 3 was used until 2006.

In 2006 we completed the framework by filling all the gaps that were still there. Version 4 was introduced. Because the framework was now complete, we decided to create a new and complete IAF reference manual.

In 2009 we injected some additional best practices into the framework and labeled it version 4.5. This is the current version, which is the basis for this book.

Chapter 2
IAF's Architecture

2.1 Introduction

Explaining IAF must start with the basics, the core elements of the framework. Actually, our aim is that you understand IAF's own architecture. Once you understand IAF's structure and underlying ideas it will be easier to apply it to the specific situation you are in. This chapter is all about helping you understand the architecture behind IAF.

IAF applies the basics of general construction methods. All construction methods have a common approach. They address questions in a specific order. The order is expressed as interrogative pronouns: Why, what, how, with what. There are reasons for the sequence of the questions.

If you don't understand why you need to do something, you can't work out what needs to be done. You have to understand the context before you can start working effectively. Studying the context helps define the scope and objectives, and thus helps with staying focused. So understanding 'why' is the first thing to do.

If you don't understand what needs to be done (the requirements), you will never be able to craft the solution. You have to define the requirements before creating the solution. Once you understand the requirements you are often able to produce a concept of what is needed. So after understanding why you are doing something you need to address the 'what' question by defining the requirements (both functional and non-functional) and getting a concept of the solution.

With a good understanding of the requirements you should be able to design a logical solution to the problem, answering the question 'How will the solution look like'. In other words you structure the solution. You create the solution on a logical level to enable flexibility. All architectures will take time to implement. Circumstances as well as real life physical solutions change over time. By describing the architecture on a logical level you will be able to deal better with new insights and adapt it at the moment you physically implement a specific part of the architecture.

J. van 't Wout et al., *The Integrated Architecture Framework Explained*,
DOI 10.1007/978-3-642-11518-9_2, © Capgemini SA, 2010
Published by Springer-Verlag Berlin Heidelberg 2010 All Rights Reserved.

Finally you can decide with what physical things the solution can be realized. This implies allocation of physical things to the logical solution.

A practical example will demonstrate how this all works.

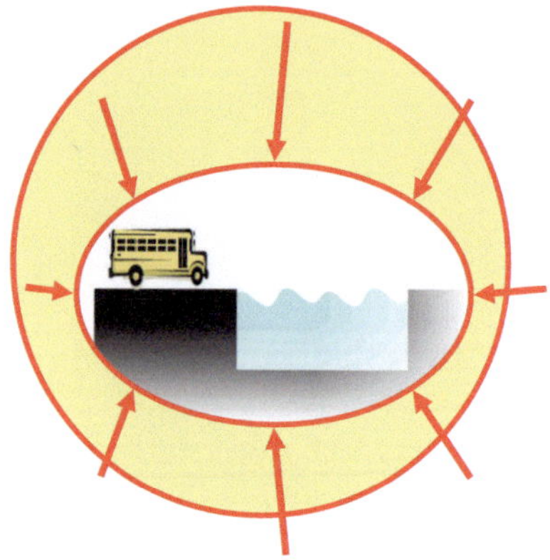

Imagine you are living in a city that has been built on both banks of a large river. There are a number of bridges crossing the river, but traffic has grown through time and there are constant traffic jams. In two years time the city is planning to host a big cultural event, and it wants to show a modern, young city that is well prepared to handle all the tourists that are visiting the event. So, the scope and context of the problem become clear. A new bridge needs to be built in the city within 2 years and it should reflect the 'young, modern' look that the city wants. The 'why' question should be clear by now.

Now we need to address the 'what' question. We need to find out what the bridge has to do. Does it have to carry pedestrians? Does it have to carry cyclists? Does it have to carry cars and trucks? Does it have to carry trains? How many of each type does it have to be able to carry during average and peak hours of usage? Which types and numbers of boats have to be able to pass under the bridge? What is the river's required water flow capacity and what would happen if that were reduced if the bridge were to have many pillars? What does the patron want it to look like to reflect the young, modern look? Once these types of questions are answered we have a clear understanding of the 'what' question. We know the requirements and are able to craft the solution.

The third main step is creating a logical model of the solution, thus answering the 'how' question. Now there is a slight snag here. Real life has shown us that there never is one solution. There always choices, and all solutions are trade-off of different aspects like cost and performance. So, in effect, if you think there is only one solution, you might have to think a little longer. There are solution alternatives that have to be considered. In this case we can identify different types of bridges that could provide sufficient river-crossing capabilities. Some of them will fit the principles we have defined regarding 'young and modern' better than others. Others might not be able to be built within 2 years. We could even

consider a temporary bridge, which would probably make a financially interested stakeholder happy, could be finished in a short period of time, avoids difficult technological studies on water flows but the patron who dreams of grandeur and eternal fame would be somewhat disappointed. In the end we present the best alternatives to the stakeholders so they can choose.

Now real life physical architecture can start. We choose the materials we need for each part of the bridge. By this time the cooperation with various construction engineering disciplines has begun. First we jointly determine what is needed for the foundation. Then we select the rebar materials and concrete. We define which steel is needed for the deck. We create the specifications the construction teams need to create the design of the bridge. We create other visualizations of what the real life solution will look like. The 'with what' question has been answered. The architecture has been designed. It can be handed over to the engineers who are actually going to build the bridge. The architect will remain involved in order to solve issues that come up during the construction phase and which might affect the starting points or principles that underlie the entire idea behind the bridge.

We are going to explain IAF's own architecture using the 'why-what-how-with what' approach explained above.

2.2 The Context: The "Why" of IAF

2.2.1 Vision

The vision we had when we started to develop IAF consisted of a number of elements. The most important goal was that we wanted to be able to provide world-class services to our clients, and were convinced that architecture was key in this. The ever increasing complexity and risk in the engagements we were working on made this obvious. We also needed a robust and mature toolset to deliver a constant quality of architecture services and a consistent experience where a client is engaged many times over a period of time. The toolset had to successfully address the alignment of business and IT. It had to be independent of a specific architect: the way we work and approach architecture should be common across all architects. In this perspective we now speak of IAF as a 'design school', with very specific style, approach and characteristics that we feel make a difference: for us as Capgemini being a global company delivering services, and for our clients ranging in size from the Fortune-500 to the local medium enterprise. In addition to this it had to provide a platform on which we could expand and improve the architecture profession. We decided up-front that it had to be based on real-life experience, and not on pure theory. We knew that we were embarking on a journey with an uncertain destination, and wanted to base that journey on things that had been proven in the field.

2.2.2 Scope

The original slogan we used in regard to IAF was: 'For a system to work as a whole, it must be architected as a whole'. This slogan nicely depicts many elements that are part of the IAF scope.

The first striking word is 'system'. What do we mean by 'system'? We have small projects that upgrade existing applications to very large programs in which we support complete post merger integrations of global companies or companies constantly reinventing themselves. All these types of projects potentially require some form of architecture. They all create or change a 'system'. Thus IAF's scope needs to cover all types of architecture engagements at all levels in an organization. Enterprise level – spanning business units –, Business unit (business domain) level and Solution level. Enterprise and Business unit level are commonly meant for supporting planning activities. Solution level is aimed at guiding the engineering of the solution.

The second important word in the slogan that is related to IAF's scope is 'whole'. Capgemini always approaches IT from the viewpoint that it has to support the business. This implies that architecture should always be justified in business terms and traceability to business requirements. Even when we are architecting a purely IT system, the business should provide the objectives and drivers for the architecture.

The third word in the slogan that is related with scope is 'architected'. IAF is aimed at the architects profession, and should only describe things for which the architect has the main responsibility. Therefore IAF does not provide support for the creation of an organization's vision, mission and strategy. These are defined as input for IAF. Some basic input that the architect usually derives from the vision, mission and strategy is contained in IAF to assist architects in collecting input if it is not there. On the other end, migration planning has also been put out of scope of IAF, because that activity is not the architect's main responsibility. In general, migration planning is a joint exercise with the engagement manager as the responsible person. IAF also tries to avoid overlap with other professions like business analysis and engineering. There are many touch points between the architects and these professions, just like there are many touch points between architects and engineers in real life construction architecture. This creates a gray area. Where does the architect stop and the engineer start? The most pragmatic answer to this question is that there is a difference in focus. The architect focuses more on how the 'system' fits into its environment. The engineer focuses more on the internal structure of the 'system', within the boundaries that have been set by the architect. In other words: the architects focuses on the behavior and non functional requirements ('black box') while the engineer on the internal construction ('white box').

2.2.3 Objectives

Through time IAF's objectives have not changed much. The framework has evolved due to increased understanding of architecture in the IT industry as a result of the pursuit of the objectives.

IAF's core objective is to provide a common way of architecting. Originally it was intended to do this within Capgemini. Nowadays more and more organizations also adopt this common way of working.

IAF also must provide a communication framework to achieve the common way of architecting. This 'common language' needs to be adopted throughout our organization and across the regions where we operate, particularly when serving global clients such as General Motors. This objective has proven to be difficult to realize – but we feel we succeeded. One word can have the same definition in multiple countries and still be perceived to be different. An example that is popular in Capgemini is the confusion we had around the term 'Business event'. In the Netherlands this was perceived as 'something that *can* happen in an organization'. In the UK it was perceived as 'something that *has* happened in an organization'. Therefore it was very understandable for the Dutch to propose basing a to-be architecture on business events. The UK architects tended to disagree. Their counterargument was: 'How can you base a to-be architecture on something that has happened in the past?'

Sometimes we have even invented new words to resolve terminology discussions. A nice example is the term 'archifact' that was used in IAF version 3 because we could not come to an agreement at that time on the usage of the term 'artifact'. Another example is the term 'scenario' which we later replaced by the term 'solution alternative'. Many US architects were confused with the term 'scenario', as they associated this term with the movie industry.

The common way of working and common language were enablers for the third objective that was defined by Capgemini. We have always had the need to staff large projects from around the world. One of the challenges in doing this was getting the right person with the right skills in the right place. IAF has proven to be a great help in achieving this objective specifically due to the common language.

The fourth main objective also comes from the large projects we work on. Managing their complexity and thereby reducing project risk is important for Capgemini because it raises the quality level of the results we deliver to our clients. Clients have the same objectives.

2.2.4 *Constraints*

One of the major constraints for IAF is related to its scope. IAF focuses on things that are the architect's main responsibility. Topics, that (a) we assist in and (b) are the main responsibility of other roles in the project, are not to be positioned within IAF. They will be covered in frameworks that the other roles use to standardize and professionalize their work.

Another constraint we have implicitly used in the development of IAF is the focus on business and IT. Real life has proven that any change in an organization should be realized by addressing a large number of topics. An acronym that is sometimes used to describe these topics is COPAFITHJ. In the preparation of any organizational change we should consider the *C*ommercial, *O*rganizational, *P*ersonnel, *A*dministrative, *F*inancial, *I*nformation processing, *T*echnological, *H*ousing and *J*udicial impact of that change. In line with the mission of Capgemini, IAF focuses on process, information and technology. However the basic structure within IAF can be used to extend the topics that are addressed. For example one client wanted to add a 'product architecture' to the framework to address commercial aspects while another client wanted a 'financial architecture' to address financial aspects.

2.3 Requirements: The 'What' of IAF

The vision, scope, objectives and constraints mentioned in the prior sections are the basis for the requirements that have been defined for IAF. This section describes the requirements behind IAF. We have chosen an informal descriptive approach of defining them, in contradiction to IAF based architectures itself, in which requirements are documented in a formal and prescribed way. We have chosen the freedom to add examples or elaborate on a topic more than we do in an architecture to help you understand the background of the requirements. In each of the sections below we address a specific requirement of IAF.

2.3.1 Requirement: Understand, Structure and Document Architecture Input

An important aspect of IAF is the requirement to provide support to help the architect understand, structure, and document the input that is needed to create an architecture. This understanding, structuring, and documenting of input is important. Things like strategy, vision, context, and scope are never standardized products. Almost all consulting firms in that area have different approaches to the topics. So what IAF needs to do is to provide the architect with a checklist of things that can be used as input. Very often the input that is relevant for the architect is scattered in multiple (large) documents and needs to be derived. It is very inefficient to have all architects working on the architecture to read all the input documents. Collecting the relevant input and documenting it will speed up the 'on boarding' of architects. Topics that are to be part of the input are:

- The strategy and vision that the architecture has to support;

> *Facts: No strategy, no architecture. No vision, no architecture.*

- The scope of the architecture;

> *Fact: When you define and agree the scope with your principal, you demonstrate to the client that you really understand the problem. This frequently leads to a modified scope (larger, smaller, shifted) because you show what the actual, real problem is.*

- The context of the solution;

> *Fact*: When you clearly recap the context, more information about the scope will emerge.

- The objective of the architecture;

> *Fact: When you don't have a clear understanding of the objectives of the architecture (the question which the architecture will answer), you will not know when your architecture is good enough. A clear objective will prevent you from going into details that are not relevant from the perspective of the architecture.*

- The principles to be applied to the solution;

> *Fact: Without principles you will not be possible to design an architecture that satisfies all stakeholders. Principles also help you to identify and resolve conflicting requirements.*

- The current state which the architecture has to take into account.

> *Fact: You will almost never architect a green field solution, in which you will have no constraints from the current state on the architecture you are designing.*

2.3.2 Requirement: As Simple as Possible

Architecture in the IT industry needs to address complex problems. Commonly we encounter organizations with hundreds of business processes and thousands of applications. This means we have to tackle very complex problems. This must not lead to a framework that is more complex than needed to solve the problem.

2.3.3 Requirement: Split Complex Problems into Smaller, Resolvable Ones

Many architectures can become relatively large and complex. A tried and tested way to solve large and complex 'configuration problems' – which an architecture is – is to split the overall problem into smaller ones that can be resolved, as long as the identification of the smaller problems is in line with ideas that you have about the overall solution. IAF is required to support this approach as we typically design architectures in response to complex situations.

2.3.4 Requirement: Cover the Breadth and Depth of the Architecture Topics Needed to Support Capgemini's Mission and Vision

Architecture is a supporting function. It is not a goal in itself. IAF needs to support the Capgemini mission ('enabling transformation') and vision ('enabling freedom'). It is to enable its clients to transform and perform through technologies. Business and IT transformation services always have been Capgemini's main focus. Therefore IAF must support them.

2.3.5 *Requirement: Support All Relevant Types of Architecture*

Construction architecture recognizes types of architecture like city planning architecture, zone planning architecture and building architecture. We also recognize different types of architecture in the IT industry. The types most commonly identified are:

(1) Enterprise architecture, aimed at supporting enterprise wide decision making and planning, and shaping the enterprise landscape;
(2) Domain architecture, aimed at supporting business unit level decision making and planning, and shaping the domain landscape;
(3) Solution architecture aimed at providing architectural guidance to programs and projects;
(4) Software architecture, aimed at providing architectural guidance to software development.

As Capgemini provides services in all these areas we need to be able to deliver all types of architecture described above.

2.3.6 *Requirement: Flexibility in Content*

Not every type of architecture requires the same amount of detail when addressing a given topic. For example interfaces might only need to be identified at enterprise or domain level, while it is very relevant to specify them in detail when working on a solution or software architecture. Also the granularity of the architecture's elements has to be variable. The topics we talk about at enterprise level (sales, marketing, HR production and finances) are often larger than the topics we talk about at solution level (order entry, stock level checking, order picking and order packing).

The content of IAF must be able to cope with these differences and should not depend on the industry sector where it is applied.

2.3.7 *Requirement: Flexibility in Process*

As Capgemini works for many different clients they encounter many different situations. Ask any Capgemini architect if they have used the exact same process to deliver an architecture twice. We promise you that they will say 'no' most of the time. For this reason we need to have process flexibility. In fact we actually need to split process and content. Often we need to be able to create similar content using different processes. We might be working together with Capgemini transformation consultants in one engagement and with consultants from another consulting firm in the other. Both groups have different approaches to transformation consulting that we have to cope with.

2.3.8 Requirement: Traceability and Rationalization of Architecture Decisions

Most architectures have to address a broad number of topics. Many topics influence each other. For example, centralizing the financial administration of 5 business units into 1 shared service center will influence the decisions on IT support that is required, which in turn will influence the infrastructure that is required. As architectures will have to be maintained over time it is very important to understand why a certain decision was made. Traceability of decisions, and the documentation of the rationales behind the decision is of paramount importance.

2.3.9 Requirement: Terminology Standardization

When you want to provide a common way of architecting, standardization of terminology used is mandatory, especially in regard to the terminology the architects use amongst each other. When they speak the same language, they can work together better. Through time Capgemini has learned that we commonly have to adapt our architecture terminology to terms that our clients have been using and are accustomed to. This in turn has led to the decision to introduce the usage of synonyms into IAF. Synonyms have formally been introduced into IAF version 4.5.

2.3.10 Requirement: Standardized Organization of Architecture Elements

Where possible we need to solve similar problems in similar ways, thus working toward the common way of architecting. By standardizing the organization of architecture elements, we will discover similar problems and enable ourselves to solve them in similar ways.

2.3.11 Requirement: Address Both Functional and Non-functional Aspects

Many architecture frameworks provide average to good support for structuring architecture from a functional point of view. They also commonly state that non-functional aspects must be taken into account. However they do not provide support for both functional and non-functional aspects. IAF must cover this, in order to develop balanced functional solutions that perform as desired; for instance, it makes a big difference if you need to support Straight Through Processing of 100 million orders a day as opposed to manually supporting 100 orders a day.

2.3.12 Requirement: Provide a Basis for Training New Architects

Development of a framework is just one step into achieving a common way of architecting. People will leave the company and new people will join. People will decide to develop their career toward architecture. IAF needs to provide a basis for its deployment by providing a basis for the creation of training material.

2.3.13 Requirement: Provide Sufficient Information for Engineers

If a building architect would deliver results that were insufficient for the engineers to build the building correctly, the architect would be sued. The same should go for IT architects. They have to deliver standards, rules, guidelines, and specifications in such a way that engineers can build the desired solution. An additional dimension for this requirement is that engineers are evolving their way of working, just as we are. When we started forming IAF, linear development was commonplace, and RUP was just starting to be used. Nowadays RUP is commonplace, and methods like XP and Agile are becoming more and more common. The different development methods have different input requirements. IAF has to cope with that.

2.3.14 Requirement: Provide Sufficient Information for Planners and Portfolio Managers

A city planning architect would also be fired if he could not deliver what the city planners needed. Enterprise and domain level architectures are mainly aimed at supporting planners and portfolio managers. Our output needs to address their input requirements. Here too we need to be flexible, as planning and portfolio management in the IT industry are not part of the business fabric yet.

2.3.15 Requirement: Take Stakeholders and Social Complexity into Account

Different stakeholders and their concerns need to be addressed and continuously managed as stakeholders have concerns with respect to the system architected. Depending on the stakeholder these concerns will differ. The architect will be working with a number of stakeholders, each with their own concerns on the result being architected. There is a need to not only consider one aspect area (such as business, applications, infrastructure, security, etc.) in isolation, but rather to see all aspect area as being part of an integrated whole. The concerns of stakeholders, especially when considered in parallel, are hardly ever limited to one aspect area only. Stakeholders will want to gain insight into these aspect areas, their interdependencies, and the possible impact of future developments on their concerns. We must be able to communicate with a possibly large and diverse group of stakeholders, addressing their individual concerns while at the same time working on a shared understanding and commitment of the result architected.

2.3.16 Requirement: Enable a Sound Approach to Solution Alternatives

Architecture in the IT industry is all about trade-offs. The best performing solution might not be secure enough, or it might cost too much. There is never one solution that perfectly answers all requirements. IAF has to provide an approach to define and compare different solution alternatives in order to support the analysis of the alternatives and decision making.

2.3.17 Requirement: Follow Open Standards Where They Add Value

Capgemini has always adopted open standards where they added value to the products that were being delivered. We have also contributed to an early architecture standard, IEEE 1003.23. This standard is now obsolete. It provided input for the famous IEEE 1471/2000 standard, which is commonly known and used in IT architecture. IEEE 1471 is now also ISO/IEC 42010. Currently Capgemini is member of The Open Group. We participate in the development of TOGAF, The Open Group Architecture Framework.

2.3.18 Requirement: Be Able to Effectively Demonstrate Completeness and Consistency

Common questions IT architects have to answer are: 'How do you know we have everything?' and 'How do you know everything is consistent?'. Many times our only answer was: 'You have provided me with the input. You know your business. Aren't you confident that we are complete and consistent?'. Of course this is the wrong answer. IT architects need to be able to demonstrate completeness and consistency. IAF needs to provide mechanisms that demonstrate it.

2.3.19 Requirement: Service Oriented Principles Have to Be Applied

Thinking in terms of service orientation has been adopted in very early stages within Capgemini. It clearly added value because it helped address a number of requirements.

Services have to be defined in such a way that they provide value to the service consumer. So the consumer has to be able to understand what the service will provide. This makes communication to the different stakeholders easier, and helps us to get decisions made.

Services encapsulate their internal structure and expose themselves through well defined, standardized interfaces. This helps manage complexity and thus supports one of the main reasons architecture has become a necessity in the IT industry – managing that complexity.

The quality of service that a service can deliver has to be well defined in order to the consumer to judge its value. Quality of service covers many non-functional aspects of the architecture.

Cost reduction is one of the ubiquitous requirements in our industry. Re-use of services is one of the things we use to reduce costs. Service orientation promotes re-use.

All the reasons above clarify why IAF needs to apply service oriented principles. Please note that we use the concept of a service not only in a technological way. We use this concept as well at business level, e.g. drilling a whole to find oil.

2.3.20 Requirement: Provide Support for Implementation Independent Models

It takes time to implement any architecture. The fact that it takes time will result in changes in the environment that could not be foreseen at the moment the architecture was created. We might want to take advantage of changes in the environment through time, simply because they might solve a problem we could not solve at the moment we created the architecture. One major example in this area is network bandwidth. Who could have imagined the speed we currently have 5 years ago? This is the reason to support 'implementation independent models'. These models show the structure of the architecture, but do not contain real life constraints. They can be used as a reference model at the time a certain part is being implemented.

2.3.21 Requirement: To Be Independent of, Yet Accommodating, Different Architecture Styles and Technology Innovations

As our industry is still rapidly evolving, different architecture styles are also evolving. Two tier client-server has been succeeded by 3-tier and cloud computing. Product oriented business organization is being replaced by customer oriented business organization. IAF has to be independent of these evolving architecture styles to be stable. On the other hand, IAF also has to be able to use the styles to create a specific architecture.

2.3.22 Requirement: Tool Independence

Different customers will have different tools to create and maintain architectures. We will have to be able to use the different tools in combination with IAF. We will not link ourselves to one tool environment. Capgemini has developed a meta model and certification scheme for tool vendors so they can embed IAF support in their tools.

2.3.23 Requirement: Diagramming Model Independence

IAF must not prescribe diagramming models. We need to be able to adapt to the diagramming models that are used in the customer's environment. We do however recommend that UML should be considered where appropriate because it is so widespread.

2.4 Logical Structure: The 'How' of IAF

2.4.1 Introduction

The previous section has described the requirements we have defined for IAF. Here we will describe the logical structure that has been created to fulfill the requirements.

2.4.2 IAF content

2.4.2.1 Abstraction Levels

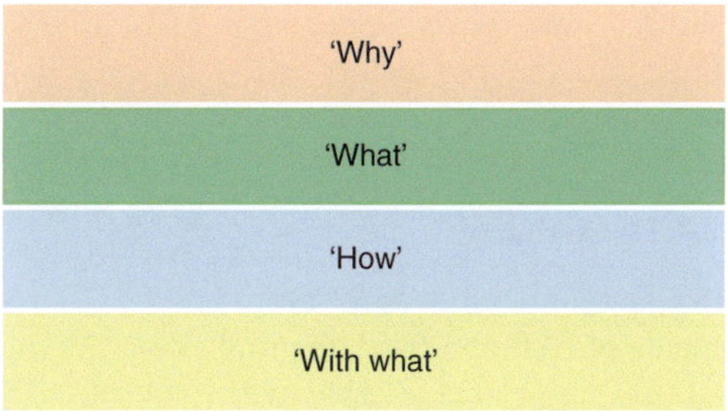

IAF recognizes abstraction levels. The abstraction levels are aimed at splitting one problem into smaller ones that are easier to solve. We follow the famous 'Why, what, how, with what' order in defining abstraction levels. First get the drivers, objectives, principles and scope right – the answer to the why question –, then understand the requirements – what services the solution has to support – , thirdly design how the 'ideal' solution will support the requirements, and finally decide with what physical components to implement the ideal solution. Abstraction levels need to be applied to all architecture topics, so they will be positioned horizontally across the topics.

2.4.2.2 Aspect Areas

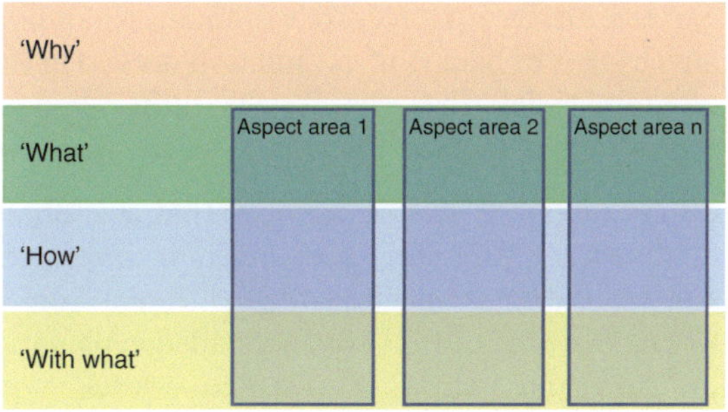

The Aspect Areas in the IAF describe a formal boundary between elements of the architecture solution that are usually considered within their own context. Each aspect area focuses on one particular dimension of the architecture, and adds information to the overall architecture. Commonly specific knowledge and background is required to be able to successfully address an aspect area. Aspect areas cover the what, how and with what abstraction levels. This is because the 'why' abstraction level contains observations and driving elements for the architecture such as strategies and trends that are applicable in all aspect areas.

Aspect areas are positioned vertically in the IAF diagram.

2.4.2.3 Third Dimension Aspect Areas

IAF also recognizes aspects that are fundamentally part of all other aspect areas, but often need to be addressed separately to ensure completeness and consistency.

Aspect areas in the third dimension commonly address topics regarding quality or non-functional aspects like security and governance, as these are the product of all aspect areas.

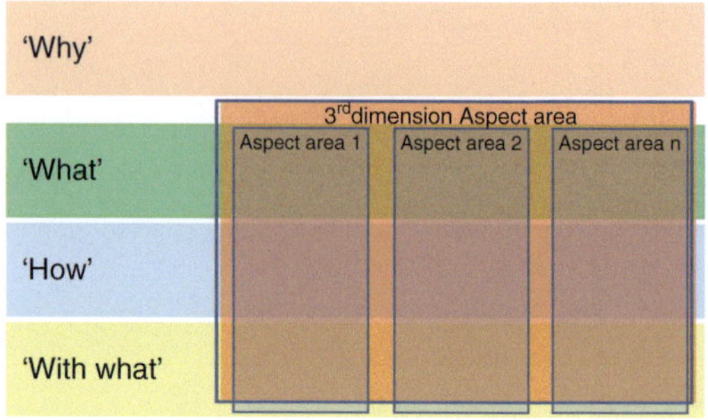

2.4.2.4 Artifacts

Artifacts are the core elements of IAF and fundamentally describe the architecture.

There are a number of core types of artifact within IAF that are essentially the same across any of the aspect areas in which they reside. This section describes these core artifacts. Other artifacts that are specific to an aspect area and abstraction level will be elaborated in Chap. 3.

Architecture Principles set out the general characteristics of the desired architecture and **why** it should be as it is. Principles are initially represented at the start of an architecture engagement; however they are often expanded and enumerated throughout the architecture process as architecture details are expanded, or as a result of better understanding of the business objectives.

Services are the architecture's fundamental building blocks. A service describes an 'element of behavior' or function needed in the architecture. The description of a service describes **what** it does, rather than *how* it is done. This implies that services are defined in the 'what' abstraction level.

Components are sets of services that are organized in accordance with the Architecture Principles and business objectives. The way IAF works with services and components is much different from many other architecture frameworks. See Sect. 2.4.2.10 for a detailed explanation. Components are defined in the 'how' and 'with what' abstraction level.

Collaboration contracts describe the interaction behavior between services and components. In effect they capture the non-functional aspects of the architecture. They document for example how often, how fast, how secure, and how controlled the interaction needs to take place.

Standards are documented statements that describe what has to be adhered to during the realization of the architecture. We often distinguish two types of standards, based on the moment they have to be adhered to. If a standard can be adhered to in the next change of the system, then it is a normal standard, and can be treated as described. If adherence to the statement has to be realized before a certain date, like with law changes, then we use the term 'rule'. Commonly standards and rules are non-negotiable. Senior business management needs to decide if they can be breached.

Guidelines provide guidance and direction (requirements) for the realization of the architecture. They should normally be adhered to. Commonly specific procedures are put in place to manage adherence to guidelines. One has to obtain waivers if it's not possible to adhere to guidelines.

Specifications describe how specific architecture components should be built, configured and implemented.

2.4.2.5 Viewpoints and Views

Views are a structured organization of the architecture artifacts in accordance with a given criteria. Views are primarily the constructs for representing the architecture (usually of structure) from different perspectives or viewpoints.

A view is the representation of an artifact or the combination of artifacts from one or more aspect areas with a specific objective. A view is a very flexible element of IAF. Depending on the architecture engagement an architect will create different views, each providing different insights. Views are very effective as a means for communicating the architecture. They are also a critical tool when analyzing the problem; by looking at the problem from a specific viewpoint we can identify areas of concern, look for gaps, etc.

Interaction Models and *Cross-references* are two fundamental Views used in IAF to show the basic architecture structure and relationships. Interaction Models typically describe the relationships between similar artifacts within a specific Aspect Area and Cross-references typically describe relationships between artifacts across different Aspect Areas. Cross-references are one of the key mechanisms for traceability and decision justification in IAF.

Other Views are selected as required usually driven by the Architecture Scope and Objectives. Views are therefore something that the architect selects based on need of the stakeholder and as such there is no definitive list of Views within the IAF.

Some views however are regularly used and are instrumental in describing significant relationships within the IAF.

IEEE 1471[1] uses the following descriptions for view and viewpoint:

A view is a collection of models that represents the whole system with respect to a set of related concerns. A view belongs to a particular architectural description. For example, a structural view of a system might include a model showing components, their interfaces and the classes comprising them, and a model of their dependencies and inheritance relationships. A performance view might consist of models for resource utilization, timing schedules and cause-effect diagrams. We use terms like

[1] IEEE Computer Society (1999) IEEE P1471 Recommended Practice for Architectural Description. IEEE, US.

'operational view' and 'performance view' where others have used terms like 'operational architecture' and 'performance architecture.'

A viewpoint captures the rules for constructing and analyzing a particular kind of view. It is a template for a view which can be reused across many architectural descriptions. The term 'view type' was considered as an alternative for viewpoint because of the strong analogy of view and viewpoint to instance and type; but we chose 'viewpoint' because of its use in existing standards and the requirements engineering literature.

TOGAF version 8[2] and 9[3] use the following definitions:

View: A 'view' is a representation of a whole system from the perspective of a related set of concerns. A view is what is seen from a viewpoint. An architecture view may be represented by a model to demonstrate to stakeholders their areas of interest in the architecture. A view does not have to be visual or graphical in nature.

In capturing or representing the design of a system architecture, the architect will typically create one or more architecture models, possibly using different tools. A view will comprise selected parts of one or more models, chosen so as to demonstrate to a particular stakeholder or group of stakeholders that their concerns are being adequately addressed in the design of the system architecture.

Viewpoint: A definition of the perspective from which a view is taken. It is a specification of the conventions for constructing and using a view (often by means of an appropriate schema or template). A view is what you see; a viewpoint is where you are looking from – the vantage point or perspective that determines what you see.

IAF uses views and viewpoints in the same way that IEEE 1471 and TOGAF do. Often we define the stakeholder and the concern the stakeholder has along with the description of the view. We do not prescribe modeling or diagramming techniques in the viewpoints as that would be in contradiction with our requirement regarding diagramming model independence.

2.4.2.6 Solution Alternatives

It is most common that a single solution does not exist that will meet all stakeholders requirements. IAF supports a technique to investigate different solution alternatives and to discuss these with the stakeholders. The place where this should be considered is in the abstraction levels 'How' and 'With what' because these levels are the places where decisions are made regarding the structural elements of the architecture. Commonly solution alternatives are defined per aspect area, especially at the logical level. This is done to simplify the analysis of the different alternatives. Of course the solution alternatives per

[2] The Open Group (2007) TOGAF Version 8.1.1 Enterpise Edition. The Open Group, US.

[3] The Open Group (2009) TOGAF Version 9. The Open Group, US.

aspect area can be merged into one overall analysis of the solution alternatives for the whole architecture. There are two basic approaches to solution alternatives, the 'fast track' and the 'full analysis' approach.

Within each approach you need to define the criteria that are used to compare the different alternatives. After that the different alternatives need to be identified. It is best practice to base alternatives on architecture principles that have been defined. That enables you to rationalize the identification of the solution alternative, and the scoring against the defined criteria and principles.

The fast track approach scores each solution alternative against each criterion. The amount in which the alternative fulfills the criterion determines the score. The solution alternative that fits all criteria the best, wins.

The full analysis approach enables the usage of relative weights for the different criteria, thus making some criteria more important than others. The table below shows how it works.

Solution alternative	Criterion 1			Criterion 2			Criterion *n*			End result
	Weight	Score	Result	Weight	Score	Result	Weight	Score	Result	
Alternative 1	3	3	**9**	2	3	**6**	1	1	**1**	***16***
Alternative 2	3	2	**6**	1	3	**3**	1	1	**1**	***10***

This approach takes more time because you do not only have to agree the criteria and scores, but also the weight of each criterion.

Solution alternatives obviously should also take the different interests different stakeholders have into account. For example, centralization might be in the interest of the corporate staff departments, whilst being strongly opposed by business unit management because centralization implies loss of control for them.

2.4.2.7 Domains

Architectures can become relatively large, simply because they have to describe many services and components. An enterprise level architecture can easily contain hundreds of services and components. It is especially difficult to communicate and visualize services, as they are the fundamental building blocks of the architecture, and therefore the most abundant. Architects using IAF have implicitly solved the communication and visualization challenges they had with services by grouping them together in ways the stakeholders can relate with. They often used the term 'domain' or 'segment' to describe the groups. As of IAF 4.5 we have formalized the usage of domains, especially in the 'what' abstraction level, as that is where services are defined. There has been much debate regarding this subject, as many people argue that grouping services into domains implies creating a structure, and thus is part of the 'how' abstraction level. There is a fundamental difference between the way we use domains and the way we construct components.

Domains are based on things we want to communicate and stakeholders can relate with. Common examples of domains are business units or geographical locations. The intention of domains is to visualize and communicate services so they can be validated by stakeholders.

Components are constructed on the basis of architecture principles, which can be very different from the basis used for domains. An example is architecture principle 'buy before build'. This implies that we should group our services in such a way that they reflect what we want to have in a package we are potentially going to select.

2.4.2.8 Synonyms

For a long time we did not have a formal mechanism to document the terms we use to communicate artifacts to non-architect stakeholders. This has lead to situations in which architecture teams caused confusion due to incorrect usage of terminology. As of IAF version 4.5 we have formally introduced the usage of synonyms. The IAF glossary has been extended to allow the definition and usage of synonyms. This can be done on a per project or per client basis. Another advantage of synonyms is that it makes it easier to link to terminology that is already being used in the organization.

2.4.2.9 Mechanisms

Wikipedia[4] describes the term 'mechanism' like this:

A ***mechanism*** *is some technical aspect of a larger process or mechanical device, or combination of parts designed to perform a particular function. Sometimes an entire machine may be referred to as a mechanism. Examples are the steering mechanism in a car, or the winding mechanism of a wristwatch.*

The term 'mechanism' was used in IAF version 1 and 2 to describe parts of the overall architecture that provided a distinct function. Often they consisted of combinations of artifacts from multiple aspect areas. The mechanisms were even described in mechanism catalogues. The usage of the concept mechanism has been less prominent in the current versions of IAF. This does not mean that they cannot be used.

Common and current usage of mechanisms is often within quality related areas. Mechanisms that ensure specific quality aspects can be described and even re-used in different parts of the architecture. Examples of mechanisms that could be described are a high availability mechanism that prescribes the different services and components that need to be used to achieve a certain level of availability, like synchronous replication and hot standby. Another example could be the use of biometrics mechanism for implementing strong authentication as opposed to weak authentication based on the combination user-id + password.

---

[4] Information available via Wikipedia. Http://en.wikipedia.org. Accessed December 2008.

2.4.2.10 Creating Components

Many architecture frameworks take a top down approach to the creation of the architecture. They start high level, and decompose down to the level required to document what the architecture consists of, much like in the figure below. This approach has advantages and drawbacks.

The main advantage is that stakeholders can easily relate to the structures and therefore easily validate them.

The main drawbacks of this approach are: (1) It's not that easy to define and analyze solution alternatives, as thinking is guided and influenced by the hierarchical structure that is being created. The structure makes it harder to think out of the box. (2) The architect is implicitly combining the 'what' and the 'how' question, because he is defining the structure along with the definition of the requirements. This contradicts the requirements we intend to meet within IAF.

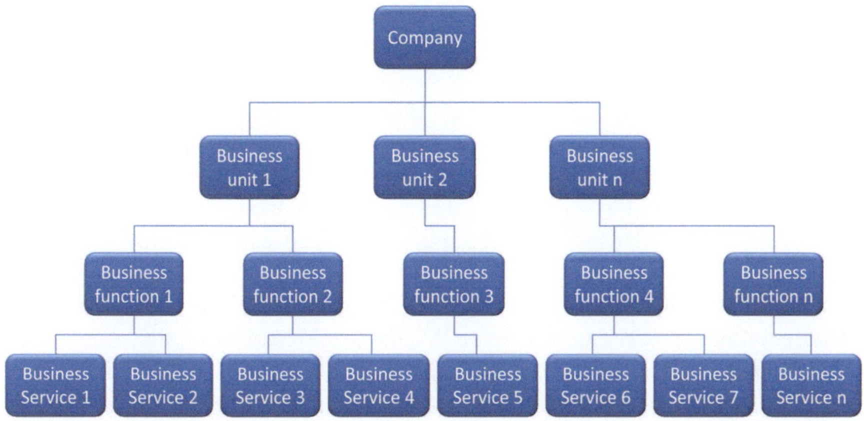

IAF takes a different approach. First we define the services at the level of detail required without explicitly putting them into a hierarchical structure. Then we define grouping criteria that are based on the architecture principles. After that we create components by grouping the services into components based on the grouping criteria. The figure below visualizes the IAF approach.

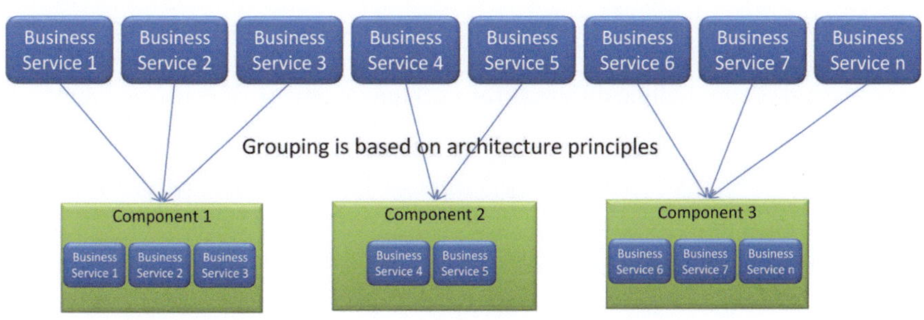

Advantages of the IAF approach are that it is easy to define and create solution alternatives as we are not influenced by structures already created. We also explicitly split the 'what' from the 'how' question by first defining services and then grouping them. Of course there is a drawback to this approach: visualization and communication of the services is more complex. This has been solved by the introduction of domains.

A group of services is a component for which a solution as a whole exists, and that can function as a whole. In general each architecture will only contain one group for each required set of services.

2.4.2.11 Policy and Collaboration Contracts

To create an architecture that works, there has to be a balance between supply and demand. In other words, the services have to be able to supply what the service consumers demand from them. An example will clarify the importance: If a pizza restaurant can bake 10 pizza's a time, and it receives one customer that orders 8 pizzas, all is fine. If a second customer comes in and orders 5 pizza's there is a problem. To be able to balance supply and demand we need to document both of them. As stated in Sect. 2.4.2.4, the collaboration contract is used to document the interactions between services and components. This implies that they document the non-functional attributes of what the service consumer demands. To be theoretically correct there would have to be a second type of contract to document the supply side, a so called 'policy contract[5]'. Services and components could have multiple policy contracts to document their different capabilities (e.g. a service request that requires immediate response, and one that can be deferred). This would lead to a jungle of services, components, collaboration contracts and policy contracts. To simplify things, IAF has decided to incorporate the attributes that describe the policy contract into the attributes of the services and components. If a specific architecture needs to, they can remove the attributes from the services and components, and introduce policy contract artifacts.

2.4.3 IAF Process: Engagement Roadmaps

IAF deliberately separates the process of architecting from architecture content, because the content is relatively stable and the process by which the engagement is run, will be different for each engagement. The process depends

[5] This term was chosen to align with the open standard WS-Policy, which describes how the capabilities of a web service can be documented and published.

on the context of the engagement: time frames, stakeholders, organizational culture, the architects team, etc will differ by situation.

We have defined the term **engagement roadmap** as '*a process pattern describing how to run an architectural engagement for specific architectural objectives within a specific client. It specifies architecture content as well as the engagement process*'. The concept of roadmap allows us to apply the line of thought from IAF in various sequences, depending on the type of assignment. Since IAF provides an artifact framework, it will provide consistency in the registration of and reasoning behind deliverables. The term 'Engagement Roadmap' is used explicitly to differentiate the process of architecture from Architecture, Product or Technology Roadmaps which describe the evolution of the architecture, product or technology.

Ideally Roadmaps are documented in the same way as patterns are. That facilitates re-use. Roadmap descriptions should have the following attributes:

Name	*[Identify the roadmap]*
Version & date	
Description	*[Provide an overview of the roadmap – an introduction.]*
Context	*[Describe the context that led to the definition of the roadmap.]*
Architecture areas covered	*[Identify which aspect areas and abstraction levels are covered]*
Design decisions & rationales	*[Provide insight into how and why the roadmap was constructed]*
Pre and post conditions	*[Help the user understand when the roadmap can be used, and what the effect of its use will be.]*
Open issues	*[Make the reader aware of things that have not been addressed in the roadmap.]*
Potential pitfalls	*[Make the user aware of potential risks or problems associated with the use of this roadmap.]*
Newly created problems	*[Make the reader aware of additional/new things that have to be addressed as a consequence using this roadmap.]*
Contacts	*[Provide information on where to get more details about the roadmap.]*
See also links	*[Links to related roadmaps, patterns and case studies that have applied this roadmap.]*
Roadmap details	*[The detailed description of the roadmap]*

A set of commonly used roadmaps can be found in Sect. 5.5.

2.5 Physical Elements: The 'With What' of IAF

2.5.1 *Introduction*

In Sect. 2.2 we addressed the 'why' question in regard to IAF. Sect. 2.3 describes IAF's requirements and thereby addresses the 'what' question. The 'how' question has been addressed in Sect. 2.4 by describing IAF's logical elements. This section uses the logical elements to describe which real life physical elements are part of IAF. An example: We described that we use abstraction levels in Sect. 2.4.2. In Sect. 2.5 we will describe which physical abstraction levels are really there.

2.5.2 *Physical Content*

2.5.2.1 Abstraction Levels

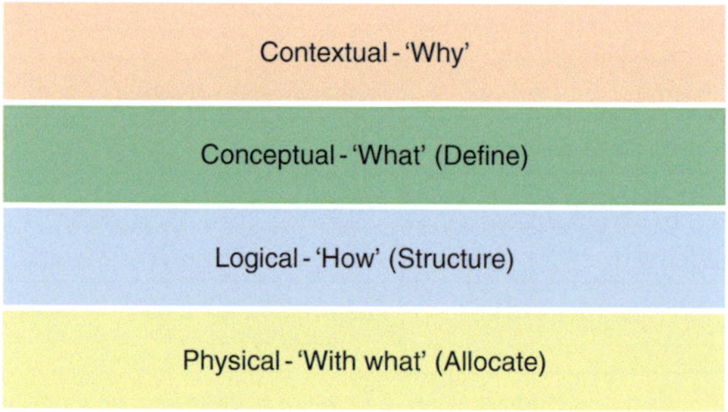

The real life abstraction levels that have been defined in IAF are fairly obvious. We have been using them throughout this chapter. The names for the abstraction levels were adopted from a large architecture project Capgemini had executed at the Bibliothèque nationale de France in Paris. The project was about implementing distributed computing in the French library. There they captured requirements in terms of 'conceptual servers'. They translated the requirements into the logical structure of the computing environment, and called the different components 'Logical servers'. And of course the next one is easy to guess – The real life servers were called physical servers.

Through time we also introduced synonyms for the terms 'What', 'How' and 'With what'. The diagram maps the interrogative pronouns with the more formal IAF name of the abstraction layers: Contextual, Conceptual, Logical and Physical. In effect the 'what' level is all about *defining* architecture requirements. The 'how' level actually creates the logical *structure* of the architecture. In the 'with what' level the logical components are *allocated* to real life, physical things you can buy, hire or build.

In the past there has been debate about defining a fifth level, which would address the 'when' question. The 'when' question is all about transformation and migration planning – when will we transform or migrate which part of the architecture. As transformation and migration planning is not the sole responsibility of the architect, and as the planning depends on many other aspects, it has not been incorporated as a formal part of the IAF model.

2.5.2.2 Aspect Areas

IAF consists of four physical aspect areas, Business, Information, Information systems and Technology infrastructure.

There are a number of rationales behind the choice of these aspect areas. The rationales are based upon 2 questions: (1) What do I need to know to deliver the overall architecture in such a way that it serves its purpose and (2) Which capabilities are required to answer the different types of questions we need to address in the architecture.

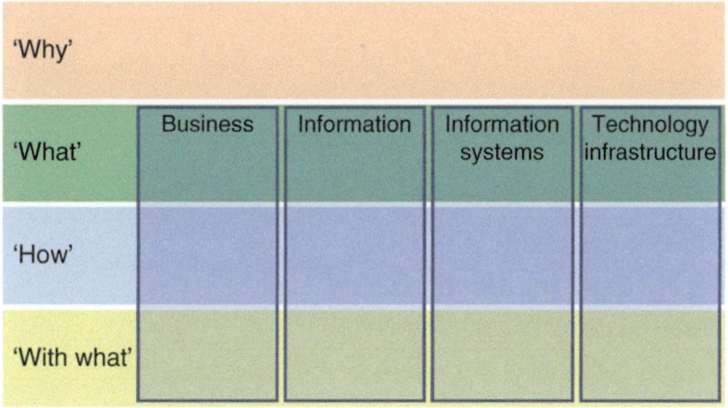

To answer the first question: IAF was originally designed to support the creation of architectures for Capgemini's business. Capgemini's business is all about business and technology transformation. So the topics we need to address are:

1. The structure of the business itself, otherwise we will not be able to understand which technology is needed to support or enable the business;
2. The way in which the business wants to process its information, as information processing is what the supporting technology does;
3. The structure of the information systems that support the business, to be able to understand which information systems have to be built and bought, along with the interfaces between them;
4. The computing systems, network technology and other infrastructural elements needed to make the information systems work.

The second question is actually implicitly answered by the first question. The capabilities a person needs to be able to structure a business are different from those needed to structure the information household of the business. In the first instance one needs to know the pros and cons of different business models and the way processes are structured within the different models. People that need to structure the information household of a company need to know what information modeling is all about. An information modeler does not have the skills that information systems people have. Information systems architects need to know the different packages that are available for a specific area, they also need to know all about interfacing mechanisms, data conversion and migration topics etc. People with information systems skills do not naturally have the capabilities to define and structure the computing systems and network technology needed to let the information systems run.

This all leads to the conclusion that the four aspect areas defined in IAF are needed to create an architecture that supports business and technology transformation, and that each area requires distinct skills which helps in getting the right architect in the right place, enabling effective communication across the borders of each architect's discipline.

2.5.2.3 Third Dimension Aspect Areas

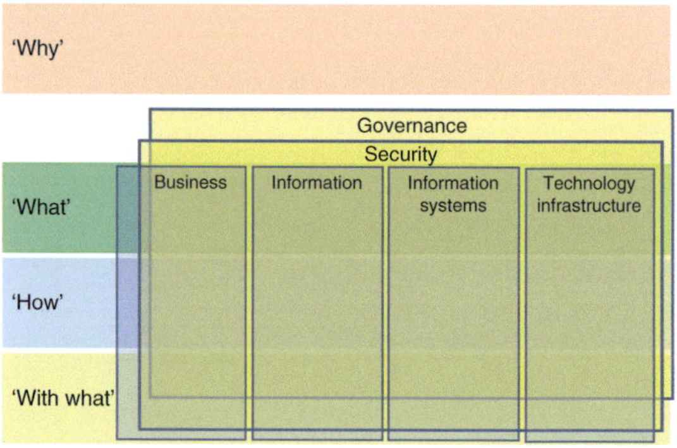

Next to the four aspect areas covered so far, IAF has included two third dimension aspect areas, Security and Governance in previous versions. Security is a topic that must be addressed holistically, across aspect areas, to ensure that all security related topics in the different areas work together to provide the desired level of security. You can enforce very tight security within an information system, but if you do not ensure that access control to buildings in which the information system is used is also at the desired level, it will be relatively easy for a hacker to enter the building and access the system through the workplace of one of the employees that has left his desk. Security architecture is also a topic that requires specific knowledge, so it also fits the rationales of the aspect area definition.

Governance, the other third dimension aspect area, has a bit of a strange name, especially if you look at what topics it addresses. Capgemini still considers the options to cover many more topics within this aspect area, including subjects like compliance or corporate governance. We have started with addressing quality of service (QoS) aspects within this area. Thus, the aspect area "governance" is all about ensuring that the desired quality of service is delivered at the defined acceptable level of cost. Of course quality of service is not only delivered by IT. There are many processes around IT that have their own information processing requirements and information systems. Simply think of topics like incident management, change management and availability management.

During the creation of IAF version 4 we have merged Security and Governance into the main aspect areas. The rationale for this was the observation that security and governance were often neglected as topics, were only addressed at the end of the process and then required the collection of additional information from the business, and at this point were often looked at only from an IT perspective. People were only focusing on the main aspect areas. The merge was done by the addition of attributes to artifacts in the main aspect areas and defining mandatory security and governance views in the relevant cells of IAF. This has the effect of both ensuring that the information can be collected from the business as early as possible, relates directly to the business needs and is treated in a holistic manner across the whole architecture.

2.5.2.4 Artifacts

As Chap. 3 will describe all artifacts per aspect area and abstraction level, we will use this section to explain where artifact types are positioned in the IAF.

The contextual level is the area where all our 'input' is positioned. The input help us understand (1) the context of the business (mission, strategy, drivers, . . .), (2) the architecture engagement (scope, objective, . . .) and (3) the architecture principles.

Services and collaboration contracts are used in the conceptual level to document architecture requirements. What services are needed and how do they collaborate? Services are defined within all aspect areas, so they can be business services or technology services.

Actually this way of documentation can be used to describe functional and non-functional aspects of anything. The service describes what can be delivered (functional aspects) and how it should behave (non-functional aspects). The collaboration contract describes the way in which it is to be delivered in terms of the communication mechanism to be used and the syntax and semantics of how it can be requested. The communication mechanism effectively defines how fast, how secure, how often etc things can happen. An example will clarify this. If you were in a conversation and you were asked what your age is, then nine out of ten times you would answer the question within a few seconds. This is an example of two services executing a collaboration contract with each other. The requested and delivered service are: 'Collect age' and 'Provide age'. The communication mechanism is sound waves generated by vocal chords. Syntax and semantics are the English language. The communication mechanism implicitly defines behavior: you know the other expects an answer within a few seconds. You also know you can lie about your age, and the

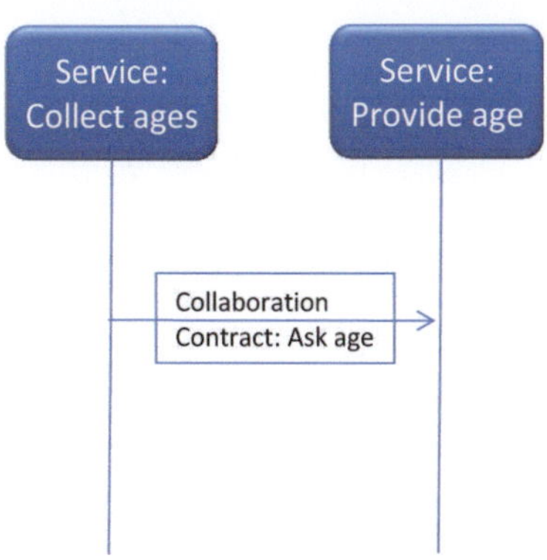

other might not mind. However, if we used another communication mechanism, your reaction would be different. If the question was asked in an email, you might answer it. You have the choice not to. You can also wait a week before you answer. The requestor knows that. And you can still lie about your age.

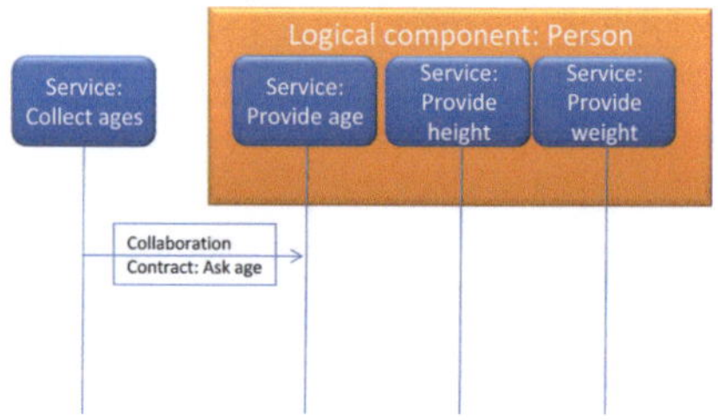

Components are positioned in the logical and physical levels within IAF. They are sets of one or more services, represented either in a logical or physical manner. Each main aspect area contains components. Components also have collaboration contracts between them, as they are sets of one or more services and services have collaboration contracts.

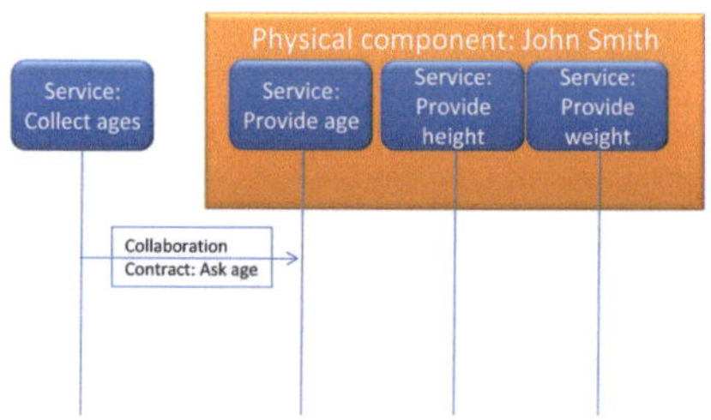

Standards, guidelines and specifications can be relevant in every aspect area. As they are key deliverables that are to be used to guide realization of the architecture, they are positioned in the physical level. So IAF identifies business standards, information standards, information systems standards and technology infrastructure standards. Where relevant you can also define security and governance standards. Guidelines and specifications are treated in the same way.

2.6 Recap: IAF's Meta-meta Model

This paragraph brings several topics from the previous paragraphs together to show how they are linked. The meta-meta model depicted in the figure visualizes the relationships. Services are defined in the conceptual level. Interaction between services is documented in collaboration contracts. Services in different aspect areas will have relations with each other. These relationships are commonly documented in cross-references. Services do not need to have one-to-one relationships with services in other aspect areas. It is not uncommon to encounter one-to-many and even many-to-many relationships.

Services are grouped into logical components. Grouping is based on principles. Grouping always implies trade-offs, which we assess using the architecture principles. Different groupings can be made and compared with each other. The name we use for a set of groupings is a **solution alternative**.

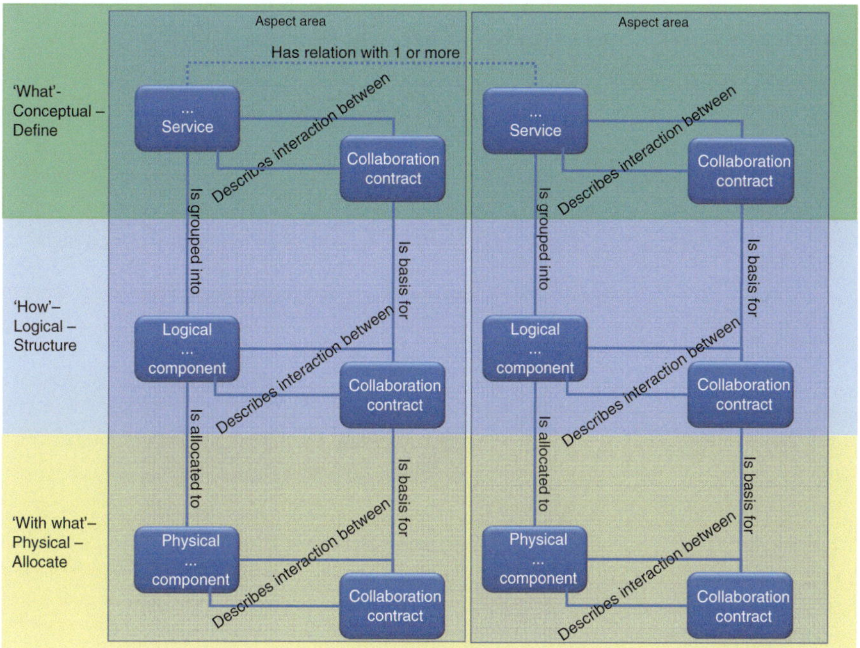

The collaboration contracts between services are the basis for collaboration contracts between components. Collaboration contracts between components can be the result of merged collaboration contracts between services, if their characteristics allow them to be merged. If they cannot be merged, then we can conclude that there will be two 'interface types' between the components. A simple example is one interface for single, high priority service requests, e.g. airline ticket bookings. The second interface type could then be grouped requests for lists of bookings done during the last 24 hours. Collaboration contracts in one area also form the basis for the collaboration contracts in other areas. A business area collaboration contract could define the maximum business response time for a service request to be 3 seconds. We can use that as the basis for the response time for the IS services that support the business service. We could assume that IS processing would take 2 seconds. That implies that the maximum infrastructure response time would have to be 1 second.

Logical components are 'allocated' to physical components. What does this 'allocation' actually mean? Well, in its essence the mechanism is simple. Logical processes are mapped to the real life physical parts of the organization that will be executing the processes. Logical IS components are allocated to products that have been selected to implement them, or we have decided to build them in a specific physical environment like .NET or Java. Logical TI components like a server, mobile workstation, SAN or backbone switch have been allocated to the real life physical products with which they will be implemented.

This basic approach and meta-meta model has proven to work in all architecture aspect areas. It keeps the overall architecture as simple as possible and ensures traceability across aspect areas.

Chapter 3
IAF's Aspect Areas Explained

3.1 Introduction

While Chap. 2 presented IAF and its aspect areas, this chapter focuses on IAF's artifacts and architectural views. It is based on the Integrated Architecture Content Framework (IACF) which is a formal collection of all artifacts and views. All artifacts within IACF will be discussed and defined in this chapter. The collection of views explained consists of views we encountered frequently throughout the years. An exhaustive listing of views makes no sense, due to the large number of potential stakeholders and concerns who might need their own specific presentation of the architecture.

We will describe artifacts and views, provide examples, and give guidance in regard to their usage. However we will not explain all attributes of each artifact, as they can be found in our IAF reference manual.

Next to the four core aspect areas, IAF also explicitly recognizes two additional aspect areas, covering the two disciplines "Governance" and "Security". These aspects (a) are common across all the other aspect areas, (b) represent a set of requirements that are driven across all core aspect areas, and (c) may significantly change the architecture structure across one or more core aspect areas.

For the sake of covering all parts of IACF, the Contextual Layer will be also addressed in this chapter, although this abstraction level is not an aspect area itself but provides generic input for all aspect areas.

3.2 Contextual Artifacts and Views

3.2.1 Overview

The Contextual Layer is about understanding the WHY question. It sets the stake in the ground for the rest of the architecture by providing context. One of the challenges we often encounter is that the contextual information we need to know is scattered throughout many documents. In addition, the status or validity

J. van 't Wout et al., *The Integrated Architecture Framework Explained*,
DOI 10.1007/978-3-642-11518-9_3,

of information we find is often unclear, leading to validation activities with relevant stakeholders while gathering the information. These validation activities usually help in getting buy-in for the architecture work that will follow.

Another challenge we have to address is the fact that the contextual information we need or can get to, differs per organization. Therefore the artifacts we describe in this section should be regarded as a checklist of topics that can be part of contextual information. They do not always have to be present. Of course there are some topics that always need to be addressed, e.g. starting an architecture without architecture objectives and principles would not be a wise thing to do. We will indicate which artifacts are critical.

Just to make sure, we re-iterate that many of the topics described here are *input* to the architecture process, created by business strategists. It is our task to select the relevant parts and transform them into relevant drivers, objectives and principles we need in our architecture work.

3.2.2 Business Vision and Business Mission

The business vision defines the desired or intended future state of a specific organization or enterprise in terms of its fundamental objective and/or strategic direction. The business mission defines the fundamental purpose of an organization or an enterprise, basically describing why it exists and how it supports the move toward achieving the vision. More information about the differentiation between vision and mission can for example be found on Wikipedia.

Business vision and mission statements are often used to support programs of major change. For architecture they provide a strategic goal and a means to validate many of the architecture objectives. Vision and mission statements also often help shape and validate architecture principles. It is important to collect and validate the vision and mission in architecture engagements that support business transformation, as they will help decision making in the restructuring of the organization.

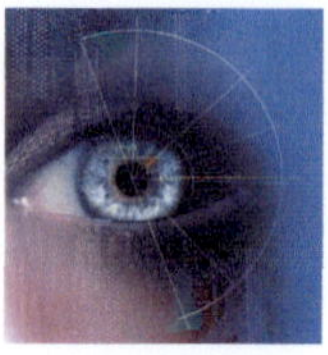

Capgemini's business vision statement is: 'Capgemini will lead the way by providing clients with insights and capabilities that boost their freedom to achieve superior results.'

Some other examples of business mission statements are:

- 3 M: 'To solve unsolved problems innovatively.'
- Mary Kay Cosmetics: 'To give unlimited opportunity to women.'
- Merck: 'To preserve and improve human life.'
- Wal-Mart: 'To give ordinary folk the chance to buy the same thing as rich people.'
- Walt Disney: 'To make people happy.'

3.2.3 Business Strategy

The business strategy provides direction, including describing how an organization wants to achieve its business vision within a given timeframe and to some extent how it can be achieved (key actions). It is the 'what and how' translation of the vision.

The business strategy is most important to the architecture's long and short term goals. The ideas expressed in the architecture must hold for a period of time that is at least as long as, and preferably longer, than the usual planning horizons.[1] That's why as a minimum we must explore that part of the planning period that is more or less clear, and the business strategy contains that. Therefore architecture scope and objectives and thus the whole architecture engagement should be aligned with the business strategy.

A business strategy is not always available, as it can be implicit, or confidential information. However if you are working on a business transformation program it is important to understand the business strategy, so hunt it down, e.g. by interviewing key executive stakeholders.

Examples of business strategy statements:

- Global governance with regional flexibility
- Increase in market share is more important than increase in margin
- Concentrate on core activities
- Diversify to gain market share

3.2.4 Business Drivers

There are different definitions for business drivers. Three of the most common ones are:

- The tasks, information, and people promoting and supporting the goals of the enterprise.
- The requirements describing what the business wants (e.g., more quality data, faster response to queries).
- The burning platform: A problem in the business or its environment that is important enough to spell the difference between success and failure for an organization.

We usually search for statements that meet the third definition, the important problems, as we should try to solve them as part of the architecture outcome.

[1] 'The sins of the architect are permanent sins' – Frank Lloyd Wright.

Some business driver examples:

- **Provide direct information access.** Provide increased access to information including direct access to government information and services in response to the customer, both internal (employees) and external (citizens), requirements.
- **Ensure accurate and timely service delivery.** Improve customer service and satisfaction through delivery of measurable timely and accurate services.
- **Provide high quality end products.** Develop and provide end products that satisfy customers' demands and fulfill their expectations.
- **Increase service delivery mechanisms.** Provide increasingly varied service delivery mechanisms (e.g. self-service, face-to-face, phone, internet) in response to customers' demands.
- **Reduce traffic jams and travel time, and improve work-life balance.** Capgemini responds by developing mobility strategy and changing their notion of 'location where you do your work'.
- **Public distress about top-management bonuses.**

3.2.5 Business Objectives

Business objectives typically identify the planned outcomes to an enterprise's business drivers, based on taking advantage of opportunities and mitigating threats. They describe what the organization wants to achieve, typically within a specified timeframe. Business objectives are not necessarily totally financial but may include organizational aspects, changes to their image or market etc. If not explicitly available, business objectives can usually be found in various sources, e.g. in strategy papers, business cases or charters for change.

The architecture engagement must be closely aligned to the business objectives and should therefore demonstrate its contribution to business drivers and strategy.

One important aspect of business objectives is the ability to measure whether an objective was met. Hence an effective business objective should usually contain:

- An observable and measurable goal
- Level of performance
- Conditions

Some good and bad examples:

Good:

- **Keep support costs to the projected level, $3.4 million for the coming year**
  This is an effective objective. The observable and measurable goal pertains to controlling expenses, the condition is the coming year, and the level of performance is $3.4 million.

- **Generate $25 million in sales between January and June**
  This is an effective objective. The observable and measurable goal pertains to generating revenue. The condition should be met between January and June, and the level of performance is $25 million.
- **Receive ISO 9000 certification by June of next year**
  This is an effective objective. The observable and measurable goal pertains to complying with the industry regulation ISO 9000. The condition should be met by June of next year. The criterion is the same as the goal: receive certification.

Bad:

- **Improve goodwill**
  This is not an effective objective because it does not explicitly generate revenue, reduce expenses, or comply with a regulation.
- **Contain support costs**
  This is not an effective objective. Although it pertains to a reduction in expenses, this does not explicitly state the reduction's extent or the conditions under which the reduction would occur.

Like business goals, business objectives can be described in a hierarchy.

3.2.6 Business Case

Business cases can range from comprehensive and highly structured, as required by formal project management methods, to informal and brief. This description of an initiative or event assists in the analysis or decision making process, like a project's justification. Business cases typically cover:

- Description of initiative;
- Background;
- Estimate of costs and revenues;
- Description of benefits;
- Gap analysis;
- Expected risks;
- Options considered (with reasons for rejecting or carrying forward each option);
- High level plan of approach.

Like business objectives, drivers and strategy, the business case is used to set up and clarify the architecture engagement.

Business case information can be confidential. As with business strategy this type of information is more relevant if you are working on a transformation program, creating an enterprise level architecture. Solution architectures might be accompanied by a business case, especially if Prince2 is used as the project management method, in order to justify the investments within the project's scope in the light of the overall architecture.

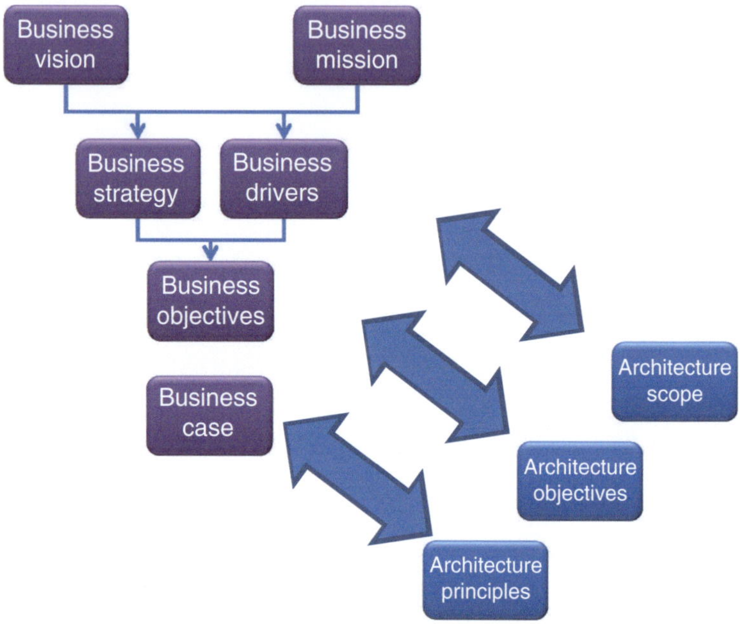

3.2.7 *SWOT Analysis*

This is a straightforward view of the organization's position in terms of **S**trengths, **W**eaknesses, **O**pportunities and **T**hreats. The SWOT analysis is used as input while setting the architecture scope and objectives.

An example from a large retailer:

Strengths:

- Acme is a powerful retail brand. It has a reputation for value for money, convenience, and a wide range of products all in one store.
- Acme has grown substantially over recent years and has experienced global expansion (for example its purchase of the United Kingdom based retailer All-Here).
- The company has a core competence involving its use of information technology to support its international logistics system. For example, it can see how individual products are performing country-wide, store-by-store at a glance. IT also supports Acme's efficient procurement.

- A focused strategy is in place for human resource management and development. People are key to Acme's business and it invests time and money in training people, and retaining and developing them.

Weaknesses:

- Acme is the world's largest consumer goods retailer and control of its empire, despite its IT advantages, could leave it weak in some areas due to the huge span of control.
- Since Acme sell products across many sectors (such as clothing, food, or stationary), it may not have the flexibility of some of its more focused competitors.
- The company is global, but has a presence in relatively few countries worldwide.

Opportunities:

- To acquire, merge with, or form strategic alliances with other global retailers, focusing on specific markets such as Europe or the Greater China Region.
- The stores currently only trade in a relatively small number of countries. Therefore there are tremendous opportunities for future business in expanding consumer markets, such as China and India.
- New locations and store types offer Acme opportunities to exploit market development. They diversified from large super centers, to local and mall-based sites.
- Opportunities exist for Acme to continue with its current strategy of large, super centers.

Threats:

- Being number one means that you are the target of competition, locally and globally.
- Being a global retailer means that you are exposed to political problems in the countries you operate in.
- The cost of producing many consumer products tends to have fallen because of lower manufacturing costs. They have been reduced due to outsourcing to low-cost regions of the World. This has lead to price competition, resulting in price deflation in some ranges. Intense price competition is a threat.

3.2.8 Competitor Analysis

Describes the (main) competitors of the organization in terms of

- A SWOT analysis
- Their performance in the market (benchmarks)
- Their perceived or real position in the market (leaders, followers etc.)

The competitor analysis will typically assist in determining architecture scope and objectives and also in setting out the principles. It is obvious that the competitor analysis is more important for enterprise level engagements than it is for solution architectures.

Key industry success factors	Weighting	Competitor #1 rating	Competitor #1 weighted	Competitor #2 rating	Competitor #2 weighted
1 - Extensive distribution	0.4	6	2.4	3	1.2
2 - Customer focus	0.3	4	1.2	5	1.5
3 - Economies of scale	0.2	3	0.6	3	0.6
4 - Product innovation	0.1	7	0.7	4	0.4
Totals	**1.0**	**20**	**4.9**	**15**	**3.7**

Source: Wikipedia

3.2.9 Organization Model

A representation of the organization. It typically takes the form of an organization chart and is useful for determining hierarchical connections, key reporting lines and stakeholders. In conjunction with a cultural analysis, the model will indicate the positioning of key stakeholders.

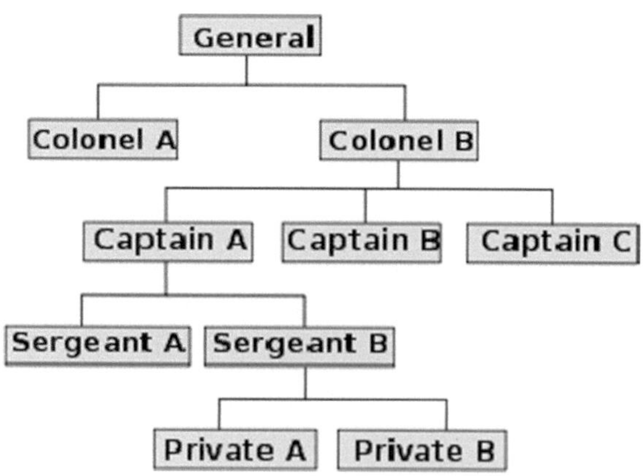

This model is also used as a current state organization model if the architecture is aimed at re-designing the organization. This is an indication that we use it mainly in enterprise level architecture engagements.

3.2.10 Culture Analysis

This is a description of the (management) culture within the organization. The most important aspect you need to understand here is the way decisions are made. If you are working in an autocratic organization in which the boss is the one that makes all of the decisions you need to go to him/her to get them. Organizing a workshop with the objective of making decisions would not be the smartest thing for you to do. On the other hand it would be smart in an organization that makes decisions based on consensus.

There are several recognized types of culture in the literature. One of the simple ones distinguishes 3 types. The *autocratic* culture is the one in which the boss makes all decisions. In the *managerial* culture decision making is delegated throughout the different management levels. Often the types of decisions that a specific management level can take are documented to ensure compliance. The *functional* culture shows true collaborative decisions, in which all relevant parties are involved. One often encounters this culture in highly specialized organizations in the science or high tech sector.

Adapting the way you do your work to the culture you are working in is critical for success of the architecture. So never forget this topic. It is relatively easy to distinguish which type of organization you are working in. Architectural engagements often bring organizational changes with them, leading to conflicts or even deadlocks. Knowing the culture of the organization helps you successfully cross these minefields.

3.2.11 Capabilities

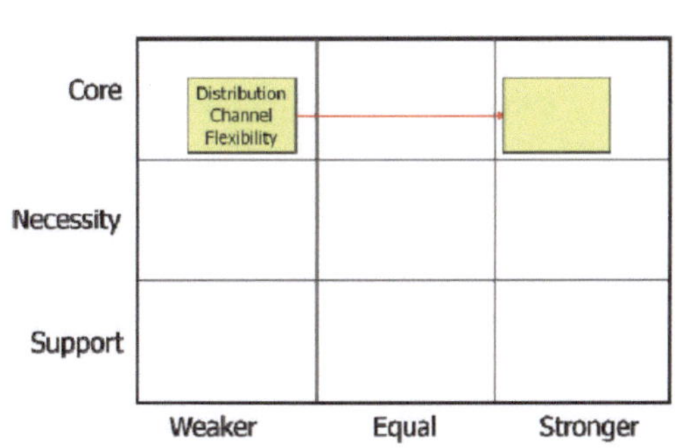

Management consultants often use the term 'capabilities'. They translate vision, mission and strategy into a set of capabilities that are required to achieve the objectives. The capabilities are often visualized in 'Boston squares' or in the extended version, the '3-by-3 grid' as shown in the figure. These grids illustrate where a capability is now, and where it needs to go to achieve the objectives.

Examples of capabilities are:

- Capability to support new technologies
- Capability to respond to change (business, technical and social) in a timely fashion
- Capability to introduce appropriate skilled resources
- Capability to produce products of a certain type
- Capability to fulfill orders

Understanding where the organization wants to go with which capabilities will help you to create an architecture that is aligned with the capabilities transformation. Capabilities are commonly more important in enterprise level engagements.

Note that the term capabilities is also sometimes used as a synonym for what IAF terms business activities, for example in IBM's Capability Modelling and Microsoft's Motion.

3.2.12 Risks

Risks are potential events of whatever nature that could impact the architecture engagement. Risks can be regarded as additional constraints on the architecture engagement e.g. upcoming organizational changes, other programs and initiatives running in parallel, or the use of unproven technology. We seldom see an architecture engagement that does not have to take risks into account. So spend time on identifying, validating, and defining measures to manage and mitigate risks.

3.2.13 Operating Model

An operating model describes how an organization operates across both business and technology domains, focusing on what is important for the organization. Typical examples are:

- The **enhanced Telecom Operations Map** (eTOM), published by the TM Forum, is a guidebook. It is the most widely used and accepted standard for business processes in the telecommunications industry. The eTOM model describes the full scope of business processes required by a service provider and defines key elements and how they interact;
- IBM's **Insurance Application Architecture** links business strategy to IT, providing a collection of more than 200 business processes and 700 individual business activities that represent insurance industry-wide best practices;
- IBM's **Information FrameWork** identify and define data, process and software component requirements of a universal financial institution, operating in an international environment;

- The **Information Technology Infrastructure Library** (ITIL) is a set of concepts and policies for managing IT infrastructure, development and operations.

Besides being a possible foundation for transforming business, the operating model is an important tool in the dialogue between business and IT.

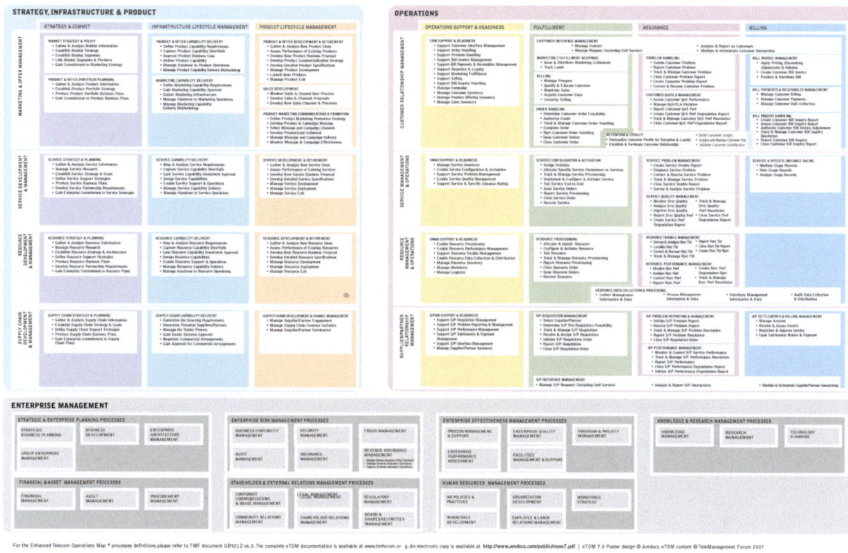

eTOM

Operating models that you encounter in the contextual phase are commonly models that the organization wants to adopt, as in the examples above. Use them as a reference model that provides guidance and input for the architecture.

More information on the interplay of the operating model and Enterprise Architecture can also be found in Dr. Jeanne W. Ross' book 'Enterprise Architecture as Strategy'.

3.2.14 Stakeholders

Stakeholders are decision makers and/or sources of information for the team on drivers, objectives, and constraints. Understanding and addressing stakeholders, their concerns, interests in, and position to the engagement is crucial to ensure success.

There are many types of stakeholder analysis techniques available. One technique differentiates between three types of stakeholders:

- **Primary stakeholders** are those ultimately affected, either positively or negatively by a corporation's actions.

- **Secondary stakeholders** are the 'intermediaries', that is, persons or organizations who are indirectly affected by a corporation's actions.
- **Key stakeholders** (who can also belong to the first two groups) have significant influence or importance in a corporation.

A second technique is to classify the different stakeholders and position them in the grid shown below. The classifications are: Power (high, medium, low), support (positive, neutral, negative), and influence (high, low).

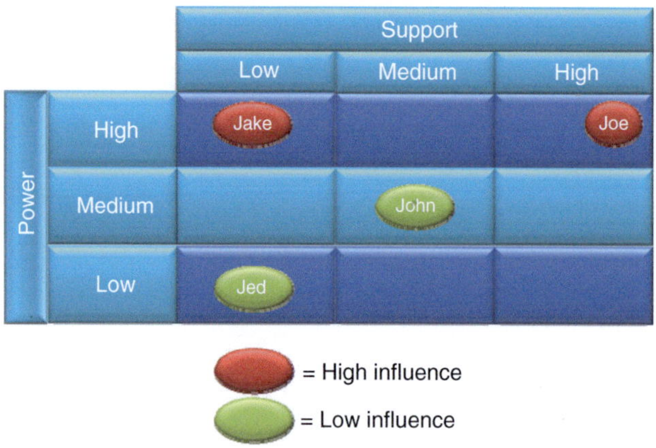

Creating an architecture without doing some form of stakeholder analysis is like trying to bake a cake without flour. You need to know who may support you, and who is hostile. In many cases there is at least one of each of them in any project. Try to understand their hidden agenda. Why do they oppose the intended change? Why is he rushing/delaying certain decisions? You will find that stakeholders will act as any human being, and that they will have their own motivation for behaving the way they do – regardless their organizational level. This often leads to your understanding of additional topics to take into account. These may be either of a personal nature or based on a passed experience. Both are important to know: If you are aware that somebody is scared of losing his/her job, or thinks the changes that will come will block his/her career, you can address those concerns. If issues in the past have caused the person to oppose the change you might just have stumbled on a new risk you will have to manage.

3.2.15 Context Diagram

The Context Diagram is usually a high-level picture, illustrating the main parts of the enterprise and its interaction with external entities in the environment. It describes the business in its context along with relevant business topics. Context diagrams are a very good means of communication to introduce the area of change to people that are new to the organization or project. You can also use them to show relevant external interfaces for the systems that are in scope of a solution architecture. Context diagrams are not critical to the architecture, but will contribute – as a communication tool – a lot to its success.

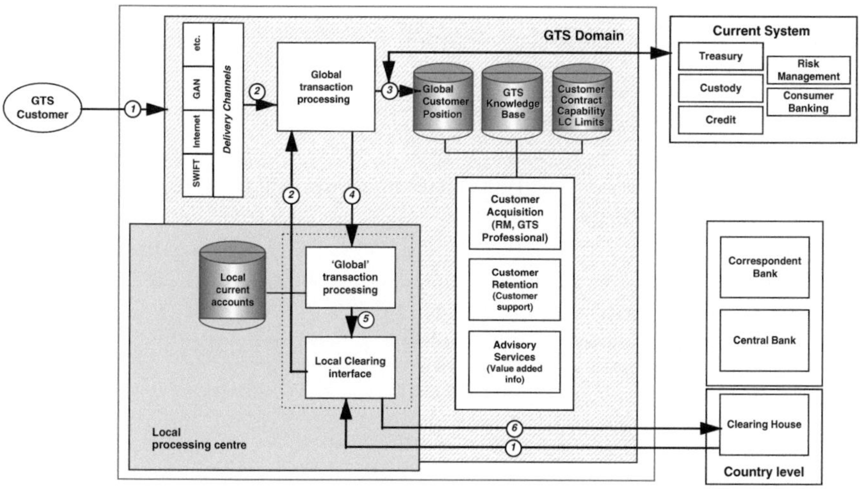

3.2.16 Policies

Policies can be of two forms:

1. A 'container' of multiple related principles, guidelines, standards, and patterns;
2. A short statement of principles that outlines and guides future decisions.

A 'security policy' is a good example of the first type. It can be very extensive and contained in multiple documents and repositories. Policies of this type should not be directly referenced. The references instead should be to the specific document or repository that contains the relevant information.

The second type of policy must be referenced as a policy.

It is mandatory to investigate and document which policies have to be adhered to. Often policies are there for compliance reasons. You could threaten the existence of the organization by not adhering to relevant policies.

(Enterprise) Architecture is used more and more as a tool to successfully steer organizational change. As with power comes responsibility, architecture needs to take all relevant policies into account.

3.2.17 *Architecture Objectives*

Architecture objectives (a) set out outcomes/deliverables of the architecture against business objectives, (b) communicate issues the architecture engagement will address, (c) shape the architecture engagement's roadmap, and (d) cover the level of analysis required to achieve a satisfactory level of confidence in the outcomes.

Different types of business issues require different types of architectures and architecture engagements.

If you do not understand the architecture objectives, it will be difficult for you to communicate them to your primary client. They will not be aware of what they are actually asking for, and will be surprised by the outcome, maybe even to the extent that they will terminate the assignment. So always define the architecture objectives and agree them with the key stakeholders. This is essential expectation management. A second reason for really understanding the architecture objectives is that it helps you to determine what needs to be done with which level of detail. It also helps you to determine what you can leave out of the architecture.

Some examples:

- Support the merger of the finance function of two companies → a business transformation which will have to address all IAF areas;
- Select and implement a package for CRM → understand just enough of the processes to be able to determine what has to change to accommodate the package. Gather requirements in terms of Business information services and their collaboration contracts. Focus on interfaces and redundant data;
- Provide a structural basis for portfolio management for the coming 10 years → a true enterprise architecture that will be used for scoping of programs;
- Support the decommissioning of legacy software → defining the order in which the legacy can be replaced.

Be aware that the objectives might not be obvious immediately. For example in one engagement the objective initially was thought to be the design of an information integration hub, but following further conversations with key stakeholders the key objective was found to be getting various contributors and consumers of information to be shared to understand that they could share the information without compromising their intellectual property.

3.2.18 *Architecture Principles*

An architecture principle is a statement of belief, approach or intent which directs the formulation of the architecture. It does not have to reference architecture artifacts or structures explicitly. They rather express the intention of the architecture. Principles are typically (a) owned and validated by particular stakeholders, (b) a starting point and guidelines for any architecture development, (c) used to manage the inevitably conflicting requirements and (d) do have a priority.

Solution alternatives and their selection will rely on prioritized principles to be able to advise on the best solution. You will also frequently encounter conflicting requirements, and even conflicting principles. Again priorities will help you out because you have determined up front what is the most important among all those very important principles.

Architecture principles are typically derived from business vision/mission/strategy/objectives/drivers and any corresponding architecture assumptions, scope, constraints, and objectives.

Example:

Principle name	Relationship fulfillment
Description	Value propositions will be generated and owned by retail division and supported by IT solutions to enable customers to have a mutually fulfilling relationship with the bank
Motivation	Ensure the bank provides the required products and services to meet the evolving needs of the customer The bank's migration from product centric to a customer centric focus
Implication	Understanding the immediate (support/tactical) and lifetime (strategic/visionary) needs of the customer Recognize the customer's choice to upgrade to a different engagement with the bank on a user pay basis Ability to monitor customer attrition
Assurance	Customer satisfaction will be monitored along with retention levels
Priority	Medium

3.2.19 Architecture Constraints

An architecture constraint is an assertion of a fact that cannot be circumvented and is recognized as having an impact on the engagement. It thus MUST be followed to ensure that the organizational and IT strategy/aspirations and the architectural objectives can be met. A constraint is similar to architecture principles but it has no weighting as it cannot be violated and thus there is no need to evaluate conflicting constraints. It can be related to time, money, quality, resource use, or availability. Architecture constraints provide the basis to ensure that project activities are channeled so as to respect the limitations imposed. Therefore always investigate which constraints need to be taken into account.

Examples:

- IT investments cannot exceed €12 million per year;
- The architecture must be implemented by January 1, 2010 or our business license will be withdrawn;

- Every piece of equipment must fit in the cargo elevator, otherwise it cannot be deployed on the 7th floor.

You need to be careful to identify those constraints which might need to be circumvented (for example, 'you can only use TBQ software', as it might not do what is required) – these are either not well enough defined or are high priority principles and as such negotiable.

3.2.20 Architecture Scope

An architecture scope should be defined to ensure complete coverage of the relevant business issues. It determines the level of granularity and detail for each of the aspect areas to be covered and ensures that the appropriate expectations are set for stakeholder agreement. It controls the architecture engagement and ensures that all architecture activities are focused on the correct business issues.

The architecture scope is a mandatory contextual artifact, because it manages expectations and provides a means to cure that ugly sickness called 'scope creep'. If you agree the scope up front you will be able to ensure you get sufficient resources and/or time if the scope of the engagement expands, and believe us, this will happen. We advise you to also explicitly define what is out of scope. This helps tackle problems later on that are the result of implicit assumptions people always have. You avoid hearing the 'I thought that was in scope' phrase from your primary client.

Example:

In scope	Out of scope
All business services related to finance, personnel, and production	All business services related to sales and transport

3.2.21 Architecture Assumptions

An architecture without assumptions is like rain without raindrops. They always exist together. You will always have to identify and communicate assumptions, simply because it will be the only way to progress with the architecture.

Assumptions are a means to allow activities to continue even though validated information is not available. However these assumptions must (a) be reasonable, i.e. they will have a high probability of being true, (b) have general agreement with the relevant stakeholders, (c) have an owner who will be responsible for validating the assumption, and (d) have a lifecycle which must be defined in terms of risk, resolution, and timeframe.

Although writing down assumptions is usually seen as a bordensome activity, it clearly helps support future discussions on design decisions taken in the past, as design decisions are usually based on a degree of uncertainty.

But beware: They should (a) NEVER be the architect's own assumptions and (b) ALWAYS be approved and communicated. They have to be agreed upon by relevant stakeholders. As assumptions mostly are wrong they are an excellent weapon to blame architects with things that are going wrong. If you get one million transactions per minute and thought you would get one thousand you should not be the person that gets blamed for the website going down.

3.2.22 Technology Strategy

Technology strategy is concerned with identifying the direction, means, and key actions to achieve the organization's technology objectives through the use of information technology. If you are working on a technology project and don't know the technology strategy, you will be making implicit assumptions.

Often the technology strategy will tell if the organization prefers a single vendor approach above a multi vendor one, or the other way around. It will tell which direction is intended with regard to technology change. The technology strategy can also be embedded in the organization's standards, rules and guidelines.

Examples of technology strategy statements:

- Improve efficiency through a one stop shop with vendor X;
- Reduce cost by explicitly adopting a multi vendor technology approach.

3.2.23 Standards, Rules and Guidelines

In Chap. 2 we described that the architecture activities create standards, rules, and guidelines (SRGs). Often there already are SRGs that must be adhered to. Select the SRGs that are applicable to your engagement. Always do this. How would you feel if you had created a set of SRGs that people didn't use . . . like an architecture not being used during the development phase.

Just as we create SRGs for the different aspect areas, you can expect to find SRGs for the same topics.

Aspect area	SRG examples
Business	Separate orchestration from processing Always utilize the front – mid – backoffice structure
Information	Conform to XBRL standards where possible
Information systems	Oracle must always be considered in package selection J2EE unless ....
Technology infrastructure	AIX is the Unix standard Microsoft office is the office automation standard Migrate to IPv6 before 1-1-2010
Security	Implement Jericho style security Strong authentication is default
Governance	ITIL v3 compliance

3.2.24 Project/Program Portfolio

An insight into current/planned projects, programs, and other initiatives is crucial for the understanding of current forces that have a direct or indirect impact on the architecture engagement, its stakeholders, or relevant environment.

Example:

In parallel with our architecture engagement, another program improves project management up to CMMI level 2. We need to anticipate that (perhaps halfway) our engagement has to be run at CMMI level 2 as well. This might not only impact the PMO processes of the engagement itself but also the (target) organizational parts and processes set up by the engagement. As you can imagine this might have a huge impact on our activities, timelines, and budget.

3.2.25 Current State (Baseline) Architecture

If you don't know where you are now, how can you determine what you need to do to get where you want to go? Of course we do not need to capture the baseline architecture in the same level of detail as we will for the future state (target) architecture. 'Just enough' is the credo here. And of course, we will give the architect's standard answer to the question 'what is just enough?': it depends. Most of the time however we encounter the following topics in a baseline architecture:

- Business process information – which ones are there;
- Information models, hopefully including ownership;
- Applications landscapes, including interfaces, and hopefully non-functional information regarding availability, transaction volume, peak usage characteristics and performance;
- Infrastructure landscapes, including interfaces.

It can also be very useful to have an understanding of licensing and maintenance agreements, especially in solution architecture engagements. These licensing arrangements are for software and services as well as maintenance arrangements for hardware and services. Insight into the cost structure might help to make certain decisions regarding solution alternatives. In addition an overview of the license agreements' lifespan is valuable input for optimizing the migration planning.

3.2.26 Contextual Views

The views we define in the contextual layer are used to validate artifacts. They will contain a subset of the attributes of the artifacts. Some examples of contextual views are:

- Business strategy view;
- Business drivers view;
- Risks view;
- Assumptions view.

3.2.27 Contextual Level Wrap-Up

It seems mind boggling, doesn't it? Two dozens of different topics to think about, work on, and validate to enable yourself to start with the architecture. And yes, it is a lot of work. On the other hand, we are convinced that you will agree that all of these topics make sense, and will provide guidance to the architecture work. 'Garbage in – garbage out' is very applicable here. Allocate sufficient time to work on the contextual material. Be genuinely interested in your engagement. In our experience it can take up to 40% of the project duration to get the contextual material in the state it needs to be. Manage expectations regarding this and make the gathered contextual information (and therewith related work) visible. Stakeholders are often not aware that all these preparation oriented topics are required, and they may feel uneasy because they do not see results in the early stages of the engagement. However, it is worth noting that many businesses gain real value from this effort, finding that the output from the contextual work for the first time gives them a clearly defined and structured understanding of their business or IT, especially through the goal hierarchy, the organization of architecture principles, and the baseline architecture (e.g. application landscape).

3.3 Business Architecture

3.3.1 Overview

The business aspect area describes the business architecture in terms of business subjects like business goals, activities, roles, and resources. The outcome of the business aspect area is a series of business architecture components that describe processes, organizations, people, and resources.

Business architecture in IAF focuses on:

- Creating a complete and consistent set of business requirements, documented in terms of business services and their collaboration contracts;
- Defining criteria to be used for grouping services at logical level;
- Grouping business services into different logical component types: process components, organization components, governance components. If desired, actors can be defined by grouping roles;
- Allocating logical components to real life physical business organization units, job descriptions, etc. in the physical level;
- Creating the business implementation guidelines. They contain the objectives and constraints regarding implementation from a business viewpoint, thus providing guidance to migration and implementation planning.

3.3.2 Business Conceptual Artifacts

Beside business services and their collaboration contracts we have defined a number of specific artifacts for the conceptual business architecture. Most of the specific artifacts are aimed at understanding the business in such a way that the definition of a complete and consistent set of business services can be validated. Experience has shown us that different organizations prefer different starting points for business service definition. Some prefer to start with the definition of business objects. Others prefer to start with business roles.

To explain the different approaches to business service identification we will initially describe the artifacts and then elaborate on the different approaches.

A *business object* is a physical resource used by the business that is significant to the architecture. Typical business objects are containers & trucks (transport industry), oil & steel (manufacturing industry), and contracts & money (financial industry).

Object contracts describe how business services use business objects, e.g. reading, writing or transforming an insurance proposal.

Business event. In computing an event is an action that is usually initiated outside of a system and has to be handled by the system. Business events therefore are actions that the business and its supporting IT must react on. Examples of business events are 'order placement of an article by a customer', 'request of a quote by that same customer', or 'the receipt of a payment from a customer via the bank'.

A *business activity* is a business task or group of business tasks that are undertaken by the business to achieve a well defined goal. Business activities are a description of WHAT the business does in order to meet its goals. They are implementation independent (i.e. independent of any organizational structure or process) and have clearly defined objectives in transforming an initial state to another state. A typical business service in the oil industry would be 'interpreting geographic data to find possible oil reserves'.

Business goals describe what the business needs to achieve in order to fulfill its business objectives. A business goal is an implementation independent, fundamental, and unique contribution to the business mission. The business goal is the 'WHY' objective for any business activity.

Business goals provide a reference baseline for comparing current state and future desired state.

They support the definition of results related targets for the organization. The goal of 'interpreting geographic data to find possible oil reserves' is probably 'finding new oil reserves'.

A *business role* performs a business activity. Roles may also have accountabilities for goals (although there will be corresponding governance activities for those goals). Roles should not be associated with people or systems as people have multiple roles. Roles are independent of implementation but are still needed to support the activities. Roles relate to specific activities and support the same business goal as the activity.

3.3.2.1 Business Service Identification

A Business service characterizes a unique 'element of business behavior' in terms of a business activity, undertaken by a specific role that together support a specific business goal. Business objects are used by business services. The way they are used is documented through object contracts. Business events trigger business services, which in turn can trigger other business services to provide the requested result. All these artifacts have been defined to meet two requirements. The first is to be able to demonstrate completeness and consistency. The second is to accommodate different customer preferences toward describing the business.

Experience has proven that combining activities, goals and roles to define services leads to a complete and consistent identification of the services. Because if you start with one of the three and use the other two to check and amend the identified services, you end up with a triple check, which incorporates what has to be done, why it has to be done and who will be doing it. This understanding will then help to define IS and TI services as well.

Business events and business objects are often used to assist in the identification of business activities.

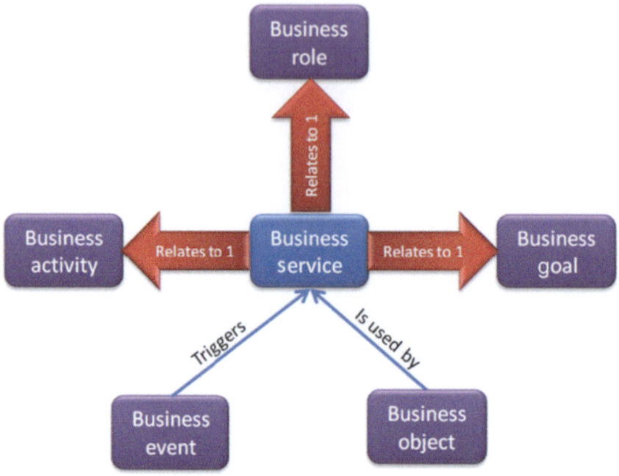

There are a number of orders in which the different artifacts can be used to identify business services. Five of the most common ones are described below.

Business Object Based Approach This approach starts with identifying business objects and determining which activities can be derived from these objects. So business object 'paper order' could result in business activities 'accept order', 'verify ordering customers credit', 'register order', etc. The business object 'stock item' could result in the activities 'validate stock item quantity', 'collect stock item', 'register new stock item', etc.

This initial list of business activities is the basis for further double check and amendment. Very often we define business roles as a second step. We determine which activities can be related to a business role, check if they are in the list, and add them if needed. In case of our example, we could define the role 'order picker' which executes activities 'collect stock item' and 'transport stock item to packing area'. This last activity is not present yet, and will therefore be added to the list. Finally we would define the business goals. We use the business activities and business goals to create the set of business services. Of course it will happen that missing activities, roles, and goals will be discovered during business service definition. We just add them and always check if they lead to the discovery of even more omissions.

This approach is obviously used when business objects are very important and relevant. We see this in organizations with many physical goods, like manufacturing and transportation companies.

Business Role Based Approach In contrast to the business object based approach, this one skips defining business objects and the initial list of activities related to the objects. It starts with defining roles and the activities related to each role. After that the business goals are created. The activities and goals are the basis for service definition.

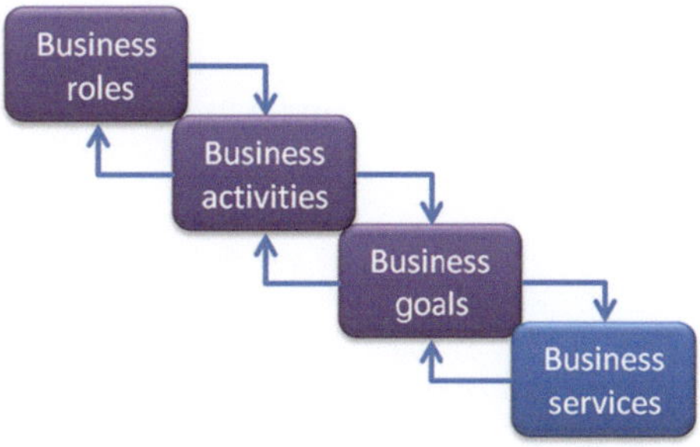

We see this approach in particular in 'information intense' organizations like the finance industry and government.

Business Goal Based Approach There are cases when a fundamental analysis of the organization is required. Often this is the fact when (a) effectiveness is a prominent driver or (b) visibility of the architecture's value contribution to a strategy is important. The business goal approach takes this fundamental approach because it focuses on **why** things are done and establishes a clear link between strategy and business services. If something does not contribute to the overall business mission, it is not needed.

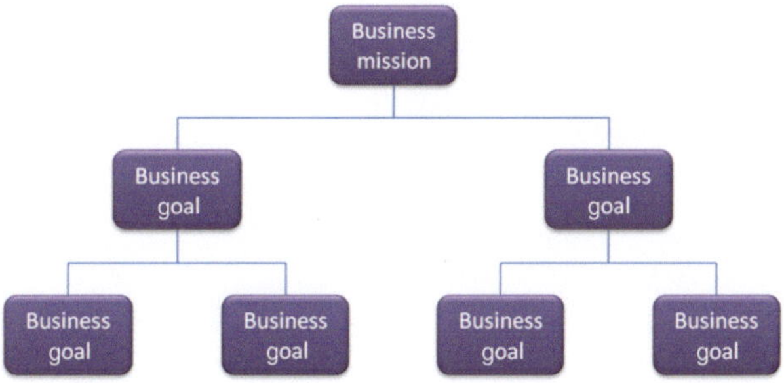

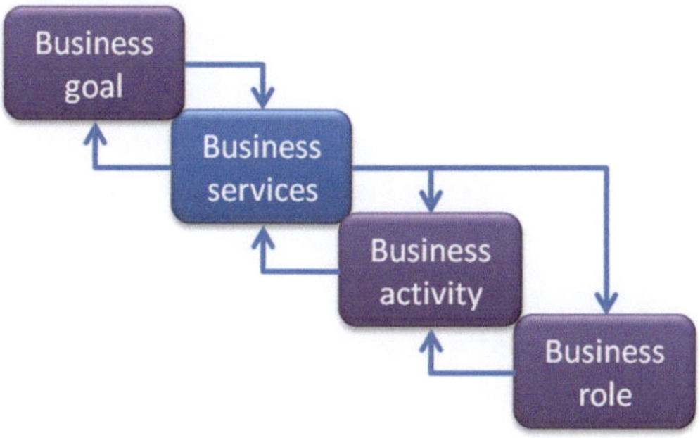

In this case we start with the creation of a 'goal hierarchy'. We determine which high level goals are required to achieve the business mission or strategy. In turn we determine which sub-goals are needed to achieve these goals at the higher level. This continues until we have reached the level of detail required to start defining business services. We derive roles and activities from the services and ensure all artifacts are complete and consistent.

An example of a goal hierarchy from the IAF course material provides good insight in what a goal hierarchy is. It describes the business goals an Eskimo fisherman has in making a living by providing food for an arctic restaurant.

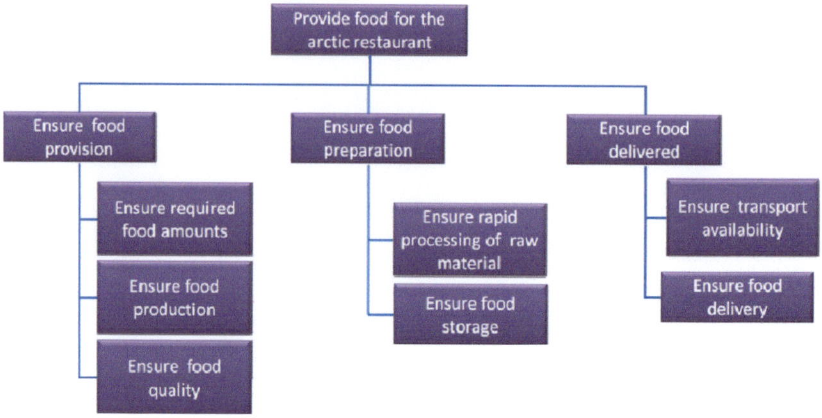

Business Event Based Approach The business event based approach is executed the same way as the business object based approach. The difference is that we start with identifying business activities based on identified and defined business events instead of business objects. As events are very often limited to those events that enter the organization, we use business roles to determine the activities that are not exposed to the outside world and use business goals to check for completeness and consistency.

Event modeling and the event based approach are commonly encountered in organizations, that (a) are value chain oriented and have chosen to work with end-to-end value chains like 'book to bill' and 'build to order', (b) focus on straight through processing, or (c) have activities that are more passive or activities that strongly depend on external events.

Business Process Based Approach The business process based approach is the most appropriate when a customer is very process oriented, especially if he already has future state or baseline process models available.

Process steps can be seen as candidate business services. If you can link a 'one activity, one role, and one goal' – combination to a process step, the process step complies to the criteria of a business service, and you can document the service. However if the criteria cannot be met, you might need to split the process step – or merge it with another one – to find a 'true' business service.

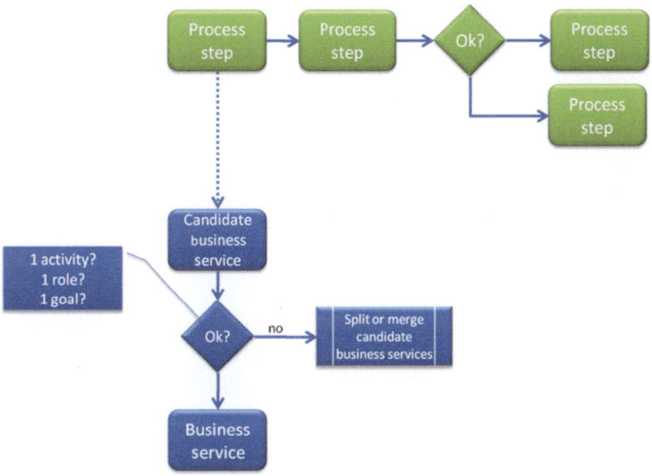

Why do this re-engineering style of business service definition? It makes sure that the process steps get all the characteristics of a business service, and become service oriented. Process based organizations tend to be relatively hard to change, as process steps are closely linked together. Ensuring process steps become true business services makes them relatively loosely coupled and thus helps in making an organization more flexible.

3.3.2.2 Business Goal

A business goal, as the 'WHY' objective for any business activity, defines what the business needs to achieve in order to fulfill its business objectives and ultimately its mission.

Examples:

Defining business goals is not always as easy as it seems. In practice it takes participants from the business a while to get used to thinking in terms of 'why something has to be done'. Besides that a lot of things have become implicit in the minds of business people, so the architect has to actually 'knowledge engineer' the business goals out of the brains of the specialists. Normally the business participants become really enthusiastic after they have gone through the learning curve. They see the value of business goals, and especially of a business goal hierarchy. Such a goal hierarchy helps to visualize the business services contribution to achieving the business mission.

3.3.2.3 Business Role

A business role ('who') performs a business activity, being responsible for the execution. Roles are associated with actors like people or systems and they usually have a many-to-many relationship.

Examples:

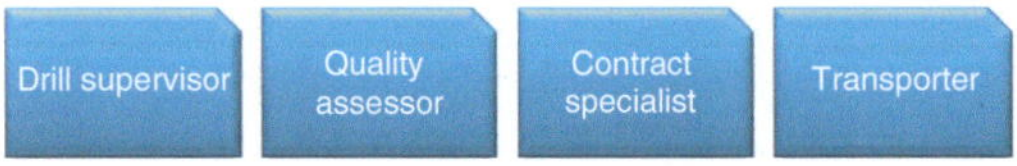

The added value of the business role concept – enabling many to many relationships between roles and actors – provides you with the option to create 'solution alternatives' for actors; you can combine different sets of roles into actors, resulting in people doing different things. Of course you do not have to do this. You can define roles that end up in having a one to one relationship with actors if you do not need to mix and match what people will be doing.

3.3.2.4 Business Activity

A business task or group of business tasks ('WHAT') that are undertaken by the business to achieve a well defined goal is called a business activity. Based on the architecture engagement's nature the granularity of business activities can differ, ranging from 'drilling a hole to find oil', 'convey consumer satisfaction surveys' to 'endorse accepted escalations'.

Examples:

Commonly business activities are the easiest to collect. People can easily tell you what they are doing. They do not always understand why they do it. They are also not always aware of the things they actually are responsible for either.

However you have to be aware of one pitfall when collecting business activities. People tend to focus on what they are doing now, not what they will be doing in the future. So if your architecture involves a large change of business activities, it might be better to derive activities from the business goals to enhance 'blue sky' thinking.

3.3.2.5 Business Event

A business event is any observable occurrence, or an extraordinary occurrence, that has significance to a business. Business events are used to 'trigger' business activities. Typical examples would be 'birthday notifications in the world of CRM', 'marriage or promotions in the world of Insurance', or 'constellations of money transfers used for detecting fraud'.

Other examples:

The artifact 'business event' has been introduced into IAF as part of version 4.5. In the past we used another construction to document business events. We defined business services that were external to the system and defined collaboration contracts between the external and internal services. Although in theory this was an acceptable approach, we still got a lot of discussion about it. So we decided to get more in line with what was happening in the industry regarding event modeling.

3.3.2.6 Business Object

A business object is a physical resource used or consumed by the business that is significant to the architecture: transport, raw materials for manufacture, etc. Business objects may be or infer information objects like client or contracts.

Examples:

Business objects tend to be the most important in industry sectors that have a lot to do with physical goods. Transport, manufacturing and retail are good examples. Listen what the business people are talking about. If their focus is on objects instead of activities, then you should consider taking the business object based approach when identifying business services.

3.3.2.7 Business Object Contract

A business object contract describes how a business service uses a business object. Different business services may make different use of a business object for example 'fleet management' will regard 'trucks' differently from a 'shipping department'.

Another example:

Business object contracts provide valuable information later on in the architecture engagement. They will simplify the creation of an information interaction model in the conceptual information architecture phase. So if you define them here with sufficient detail, you will benefit later on.

3.3.2.8 Business Service

A business service characterizes a unique 'element of business behavior' in terms of a business activity, undertaken by a specific role that together support a specific business goal. More information on identifying and defining business services can be found in Sect. 3.3.2.1.

Examples:

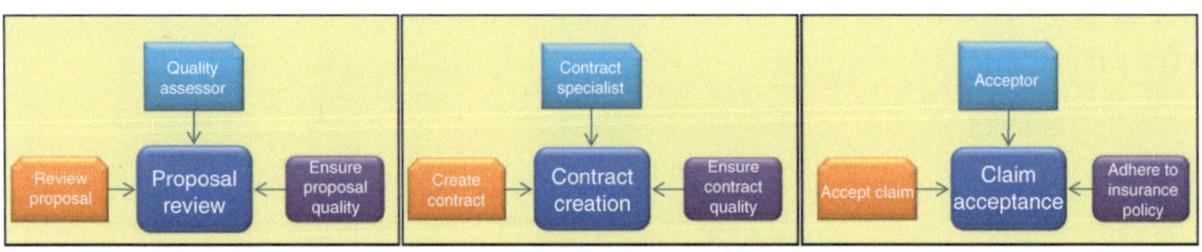

The trick behind business services is using the right level of granularity that is in line with the architecture objectives. Defining business services at the level used in the example for a whole enterprise can easily lead to the definition of thousands of services. In situations like that it might be sufficient to define services at a higher level, like 'order management' and 'claims processing'. There is no straightforward answer to granularity. One rule of thumb is to stay as high as possible, simply because that will make the architecture less complex. You can also consider to 'zoom in' on specific areas that need more attention because they are more complex or make the difference between successful and failing companies. 'Zooming in' is done by defining services at a more detailed level in that area. However by doing this you have to manage the risk that people will get confused about the granularity and start discussions. Therefore communicate clearly and frequently why you are combining different granularity levels in your architecture.

3.3.2.9 Business Domain

Value chains (or parts of them), parts of an organization, and other subject areas of a business can be positioned as business domains. Usually they consist of a collection of business services contributing to a joint, certain higher business goal.

Example:

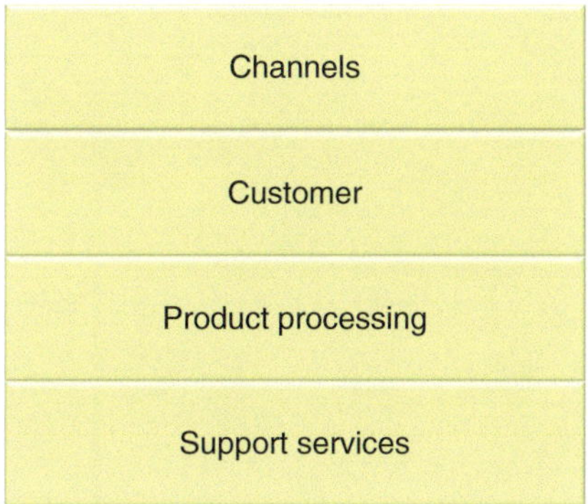

Sect. 2.4.2.7 describes reasons for having business domains. It is important to choose domains that stakeholders can relate to, especially because it is a best practice to use them as background while communicating. This background provides an anchor point for readers. This context helps them understand what you are communicating more easily.

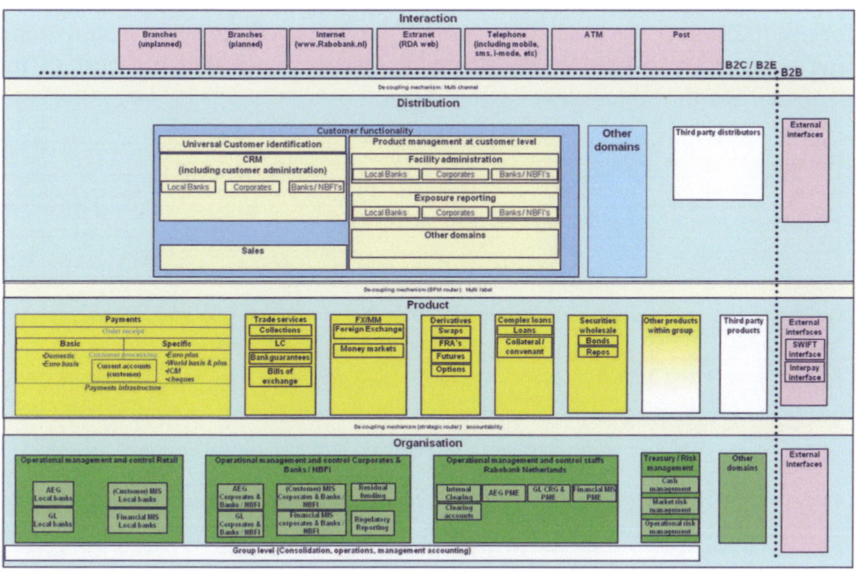

This is the domain model for a large bank. In the next figure it is used as a background to show how a process will flow through the various parts of the system.

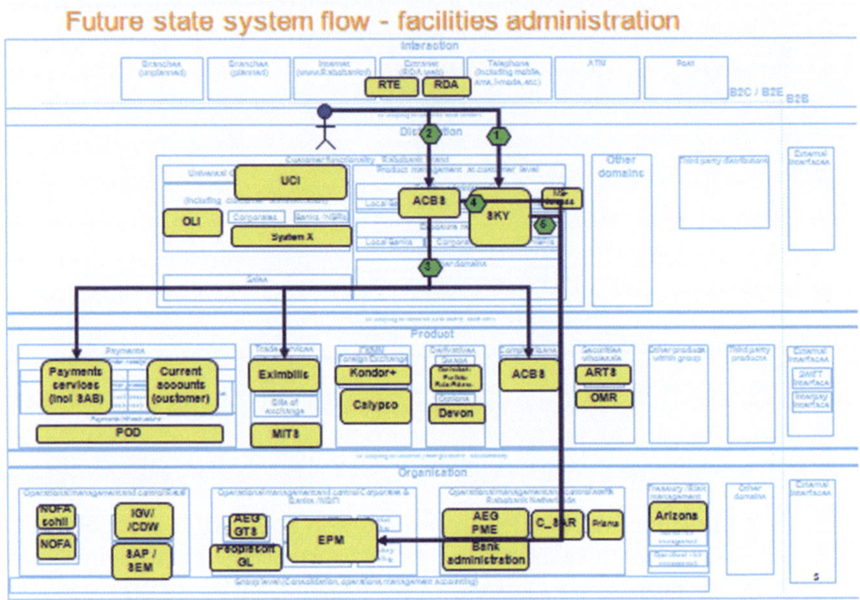

3.3.2.10 Business Service Collaboration Contract

Business services interact with each other. These interactions and their nature are described in business service collaboration contracts. They form the basis for negotiating service level agreements. To understand the depth of collaboration contracts you need to see some of the attributes that are part of the template. See the table below.

Description	*Describe the collaboration contract*
Result	*Describe the outcome that will be exposed to whom it concerns*
Throughput	*Describe the average required throughput*
Throughput period	*Describes the throughput period.* <second/ minute/ hour/ day/ week>
Growth	*Describe the expected growth in percentage.* %
Growth period	*Describes the growth period.* <second/ minute/ hour/ day/ week/ month/ year>
Service window	*Opening hours, describes when the service should be available*
Peak profile short term	*Describes the peak profile for the short term period.* <standard office/ morning peak/ afternoon peak/ flat>
Peak profile long term	*Describes the peak profile for the long period.* <standard week/ month end peak/ month begin peak/ mid month peak/ flat/ quarter end peak/ year end peak/ something else>
Characteristics	*Describe the characteristics of the contract.* <immediate response required/ delayed response possible (within response limits)/ transactional/ batch/ conversational>
Response requirements	*Describes the normal time a service/component request should response.* <<1 second/ >1 <5 seconds/ > 5 seconds < 10 minutes/ >1 hour < 1 day/ < 1 week>

Quality of information required	*Describe the required quality of the information. Should the response be real time, info must not be older than 1 day or 1 week, etc.*
Contract control requirements	*Describe the control requirement of the contract.* <control required every time the contract is activated/ logging of contract activation & results insufficient/ no contract control requirements>
Result control requirements	*Describe the result requirement of the contract.* <no result control required/ result control based on periodic checks/ result control required every time the contract is supporting>
Importance	*Describe the importance of the contract.* <failure allowed if only quality degrades/ must complete within response times>

It is important to document these attributes as much as possible, as they are the basis for all collaboration contracts down the line, especially when developing solution architectures. This is especially so for solution architectures. It will not always be possible to get all this information for enterprise level engagements. Try to focus on throughput and growth, together with service windows in that situation. Most of the time that will be sufficient. If you cannot get the information, use the good old architect's solution: make assumptions and get them validated!

3.3.2.11 Business Interaction Model

The business interaction model illustrates business services and their interaction and therefore usually consist of business services, their collaboration contracts, and relevant business events.

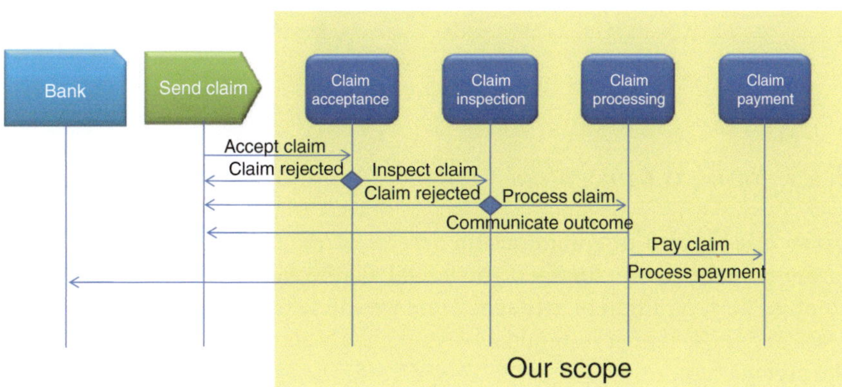

There has been much debate about this model. Is it a view or an artifact? Of course in its essence it is a view because it communicates existing artifacts. However this model is of such importance to the understanding of how the business wants to work that it fundamentally is an artifact. Thus we decided to position the business interaction model as an artifact.

Interaction models often copycat UML drawing techniques. The example diagram above is based on a UML sequence diagram, but communications diagrams or IDEF0 function models work just as well. It all comes down to personal and client preference which model you use.

These formal modeling techniques do not always work at enterprise level. Using a domain model and superimposing business services and their interaction on top of it is a well known way of creating high level business interaction models, as depicted in the figure below.

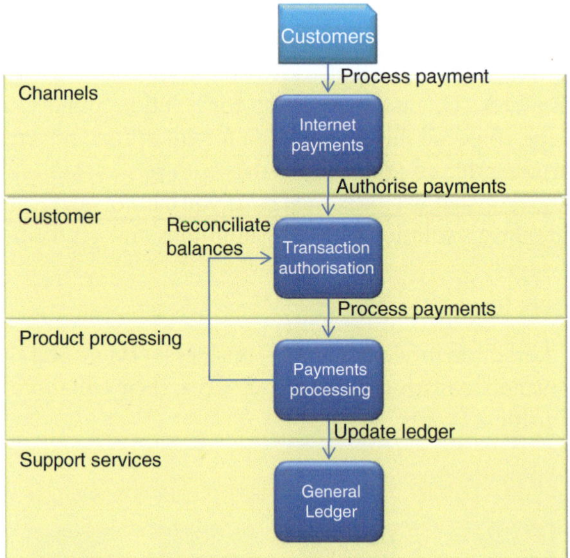

3.3.3 Business Conceptual Views

Views can be used to communicate aspects of the artifacts in the conceptual business architecture. In fact you could define views for each artifact, or combinations of different artifacts. Here we will focus on some of the common ones, and those that you should always explicitly chose to create or leave out of the architecture.

3.3.3.1 Business Domain View

Business domains have been specifically introduced into IAF to communicate topics from the conceptual business architecture. The enterprise level business interaction model in the prior paragraph is just one example. Communicating business goals by showing which business domain they belong to is just one example. Mix and match artifacts and business domains as you desire to communicate your messages.

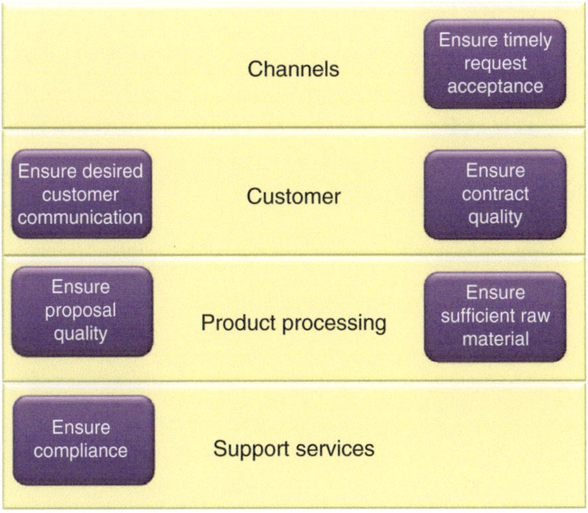

3.3.3.2 Business Service View

The business service view can be used to communicate specific aspects of business services. An example is showing which business services are in scope, and which ones are out of scope. Of course you can also use this view to communicate things like service times or expected growth percentages.

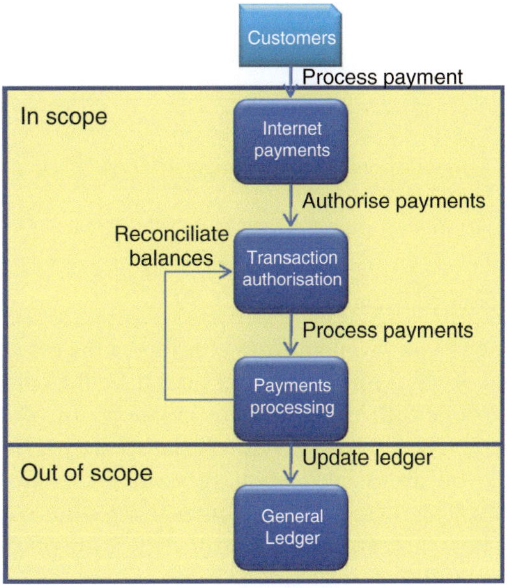

3.3.3.3 Business Service Gap View

The business service gap view illustrates the gap between the as-is and the to-be situation of a set of business services. We advise you to adopt the visualization technique below. TOGAF also uses this technique. The model and the size of its cells help you to stick to the main changes in the architecture as you are forced to headline what you are communicating.

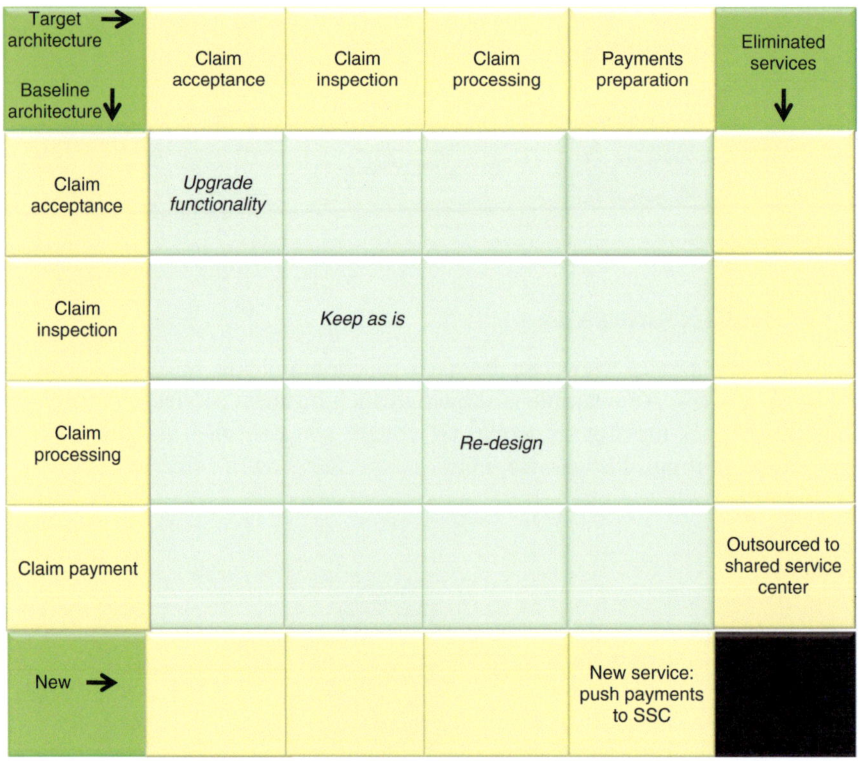

3.3.3.4 Business Service Security View

One of the two views you should always consider is the security view. In other words you should check if all business services have the correct security attributes. This can be done with a view that you create (a) for yourself to ensure the architecture's quality, or (b) to show others the security attributes so they can validate them. If you are using a tool, very often this view can be created automatically. It will show security attributes using color codes. The example on the left shows how this can work. Of course there are other ways of creating the view, as shown in the example on the right.

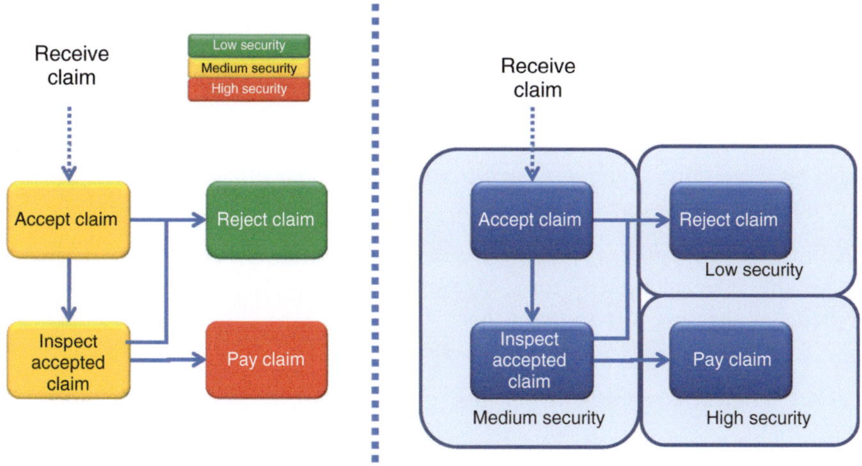

3.3.3.5 Business Service Governance View

The second view you should always decide upon is the governance view. It has the same intention as the security view, but it visualizes the different governance attributes like availability, performance, restorability etc.

Very often the governance view is also called the non-functional requirements view.

3.3.4 Business Logical Artifacts

The completion of the conceptual business architecture provides us with sufficient ingredients to create the logical business architecture. The most important thing that needs to be done is to create logical business components. The basic approach to creating components is described in Sect. 2.4.2.10. Grouping criteria need to be derived from the architecture principles and the different component types need to be created. In practice we experience that principles frequently lead to one of three basic grouping approaches. These approaches fall nicely in line with the competition strategies defined by Tracy & Wiersema in 1995. They are customer intimacy, operational excellence, and product leadership. The first two are the most common ones. Companies tend to prefer customer intimacy in the client facing parts of the organization, and operational excellence in the more back office and production oriented parts. Customer intimacy is all about effectiveness, making sure that everything the customer might want or ask is at hand.

Grouping for effectiveness regarding the customer can be done by analyzing the business goals that are related to services, and grouping the customer related ones together. Operational excellence is all about efficiency. When you need to achieve efficiency within logical business components you need to look at combinations of business roles and business activities that have strong affinity with each other. Product leadership requires focus on innovation along with ensuring a fast time to market for new products. So here the focus is on flexibility and speed. Speed is achieved through effectiveness in the production process. Flexibility is implicitly achieved by the service orientation that has been applied to the business services.

Defining the grouping criteria, derived from the principles, is still part of 'the art of architecture', along with topics like selecting the right granularity of services. Practice is the only way to learn this.

3.3.4.1 Logical Business Components

When working on a logical business architecture you commonly will have to answer a set of questions to be able to provide the information required to implement the changed business structures. The three most common topics you have to address are:

1. How are we going to deliver the desired results by grouping business services into process components?
2. How are we going to group the services into logical units of organization?
3. How are we going to group the services so they can be governed in the way desired?

These three questions can and often will lead to different groupings of the business services. An example is the easiest way to explain what you need to do here. As you can see, with just six business services you can easily come up with three different ways of setting up the logical business components.

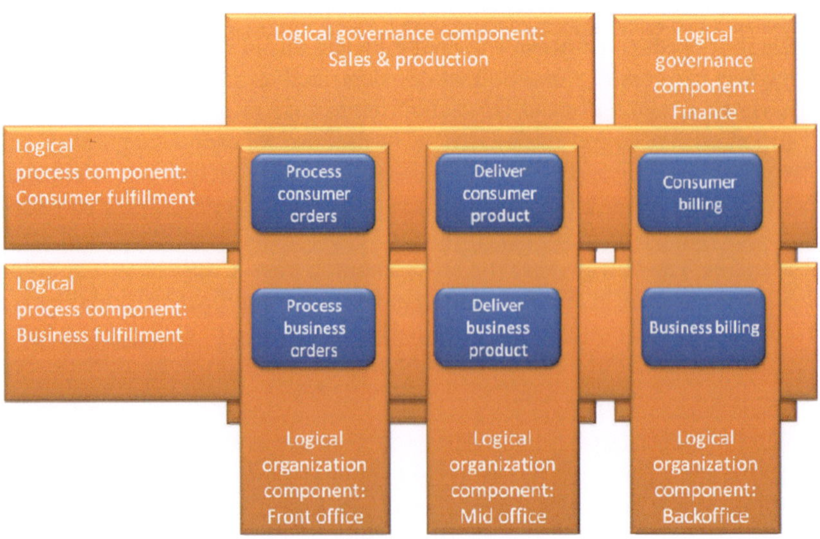

Often processes are constructed to deliver specific overall results, like in the example. There are two processes, 'consumer fulfillment' and 'business fulfillment'. They both create an end to end result, a delivered product together with a bill.

As the example shows, processes are not always the best way to organize things, it often will be better to create a logical organization by grouping services together that do similar things. The logical components front office, mid office, and back office do that.

The way business services are organized is often also different from the way business services will be governed. In the example order processing services and product delivery services are grouped together to create one unit of governance, 'sales and production'. The logical governance component contains the same services as the logical organization component 'back office'.

The example shows that logical business architecture creates three types of logical business components: process, organization, and governance. Of course the grouping criteria for all three types of components should be derived from the principles. If the defined set of principles is insufficient to derive grouping criteria, define and validate additional principles.

Process components are the easiest to construct using the approach described in Sect. 3.3.4.

Organization components are often constructed by using existing or defining logical organization elements and cross referencing business services to them, based on criteria derived from principles.

Logical organization elements → Business services	Front Office	Mid office	Back office
Process consumer orders	●		
Process business orders	●		
Deliver consumer product		●	
Deliver business product		●	
Consumer billing			●
Business billing			●

Governance components can be defined using RACI mechanisms.

3.3.4.2 Logical Business Component Interaction Model

Logical business components and their interaction are illustrated in the logical business component interaction model.

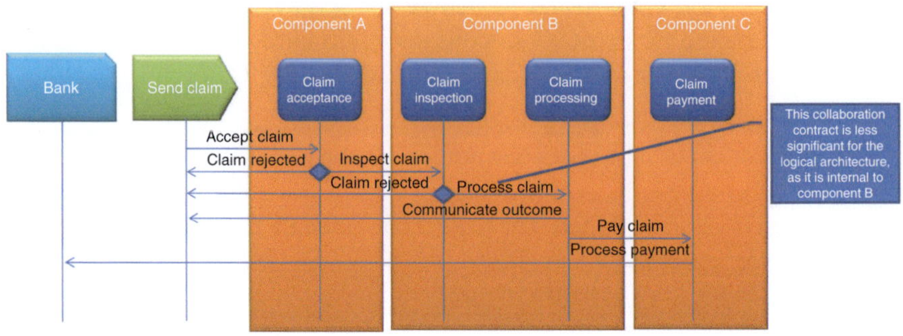

Of course this model is derived from the business interaction model. Very often component interaction models can be made simpler than service interaction models, as some of the collaboration contracts between services will become 'internal' to one component, and therefore become less important to show in this model. You just hide the internal complexity. A cleaned logical business component interaction model is shown in the figure below.

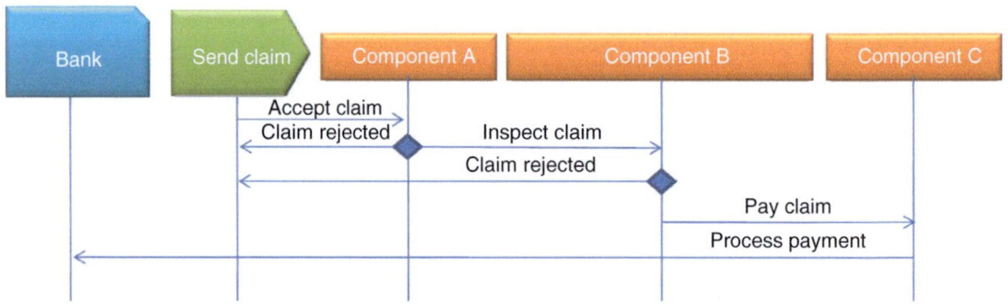

3.3.4.3 Logical Business Component Collaboration Contract

A logical business component collaboration contract documents the agreed interaction between logical business components. It is very common to encounter multiple collaboration contracts between two logical components. We advise you to check if the collaboration contracts can be merged to simplify the logical architecture.

You can merge collaboration contracts if the behavior and communication mechanisms are practically equal. Look at service windows, throughput, response requirements, etc. to determine the ability to merge.

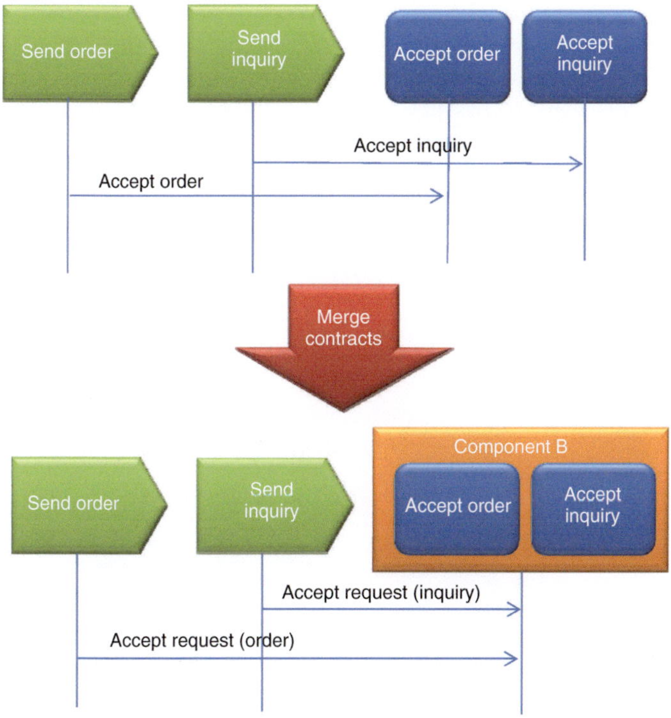

3.3.4.4 Actor

An Actor is someone/something that is performing a collection of roles.

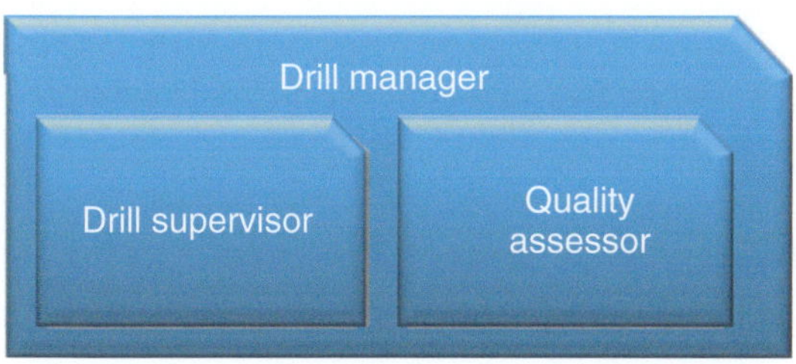

As this is another form of grouping, you should also go back to the principles, define grouping criteria and group roles into actors in such a way that your choices are derived from principles.

3.3.5 Business Logical Views

3.3.5.1 Business Solution Alternatives

During the process of creating a business architecture you will be confronted with possible directions and alternatives forcing you to make or advice on decisions. To underpin your argument it comes in handy to document these different solution alternatives (input for proper decision making on which solution alternatives to choose) and made decisions (log book). This view shows (a) different options in grouping logical business components based on different criteria, and (b) the pro's and con's of this grouping.

Solution Alternative A: Effectiveness focus, actors are able to perform all activities.

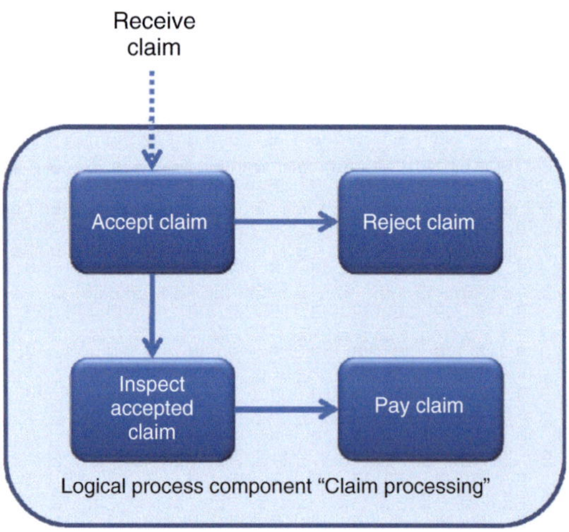

Or Solution Alternative B: Efficiency focus, actors are able to perform a small set of activities. They can focus on efficiency.

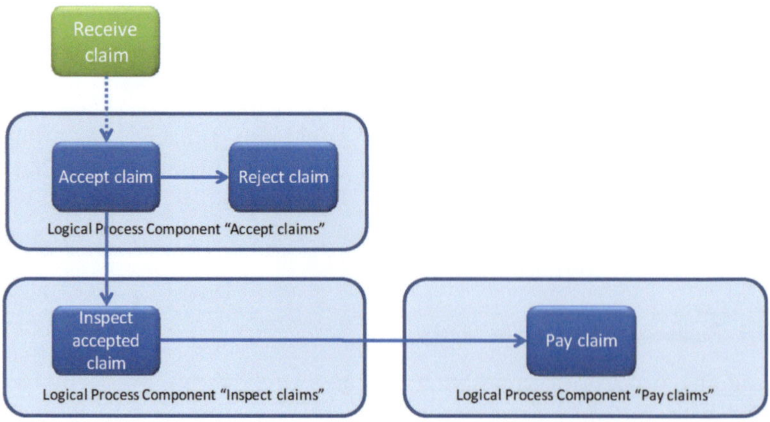

The result of solution alternatives is the agreement on one alternative that will be used as basis for the architecture.

3.3.5.2 Logical Business Component View

The logical business component view contains information about a subset of logical business component attributes relevant for communicating with a specific target group. This view mainly helps to show combinations of the different types of process components, e.g. which process components are governed the same way, or which process components have a relationship with which organization components. The figure below is an example of showing relationships between process and organization components.

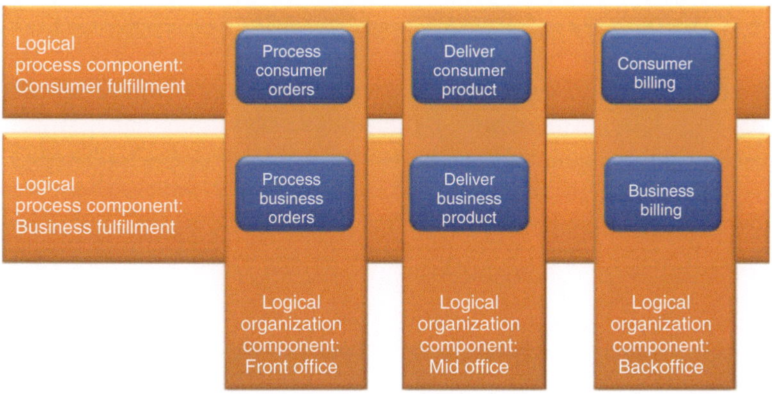

3.3.5.3 Logical Business Component Gap View

This view is useful to identify the difference between baseline and target within a logical business architecture, supporting discussions on how to reach the future state. It describes the change that is expected. See Sect. 3.3.3.3 for an example. Just exchange the business services with logical business components. Of course the gap view can be used to show what will change for all three types of logical business components. However, the process gap view is the most common one.

3.3.5.4 Logical Business Component Security View

This view provides insight into the security requirements of services within a component. Commonly color coding, as shown in the example below, is the most effective way to construct this view. We highly recommend you to always consider creating this view, as experience shows it often prevents surprises.

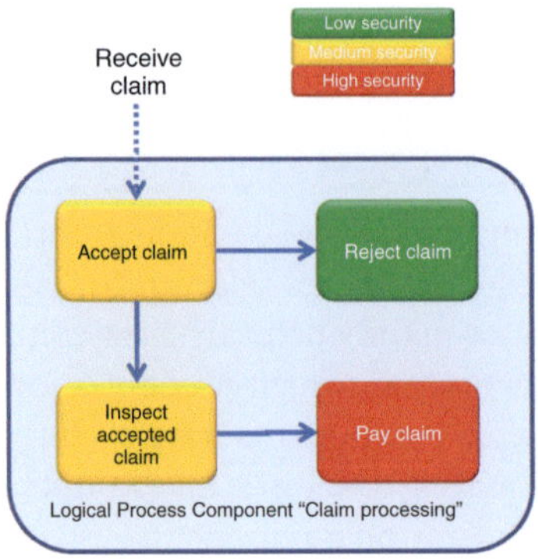

This example compares the security impact of solution alternative A (illustrated above) versus solution alternative B (illustrated below). Alternative A will lead to the whole component requiring high security as it contains a service with that requirement. Alternative B will lead to two components with medium security and one with high security.

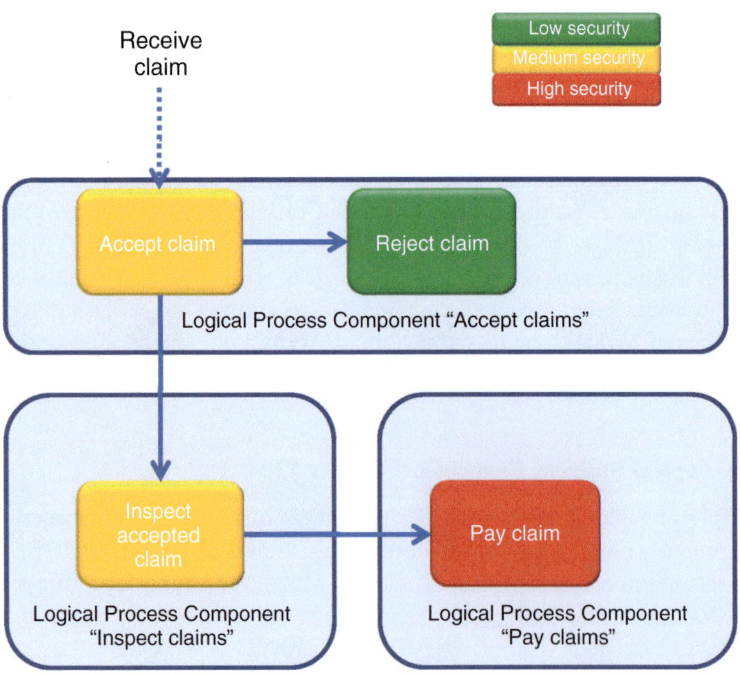

3.3.5.5 Business Design Decisions

During (and after) the project, stakeholders are interested in agreed design decisions (made during the architecture engagement) and their impacts. The view's content ensures decisions' traceability, both backwards ('why was it made?') and forwards ('what is its impact?'). A design decision is similar to a principle in its specification, operation, and use. The key difference is that a design decision is taken by the project, whereas a principle encapsulates external decisions for use by a project.

It is turning into a best practice to document design decisions in terms of architecture principles. The rationale is that you end up with one spot in which people can look when they want to understand why things were done the way they were.

3.3.5.6 Logical Business Component Governance View

This view works the same way as a security view, but provides insight into the governance attributes of a component's services. We also recommend you to consider this view, as it has proven to provide additional surprises, which you need to take into account.

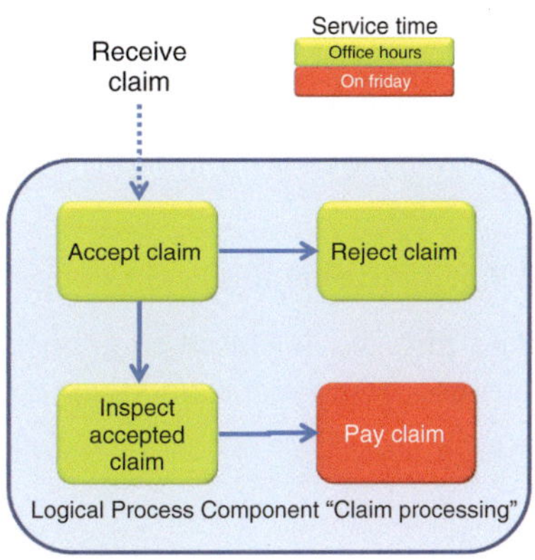

3.3.6 Business Physical Artifacts

3.3.6.1 Physical Business Component

Physical architecture is all about mapping[2] logical components to real life, tangible physical components. In this case we are talking about business components, so what we need to do is allocate them to real life physical business elements that will be responsible for delivering the services that are contained in the components.

It is very common to allocate logical organization components to physical parts of the business and then determine which logical process components will be executed by each physical organization component.

[2] The terms 'mapping' and 'allocating' are both used in this context. They are synonyms.

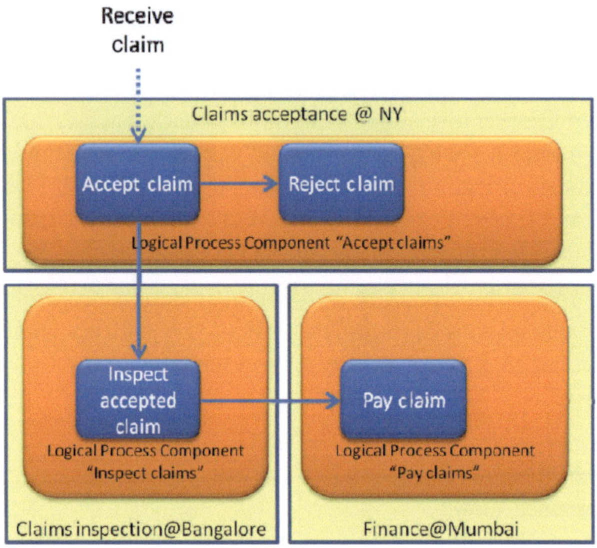

3.3.6.2 Physical Business Component Interaction Model

The physical business component interaction model visualizes the physical business components and their collaboration (contracts).

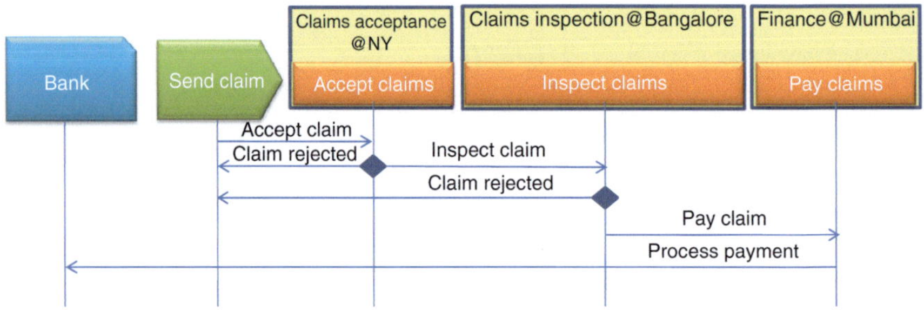

3.3.6.3 Business Standards, Rules and Guidelines

Physical business components and their collaboration are just one part of the physical business architecture. Just as important are the business standard, rules, and guidelines (SRGs). In effect they are a list of the topics that you will use to ensure a business architecture's implementation is done the way you want it to be done. In other words they are the criteria you will use to validate business architecture's implementation.

Typical examples for business SRGs are

- All financial services are to be centralized in Mumbai;
- All processes need to be modeled in ARIS[3];
- Decisions should always be based on a peer review;
- All processes should live up to the separation of concerns.

Make sure that the implementers of an architecture are aware of the usage of business SRGs. If possible, pro-actively coach them in the application of SRGs to prevent non conformance.

3.3.6.4 Business Tasks (Specifications)

Business tasks are job, role, and task descriptions, based on the identified roles and actors. They are usually required (even often requested by the human resources department) to find and align resources which will perform these business tasks.

Topic	Description
Task name	Drill manager
Location	Valdez, Alaska
Services to be delivered	Drill supervision and quality assessment
Skills required	Certified drill manager level C ISO 9000-4 qualified
Task complexity level	High
Salary level	€90–120 K

3.3.6.5 Business Migration Specifications/Implementation Guidelines

There might be circumstances in which you do not want to document the way the business should migrate in terms of standards, rules, and guidelines. The most common reason is the existence of a formal process for approving SRGs within an organization, which might take a lot of time and thus delay the architecture's implementation. In that case you can document business migration specifications and pass them on to the implementers.

Migration specifications often focus on the order in which things need to be done from an architectural viewpoint. An example:

Topic	Description
Specification	Implement claims payment before implementing claims acceptance and inspection
Rationale	It does not make sense to handle claims if you cannot pay them.

[3] http://www.aris.com

3.3.7 Business Physical Views

Many of the views described within the subchapter on logical business architecture can also be used to communicate the physical business architecture. They are:

- Physical solution alternatives;
- Physical business component view;
- Physical business component gap view;
- Physical business component security view;
- Physical business component governance view.

3.3.7.1 Business Cost View

Estimating business migration costs is a topic that just about always needs attention. Your stakeholders will be asking about costs from day 1. It has an important influence on decisions. Of course you can estimate costs from day 1 if you want to. As long as you get an OK from the primary client on the assumptions you will have to make, you should be able to proceed. We advise you to also clearly communicate how accurate your cost estimations will be. This helps to manage expectations. For some or other reason people always remember your first cost estimate. If you say it will cost 2 million during that first estimation exercise, that will stick in their mind. They will keep on referring to it later in the engagement. It is best practice to use a range when doing estimates early in the project. When you say 'It will be somewhere between 1.5 and 5 million' people tend to understand and remember much better that it is an estimate, and not a fact.

Topics to take into account when estimating business costs:

- Commercial and communications costs;
- Costs needed to change the organization, like facilities;
- Costs needed to change personnel, like training;
- Costs needed to change processes;
- Costs needed to facilitate works councils;
- Legal costs.

Cost group	Cost element	Price per unit	# units	Period 1	Period 2	Period 3	Period 4	Period 5	Period 6	Period 7	Period 8	Total costs
Commercial												
	Newsletter	1.500	1	1.500	1.500	1.500	1.500	1.500	1.500	1.500	1.500	**12.000**
	TV advertisements	25.000	4	100.000	100.000	100.000	100.000	100.000	100.000	100.000	100.000	**800.000**
Organisation												
	New building	50.000	1			50.000	50.000	50.000	50.000	50.000	50.000	**300.000**
Personnel												
	Culture training	3.000	25		75.000	75.000	75.000	75.000	75.000			**375.000**
Totals				101.500	176.500	226.500	226.500	226.500	226.500	151.500	151.500	**1.487.000**

Setting up a cost view like the one in the example anticipates different types of financial analysis that will be required. Return on investment (ROI) and Net Present Value (NPV) calculations are very common.

3.3.7.2 Physical Organization View

Sponsors and other stakeholders are interested in what the real life organization structure will look like, and what the different organization units will be doing. In collaboration with the assignment of business roles to physical actors this view can provide that insight. Related to the assignment of roles to physical actors.

Be careful when communicating these views. People can easily draw conclusions about topics like job redundancies from organization views, leading to rumors and unrest in the organization.

3.3.8 Business Architecture Wrap-Up

We have come to the end of the topic business architecture as part of IAF. We have defined and documented business requirements in terms of business services and their collaboration contracts. Business services were derived from one or more of the following artifacts in a conceptual business architecture: business goal, business role, business activity, business object, and business event.

We have created a logical business architecture by grouping these business services into three types of logical business components: process, organization, and governance.

We have allocated these logical business components to real life parts of the business, and created SRGs to ensure a business architecture gets implemented the way it is needed to.

On top of that we have created a substantial set of business views to communicate the architecture, to get it validated, and to get buy-in. It seems a good time to extend our work into the second architecture area in IAF, the information architecture.

3.4 Information Architecture

3.4.1 Overview

Business architecture focuses solely on business aspects, like processes, organization, and governance. It deliberately does not look at information aspects.

One of the main reasons for this is that we intend to reduce the complexity of the overall problem by splitting it up into smaller, less complex ones. Information architecture is all about information and communication aspects of business. Information architecture adds the information aspects to the business architecture. Information architecture starts by defining which information the business services need, create, and change to be able to deliver the defined service. Of course this information is essential to be able to understand the type of IT support required. After we understand the information processing requirements of business services, we will create a logical information architecture. We will apply principles of some specific forms of affinity analysis which might lead to refining our business architecture. This is due to information processing requirements we did not take into account yet. After that we will create a physical information architecture by allocating the logical components to physical ones and creating information architecture specific standards, rules, guidelines (SRGs) and migration guidelines.

3.4.2 *Information Conceptual Artifacts*

3.4.2.1 Information Object

An information object is the subject of communication for business services. The information object describes the information used or communicated by business information services. An information object is a source of information. It is not a description of data but rather indicates where data is used. An information object is independent of the media it is presented on. Information objects are characterized by statements that have the general form of:

A 'Blah' is a 'blur' that 'bleeps', for example:

STATEMENT: An ORDER is the request of a CUSTOMER to supply an ARTICLE.

Therefore an information object can be described by a collection of 'STATEMENTS'.

Describing information objects this way reduces ambiguity and leads to a common language that forms the basis of communication between the business and IT. It is very important to define information objects sufficiently. Many man years have been wasted on arguments about the meaning of something simple like 'customer'. Using this approach will help to build a business vocabulary or 'universe of discourse', in which all information objects are unambiguously defined. It will also help in finding synonyms (multiple words with the same meaning) and homonyms (one word with multiple meanings).

Some examples:

- A CLAIM is a request of a CUSTOMER to receive a PAYMENT based on an INSURANCE POLICY.
- A CUSTOMER is a natural or legal entity that has an existing INSURANCE POLICY with our organization.
- A PAYMENT is the transfer of funds to a CUSTOMER based on a valid CLAIM.
- An INSURANCE POLICY is a legal agreement between our organization and a CUSTOMER that states when a CLAIM can be made and how much the CUSTOMER will pay for it.

Information objects can be derived from business objects. The basic rule is that if the organization *wants to know something about* a business object, it becomes an information object. If business objects have not been defined you can use the business services as a start for defining information objects. An analysis of the business services will result in a set of candidate information objects. They are candidates because we need to distinguish between those that are essential, those that are related to specific roles, and those that have specific characteristics (object, non-object, information etc.) which differentiate them. These candidate information objects are then grouped into object type classes. The classes are: elementary, generalizations/specializations, aggregations, and classifications.

Generalizations. A is a generalization to B if the characteristics of A form a partial collection of B's characteristics. So a vehicle is the generalization of a motorized vehicle.

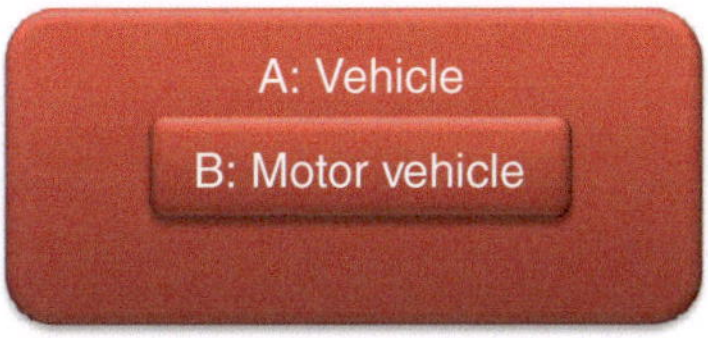

Specializations. B is A's specialization if A's characteristics form a subset of the characteristics specifying B. Thus a motor vehicle forms a specialization of vehicle.

Aggregations are combinations of 1 or more distinct object types into another object type. So A forms an aggregation of B, C… if any A element is constructed out of a B, C, … element . An example is that a maintenance check forms an aggregation of mechanic and motor vehicle.

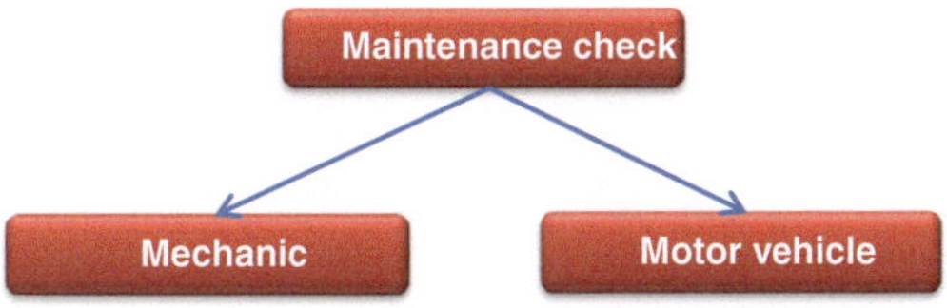

Classifications are the composition of object type classes according to a specified composition criteria. So

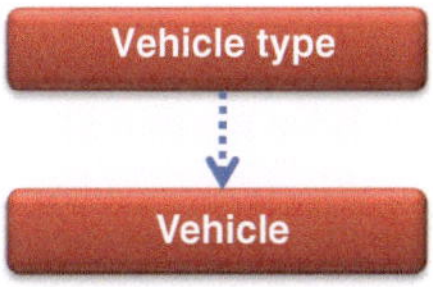

A forms a classification of B if every element of A forms a subset of B. An example is: VEHICLE TYPE forms a classification of VEHICLE.

Elementary information objects are those that do not belong to any of the other groups.

All the information objects can be visualized in an object model, see Sect. 3.4.3.1 for details.

You should not forget to add security and governance classifications to the information objects, besides defining ownership. The classifications will be used to make sure that the business information service classifications are in line with the information object classifications. Information ownership is needed to get decisions made regarding information usage, master data management, access rights, etc. Information ownership can be derived from business services that use the information (business information services, introduced in the next section).

Please note that an information object model will not be right in one pass. You will need an iterative approach.

3.4.2.2 Business Information Service

A business information service is a construct of a business service and the information objects it uses. A business service uses information objects as input (get), or changes (transform) or creates (write) them. Thus a business information service is a business service for which the relationship to information objects has been defined.

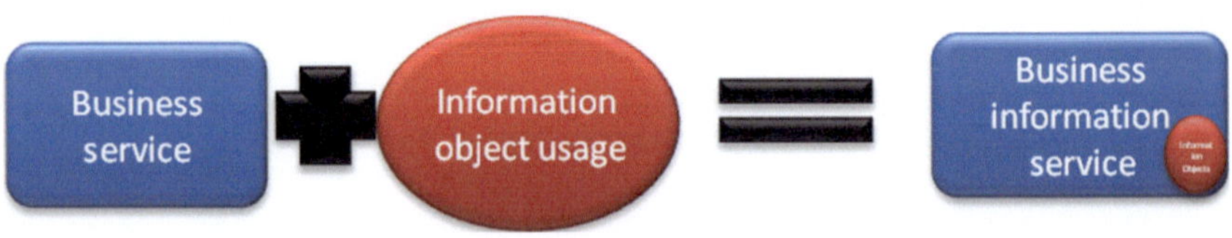

IAF purposely calls it a business information service to avoid confusion. Initially the term information service was used. In practice we discovered that many people associated the term with information objects, and not with the combination of business services and their information object usage. So be careful with terminology in this area when using synonyms.

A business information service changes the perspective on a business service. We are now looking especially at the information aspect of a business service.

3.4.2.3 Information Interaction Model

In its essence the information interaction model is a cross reference between business services and information objects. However, it is a special

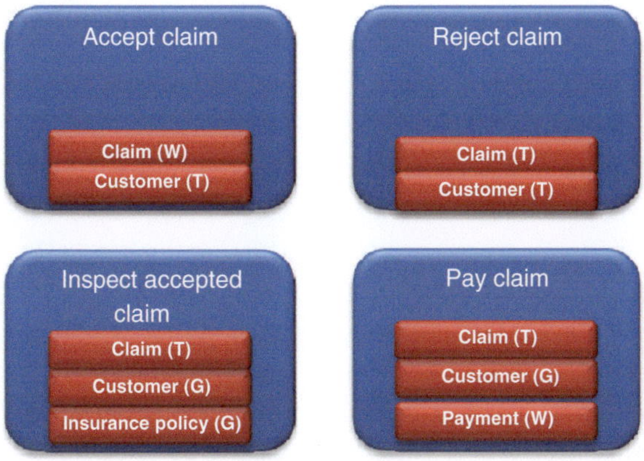

one. Instead of simply depicting that a business service and an information object have a relationship with each other by putting an 'x' in the cell, we use specific letters to depict what the usage of the information object by the business service will be. The letters we use are: 'T' (for transform) is used if an information object is changed, 'G' (for get) if the object is only read and not modified and 'W' (for write) if the object is newly created. This information is a prerequisite to create the models defined in information logical and to provide an IS architecture with sufficient information regarding information object usage by business services.

Information object → Business service ↓	Customer	Consumer order	Business order	Consumer product	Business product	Consumer bill	Business bill	Delivery schedule
Process Consumer orders	T	W		T				
Process Business orders	T		W		T			
Deliver consumer product	T	T						G
Deliver business product	T		T					G
Consumer billing	T					W		
Business billing	T						W	

In the example illustrated above business service 'process consumer orders' transforms information object 'customer' – to indicate the most recent date this customer has ordered something. The service writes an occurrence of information object 'consumer order' – as this is a new order. Finally the service transforms information object 'consumer product' – to update the amount of products that have been ordered.

The information interaction model for our claims example looks like this:

Information objects → Business services	Claim	Customer	Insurance policy	Payment
Accept claim	W	T		
Inspect accepted claim	T	G	G	
Reject claim	T	T		
Pay claim	T	G		W

The information interaction model is especially important when you are planning to create a logical information architecture as it is the major source of input for that. This interaction model provides understanding of the information exchange between business services and the shared usage of information. The information interaction model will help you in checking the completeness and scope of your architecture. If you find an empty column, you have an information object in scope, but no business services that use it. Either the information object should be out of scope or you missed some business service. A row can contain only 'Gs' and/or 'Ts'. This will mean that the information object is created by a business service that is out of scope of your architecture. In the example above this holds true for Insurance Policy. If you identify a row will no 'Gs', the information object will be used by a business service outside the scope of your architecture.

3.4.2.4 Business Information Service Collaboration Contract

Normally this is the same as the business service collaboration contract described in Sect. 3.3.2.10. If it is relevant, you can add information processing oriented attributes to the contract. For example you can indicate which objects are passed between the business information services, or indicate which messages are part of the communication. Adding this type of information to the contract is normally only done in solution level architectures. In enterprise/domain level architectures it is done in less.

3.4.2.5 Information Domain

Information domains are used to communicate information objects to any stakeholder or groups of stakeholders. The domains are groupings of information objects according to some criteria. Because you can have different criteria (for different stakeholders) you may end up with information domains that may overlap. That means an information object may belong to multiple information domains. Information domains have no additional purpose or meaning in IAF itself.

Criteria that you can consider to define the domains are:

- Ownership, who owns which objects;
- Usage, who uses which objects;
- Security classifications, how secure are which objects.

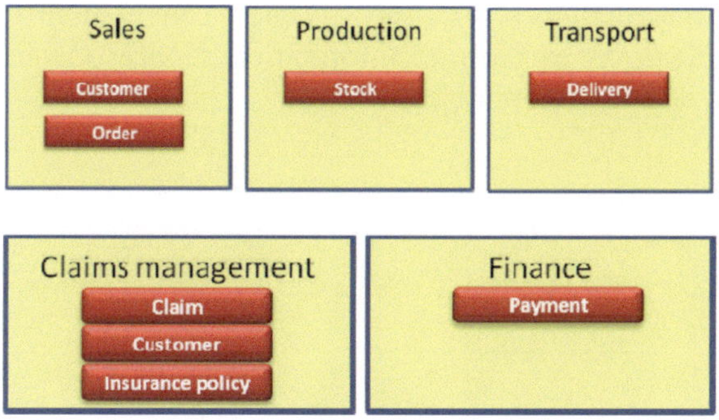

3.4.3 *Information Conceptual Views*

3.4.3.1 Information Object View

The information object view is one of the most common views in the conceptual information architecture. The way we visualize information object classifications as shown in Sect. 3.4.2.1 is used as a basis for this view.

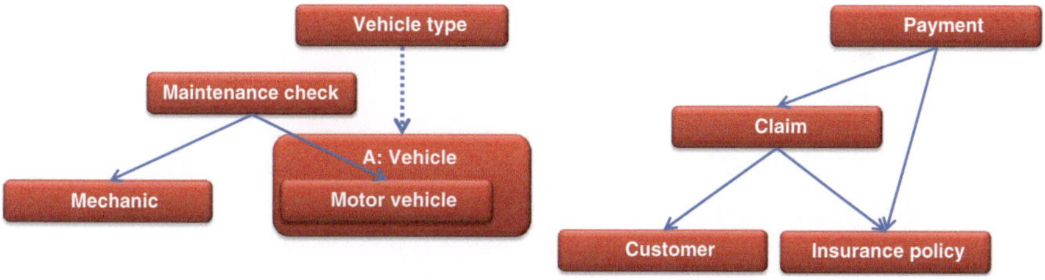

There has been much debate about the usage of data modeling techniques in information architecture. Those who oppose take the position that data modeling tends to go into too much detail for architecture – it makes communication with less technical stakeholders very difficult. They state it should happen during design. The proponents state that solution architecture does require data modeling techniques since it allows to grasp the essence of a problem. In IAF if you need to, you can use entity relationship modeling or UML data modeling techniques to create this view.

3.4.3.2 Business Information Service Security View

Very often information objects have their own security classifications, which are often determined through a formal security risk analysis, taking into account the sensitivity of the information for privacy, reputational risk, etc.

The business information service security view can be used to check if the security classifications of business information services are in line with the classifications of information objects.

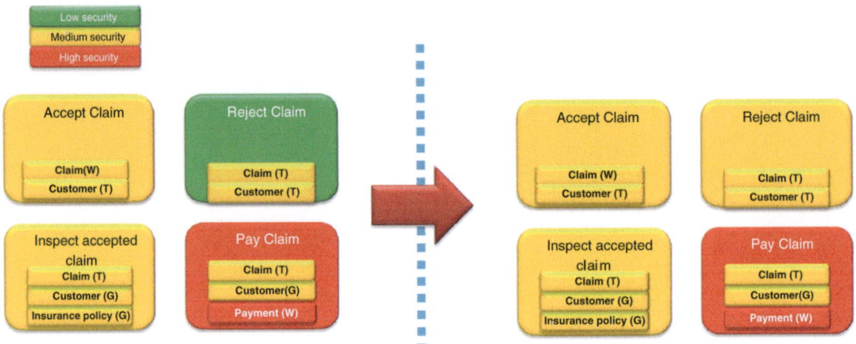

As you can see in the example we have had to 'upgrade' the security level of the business information service 'reject claim' from low to medium because of the information objects it uses. We did not have to change 'pay claim' because a business information service with high security will also be able to handle lower levels of security. Security of information objects is often expressed in terms of confidentiality, availability and integrity.

3.4.3.3 Other Views

A number of views in the conceptual information architecture are relatively obvious, and speak for themselves, as they work the same as the similar views in business architecture. A *business information service view* can be created to visualize business information services or specific aspects of them. A *business information service gap view* can be created to show the business information service gaps between the baseline and target architecture in the same way as described in Sect. 3.3.3.3. A *business information service governance view* can be used to visualize quality attributes of business information services as described in Sect. 3.3.3.5.

3.4.4 Information Logical Artifacts

Just like logical business architecture needs to define multiple types of logical components to address all required topics, logical information architecture contains two types of logical components. These component types are represented in 'structure models'. A structure model shows the components of a specific type, and the relationships between the components. There is a logical information component (LIC) structure model and a logical business information component (LBIC) structure model.

3.4.4.1 Logical Information Component

Business information services use information objects in different ways (get, transform, write). While constructing logical information components you look at the interdependencies of information objects from a business information service point-of-view. In other words you find out which business information services are necessary to get/transform/write information objects in order to get/transform/write other information objects. Clustering these information objects around their relationship to similar business information services groups will lead to groups of information objects, called logical information components.

This work is done to define which information objects have strong affinity with each other. Information objects with strong affinity should be placed close together, as they are often needed at the same time. Thus the logical information components can also be regarded as 'logical information stores'.

Creating logical information components all starts with the information interaction model we created in the conceptual layer.

Information objects → Business services	Claim	Customer	Insurance policy	Payment
Accept claim	W	T		
Inspect accepted claim	T	G	G	
Reject claim	T	T		
Pay claim	T	G		W

First, we create a new table (cross reference), with the information objects in the row and column headers. We populate the cells with the Business information service names, based on the following rules:

- If a Business information service transforms an information object, it is placed in the cell where the information object is both in row and column. In our example: 'customer' is transformed by 'accept claim', so 'accept claim' is put in row 'customer', column 'customer'.
- If an information object is used (get or transform) to write or transform another object, then the name of the business information service is put in the cell where the used object is in the row header and the written/transformed object is in the column header. In our example: as 'customer' is transformed to be able to write 'claim' by 'accept claim', 'accept claim' is put into row 'customer', column 'claim'.

After analyzing the information object usage of the business information services and populating the table we end up with the table below.

Information objects	Claim	Customer	Insurance policy	Payment
Claim	Inspect accepted claim Reject claim Pay claim			Pay claim
Customer	Accept claim Inspect accepted claim Reject claim	Accept claim Reject claim		Pay claim
Insurance policy	Inspect accepted claim			
Payment				

This is the initial LIC structure model. Now we have to re-arrange or cluster the model. We do this based on the following rules:

- When both column and row of an information object are empty, something's wrong. This would mean that the information object is not used by any business services in any way. Thus you might want to check your IIM;
- Row and column order must be kept in symmetric order, so If you move a row (or column) you need to move the corresponding twin column (or row) respectively;
- Empty rows at the end;
- Empty columns at the beginning;
- Where appropriate, derive additional grouping criteria from the architecture principles. An example is: architecture principle is 'buy before build'. Grouping criterion would then be: 'group information objects in such a way that they are in line with what packages normally provide';
- Look for columns with the same content or ones that fulfill the derived additional grouping criteria. Then see if coherent rows also have the same content or if they fulfill the derived additional grouping criteria. If this is the case, the information objects concerned are related and should be placed close to one another;
- Repeat this until the BISs are optimally clustered on the diagonal because it shows a cluster of IOs that are highly correlated via the same (group of) BISs;
- Logical Information components only can be created around the diagonal. Information objects influencing one another always belong to the same information component;
- Create Logical Information components by selecting the cells that have maximal correlation with each other and minimal relationships between them.

Analyze the model by interpreting the meaning of Logical Information components and their relationships. If you can't give the LIC a meaningful name something is wrong. Re-visit your criteria derived from the principles and refine the structure so they adhere to the criteria.

Information objects	Insurance policy	Claim	Customer	Payment
Insurance policy		Inspect accepted claim		
Claim		Inspect accepted claim Reject claim Pay claim		Pay claim
Customer		Accept claim Inspect accepted claim Reject claim	Accept claim Reject claim	Pay claim
Payment				

In our highly simplified example we would end up with 3 logical information components, one containing information object 'Insurance policy', a second containing information objects 'Claim and customer' and a third containing information object 'Payment'.

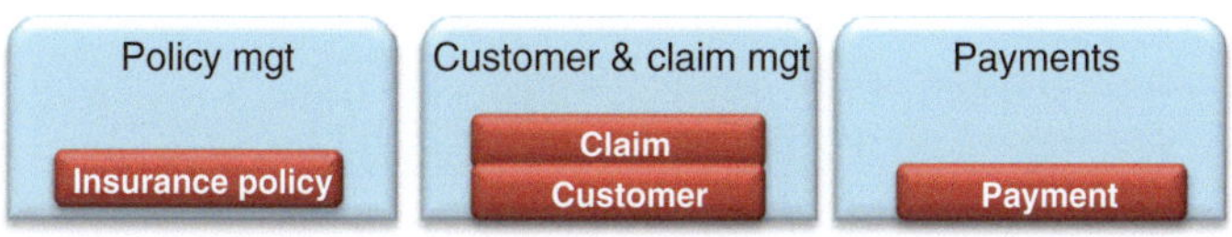

You might be thinking by now 'this can become a large exercise'. Well, that can indeed be the fact. Doing this at enterprise level can lead to tables with 200 columns and rows. There are people on this planet that can do the clustering manually, but even they prefer to use tool support (like sorting macros in a spreadsheet) to do the initial clustering.

3.4.4.2 Logical Business Information Component

Creating logical business information components works just about the same as creating logical information components.

Logical business information components are created to check if the logical business components we have defined do not violate some obvious information processing rules. The information processing rules we talk about here are: (1) You cannot use something that has not been created yet and (2) If somebody else changes something you need to use, they better change it before you want to use it. These topics have not been addressed yet, as the creation of logical business components does not take them into account.

The information interaction model is also used as input.

Information objects → Business services	Claim	Customer	Insurance policy	Payment
Accept claim	W	T		
Inspect accepted claim	T	G	G	
Reject claim	T	T		
Pay claim	T	G		W

You need to create a table with the business information services in the row and column headers. The first row and column head is fixed. It's name is '(external) input'. The last row and column head is also fixed. It's name is '(external) output'.

The cells are populated using the following rules:

- If a business information service (BIS) transforms an information object (IO), the name of the information object is placed in the cell with the row and column header that contains the name of the business information service. In our example: 'Accept claim' transforms 'customer', so 'customer' is entered into the cell with row and column header 'Accept claim';
- When a business information service writes or transforms an information object, which is used by subsequent business information services, the name of the information object is placed in the cells with the row header which has the name of the business information service that writes the information and the column headers with the names of the business information services that use the information object. In our example: 'Accept claim' writes 'claim', which is used by 'Inspect accepted claim', 'Reject claim' and 'Pay claim'. 'Claim' is placed in the cells with row header 'Accept claim' and column headers 'Inspect accepted claim', 'Reject claim' and 'Pay claim';
- If an information object is used but not created within the scope of our business information services we put the name of the information object in the cell with row with header '(External) input' and column header that has the name of the business information service that uses it. In our example: 'Insurance policy' is placed in the cell with row header '(External) input' and column header 'Inspect accepted claim';
- If an information object is created but not used within the scope of our business information services we put the name of the information object in the cell with row with header that has the name of the business information service and column header '(External) output'. In our example: 'Payment' is put in the cell with row header 'Pay claim' and column header '(External) output'.

After working through the information interaction model you would end up with a table looking like this:

Business information services	(External) input	Accept claim	Inspect accepted claim	Reject claim	Pay claim	(External) output
(External) input			Insurance policy			
Accept claim		Customer	Claim customer	Claim customer	Claim customer	
Inspect accepted claim			Claim	Claim	Claim customer	
Reject claim				Customer claim		
Pay claim					Claim	Payment
(External) output						

This is the initial LBIC structure model. Now we have to re-arrange or cluster the model. We do this based on the following rules:

- When both column and row of an BIS are empty, something's wrong. This would mean that the BIS does not use any information objects. Thus you might want to check your IIM;
- Row and column order must remain the same, so If you move a row (or column) you need to move the corresponding twin column (or row) respectively;
- Empty rows at the end;
- Empty columns at the beginning;
- Where appropriate, derive additional grouping criteria from the architecture principles. An example is: all claim handling BISs should be placed close together;
- Look for columns with the same content or ones that fulfill the derived additional grouping criteria. Then see if coherent rows also have the same content or if they fulfill the derived additional grouping criteria. If this is the case, the BISs concerned are related and should be placed close to one another;
- Repeat this until the information objects are optimally clustered on the diagonal;
- Business Information components only can be created around the diagonal. Information objects influencing one another always belong to the same business information component;
- Create Logical Business Information components by selecting the cells that have maximal correlation with each other and minimal relationships between them;

Business information services	(External) input	Inspect accepted claim	Accept claim	Reject claim	Pay claim	(External) output
(External) input		Insurance policy				
Inspect accepted claim		Claim		Claim	Claim Customer	
Accept claim		Claim Customer	Customer	Claim Customer	Claim Customer	
Reject claim				Customer Claim		
Pay claim					Claim	Payment
(External) output						

After doing the work in our example, you would end up with the table above. Three LBICs are distinguished, Claim inspection, Claim acceptance, and Claim payment. These are exactly in line with the logical business components we defined in the business architecture. That means that they do not violate information processing rules and do not have to be changed.

3.4.4.3 Logical Business Information Component Interaction Model

The interaction between the logical business information components can be derived from the interaction between the business information services. It can also be derived from the logical business components, if they are the same, as you can see in our example.

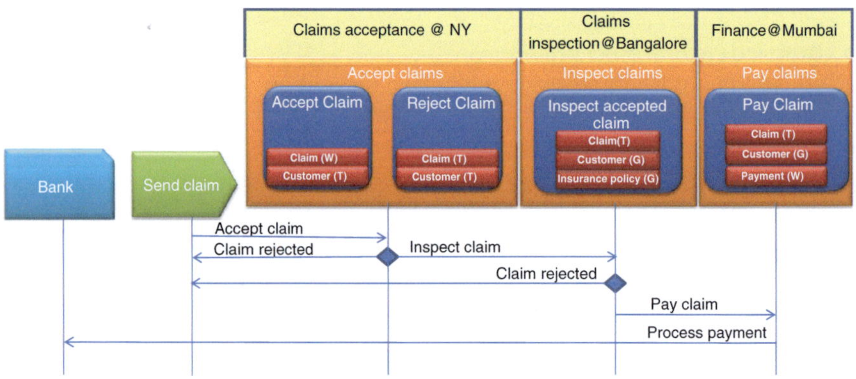

This model comes in handy when logical business components need to be changed so they do not violate information processing rules that have been described in the prior paragraph. The model is the most common in solution level architectures.

3.4.4.4 Logical Business Information Component Collaboration Contract

Normally this is the same as the business information service collaboration contracts described in Sect. 3.4.2.4. You can investigate if collaboration contracts can be merged as described in Sect. 3.3.4.2.

3.4.5 Information Logical Views

3.4.5.1 Logical Business Information Component Ownership View

One very common view that is created as part of the logical information architecture is the ownership view. Mapping business information service owners and information object owners in their components in one view provides insight into 'who uses what from whom'.

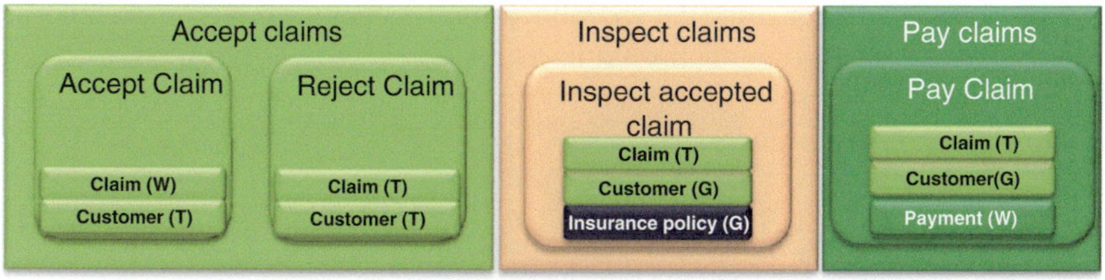

Prepare this view carefully and double check if you have got it right. Much power in organizations is based on ownership, so you can expect 'political moves' when communicating these topics. Sometimes the words 'information stewardship' are used as well to denote the accountability for the information that is used by others.

3.4.5.2 OtherLogical Information Architecture Views

Just as in the conceptual layer, there are a number of obvious views in the logical layer. *Information solution alternatives* can be created to compare and select the best fitting logical information architecture. You can create specific views on the Logical information components and Logical business information components to communicate specific aspects. *Logical information gap views* can be created to show gaps between the baseline and target architecture. *Security and governance views* should be considered, as the components that have been created might contain security or governance issues; this is especially relevant if options to use cloud computing are considered, where information might be held outside the organization. Any relevant *Logical information design decisions* should be documented as described in Sect. 3.3.5.5.

3.4.6 Information Physical Artifacts

3.4.6.1 Physical Information Component

Here we allocate the logical information components to real life physical entities that will be responsible for managing and storing the objects within the components. This could be the allocation of information components to physical locations or organizational units.

Because this is getting very close to real life, the stakeholders start to become interested. Ownership is power. Be aware of this and manage expectations carefully.

3.4.6.2 Physical Business Information Component Interaction Model

The physical business information component interaction model is derived from the one at the logical level. It shows which information will cross physical organizational boundaries.

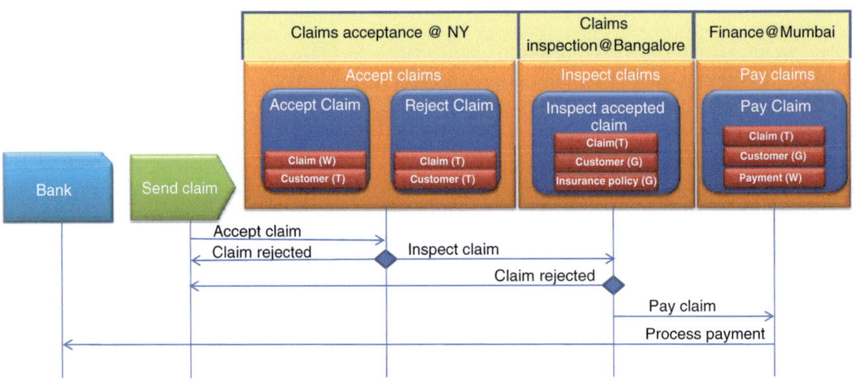

3.4.6.3 Information Migration Specifications

Just as in business architecture, there will be circumstances in which you want to pass on instructions regarding the information architecture to the implementers, without turning them into SRGs. They can address similar topics as will be mentioned within the SRGs, but will be less formal. Typical examples of migration specifications are related to the order in which different information objects need to be migrated to ensure data integrity and specifications regarding information conversion.

3.4.6.4 Information Standards, Rules, and Guidelines

Information Standards, Rules, and Guidelines (SRGs) document what the implementation of the information architecture needs to adhere to. Typical examples are:

- Policies for email, communication with external organizations etc.;
- Policies for backup, integrity, availability, confidentiality;
- Legislative rules for archive, access, audit;
- Legislative rules regarding privacy, usage of specific forms etc.;
- Information standards, corporate and/or industry specific.

3.4.7 Information Physical Views

3.4.7.1 Information Cost View

The information cost view focuses on information migration costs, like:

- Data cleansing;
- Data conversion;
- Data migration (from one location to another).

Cost group	Cost element	Price per unit	# units	Period 1	Period 2	Period 3	Period 4	Period 5	Period 6	Period 7	Period 8	Total costs
Information												
	Data cleansing@ NY (FTE)	5000	1	5000	5000	5000	5000					**20.000**
	Data Cleansing@Mumbai (FTE)	4000	4			16000	16000	16000				**48.000**
	Data Cleansing@Bangalore (FTE)	4000	4				16000	16000	16000	16000		**64.000**
Totals				5.000	5.000	21.000	37.000	32.000	16.000	16.000		**132.000**

3.4.7.2 Other Physical Information Architecture Views

The obvious views that can be distinguished here are the *Physical information component view*, which visualizes specific topics you want to communicate in that area, like big changes in physical information ownership. You can create an *physical information component gap view* to communicate changes between baseline and target. *Security and governance views* should also be considered.

3.4.8 Information Architecture Wrap-Up

We have come to the end of information architecture as part of IAF. Identifying and defining information objects was one of the first things we did. That resulted in a common definition of the things the business wants to know something about. That common definition helped us to avoid many discussions in the creation of the information architecture. It will also prevent them in the future.

After that we linked the business services and information objects, creating Business Information services. These are the minimum input needed to start with information systems (IS) and technology infrastructure (TI) architecture.

The information interaction model we created proved to be a key input for the logical level of the information architecture. Without it we would not have been able to define the information components and business information components at the logical level.

Information ownership is a topic we always need to address, either at the logical or at the physical level.

Finally we ended up with the definition of information related SRGs to ensure the information architecture gets implemented the way it is intended to be.

The business information components and information components we have created are additional input for the IS and TI architecture. They are the basis for the identification of IS services, which are deduced from the information we have gathered so far. This deduction is based on identifying which parts of the business information services in the components will be automated. This work is commonly done as a multi discipline activity. Reasons are: (1) the business architect knows what should be automated from a business point of view, (2) the information architect knows what is closely related from an information point of view, and (3) the IS architect knows what can be automated from a technology point of view.

3.5 Information System Architecture

3.5.1 Overview

By now we have an understanding of the business, its processes, organization and governance structure. In addition to that we also understand the information processing requirements the business has. We have a clear definition of the information objects so we avoid discussions in that area. What we now need to do is to define the extent and type of automated support that the business needs. Not all business information services have to be fully automated. Very often it will not be possible to fully automate them due to required human interaction, knowledge or judgement. Different technologies provide us with the option to utilize different types of automated support for the same business information service. Imagine a customer submitting a claim from a desktop computer using the internet or by sending an email. Information systems (IS) architecture is all about determining the automated support for the business, understanding the interaction between the IS Services and Components, and delivering an architecture in which it has been determined which IS systems will be bought, which ones will be built and which parts will be customized.

3.5.2 Information System Conceptual Artifacts

3.5.2.1 Information System Service

The first thing that needs to be done within the IS architecture is to define IS services. We analyze the Business information services (within the components) and define the corresponding IS services. This sounds simple, but there is a catch to it. A simple business Information service like 'accept claim' can lead to a lot of decision making. Are we going to accept claims via e-mail? Are we going to accept them via paper mail? If we accept them via paper mail does it have to be on a typed form so we can scan and OCR the claim, or do we also accept hand-written claims? Do we want to accept claims through the phone? All this decision making requires collaboration between the business, information and IS architect.

The definition of IS services might even lead to a situation in which you need to iterate back to the business architecture and define new business services. This will be necessary when you decide to define IS services that (1) require different security measures, (2) require changes to, or maybe even complete new business services and processes because you are introducing new technology, (3) have significantly different non-functional requirements. Let's work through this in an example.

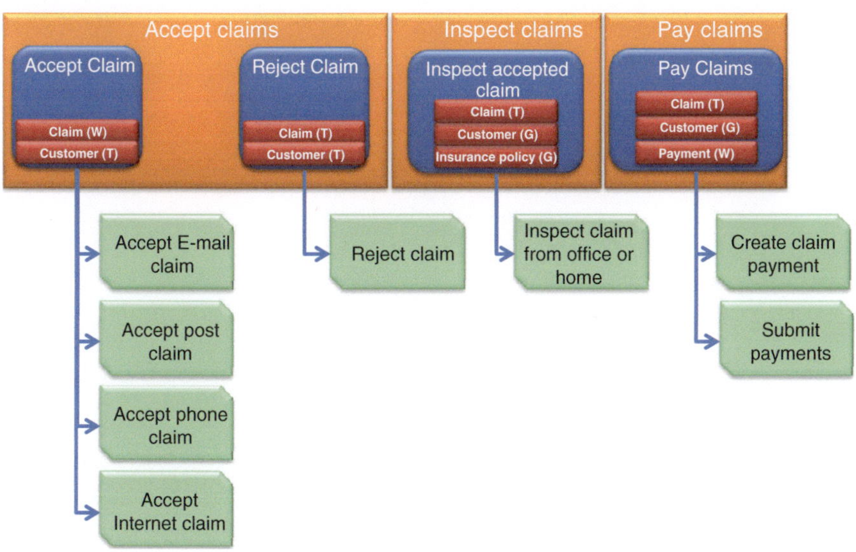

During the analysis of the Business information services, we define the IS services as depicted in the figure. We define four 'channels' through which we want to accept claims, E-mail, paper mail, phone and internet. Contextual input such as business and IS/IT strategy is helpful here, since it sets the stage for options to consider. The paper mail channel will only accept forms so we can scan and OCR them to get them in electronic format. Another thing we decide is that we want to be able to inspect claims from either the office or from home. The last thing we do is to define that we want to split the generation of payments from their submission to the bank. If we buffer the payments and deliver them in bulk the bank will give us a 15% discount on the payments processing charges.

Now we need to determine if we need to iterate back to the business architecture to change or add business services and components. Claims acceptance through e-mail and internet require high levels of security to prevent fraud. Phone acceptance requires a call center with its own services and processes. Inspecting claims from the home or from the office will not make much of a difference, as strong authentication measures (a combination of knowledge and possession) will be required in both situations to prevent fraud from inside the organization. Payment creation can be done during the day. Submitting the payments is a bulk process at the end of the day. We conclude that an iteration back to the business architecture is justified. The result is shown below.

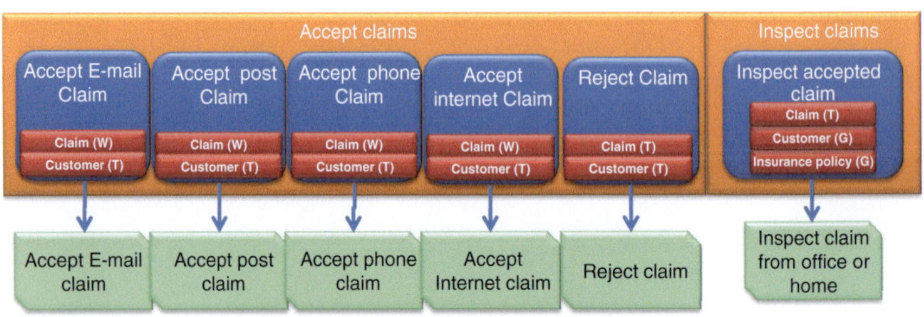

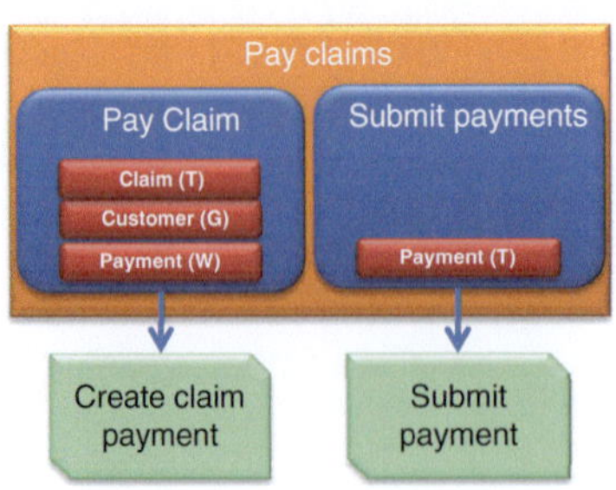

We have decided to split the 'Accept claim' business information service as well as 'Pay claim'. The 'Inspect accepted claim' business information service has not been changed. Of course we have also updated the appropriate artifacts and views to keep them consistent.

Iterating back in an IAF architecture engagement is a common activity. This is caused by the fact that we have split the overall architecture problem into smaller ones that can be answered more easily. Iterating should be carefully considered, as the different architecture teams can be working in parallel. Some will be further down the line than others. Only iterate back when you really need to.

3.5.2.2 BIS – IS Service Cross-Reference

Cross references are the main means to maintain traceability through the architecture areas. The information interaction model documents the relationships between Business services and Information objects in the information architecture. Here we need to document the relationships between the Business information services and the IS services.

	Business information services							
IS Services	Accept e-mail claim	Accept post claim	Accept phone claim	Accept internet claim	Reject claim	Inspect accepted claim	Create payment	Submit payments
Accept-email claim	X							
Accept post claim		X						
Accept phone claim			X					
Accept internet claim				X				
Reject claim					X			
Inspect claim from office or home						X		
Create payment							X	
Submit payments								X

This artifact might not seem that important to you. Its real value is later on, as the architecture is being used for impact analysis of changes. It makes that activity a lot easier to execute. So take the time to create this cross reference during the creation of the architecture.

3.5.2.3 Information System Domain

Information system domains are used to communicate the IS services. Very often Capgemini architects tend to use the same domains they have used in the business and information architecture. This to communicate the different types of services in a common way. In our claims example we could re-use the domains defined in the information architecture.

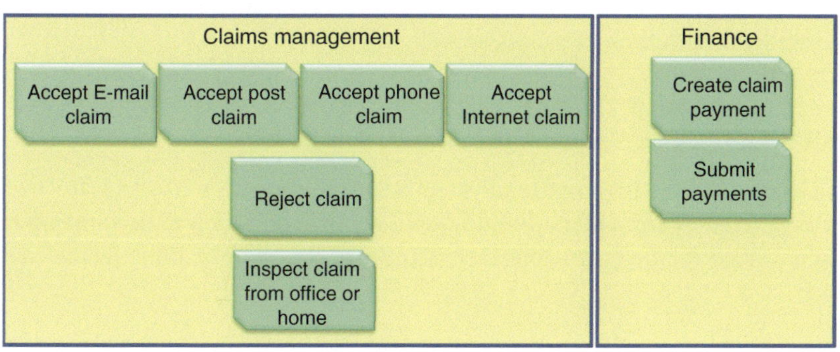

If IS specific domains need to be defined, the following criteria can be used as a basis:

- Type of technology, e.g. all internet IS services are shown together;
- Complexity of the IS services e.g. easy to create, hard to create;
- Level of automation e.g. the IS service fully automates the business information service, or partly or marginally.

3.5.2.4 Information System Service Collaboration Contract

Collaboration contracts between IS services are derived from the collaboration contracts between the business information services. Attributes like growth, service windows and quality of information can be copied from the business information service collaboration contract. Other attributes like response time, throughput and peak characteristics will have to be derived.

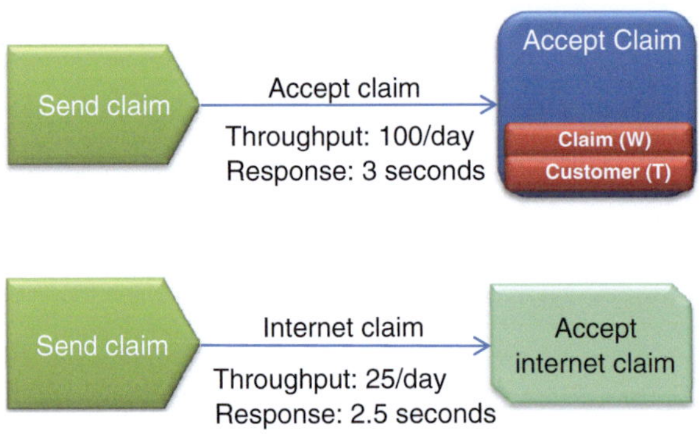

This example shows that the business expects a total of 100 claims a day. They want an initial response back to the customer within 3 seconds. Part of the claims will be submitted through the internet. The internet channel implies network latency. Therefore we derive a response time of 2.5 seconds for this specific contract.

Note: this example may give the impression that contracts are only modeled on the edges of the scope of the architecture (the interface between inside and outside); however, contracts can likewise be used to model the requirements to internally underpinning services as well.

3.5.2.5 Information System Service Interaction Model

The purpose of the Information System Service Interaction Model is to develop more clarity toward understanding the IS services and their collaboration. The model forms the basis for interface definition that will be done in the logical level.

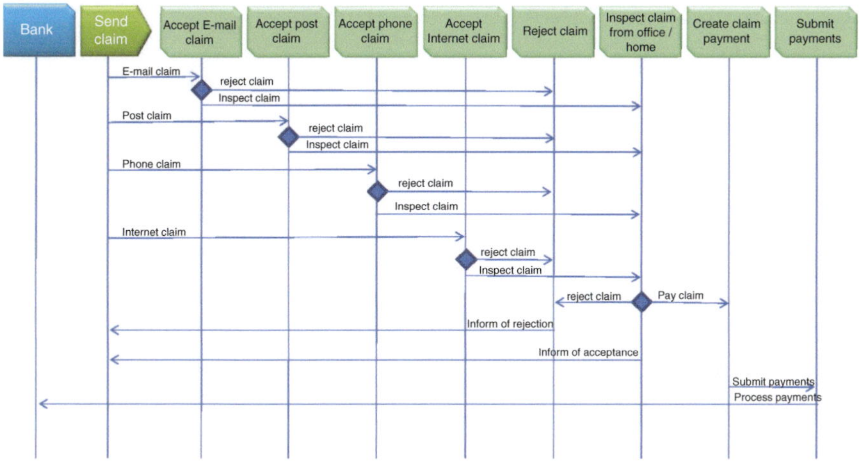

Of course the IS service interaction model is derived from the Business service interaction model. The model in the example above is a straight forward deduction from the interaction models in the business and information columns. Think of what could happen with the interaction model if we decided to use workflow or business process management tools. Then we would have to introduce an orchestrator IS service that expresses the requirement to orchestrate the interaction between the other IS services; this orchestration service then typically is delivered in TI. This service could also be the central data storage service, passing the necessary data along with the orchestration messages.

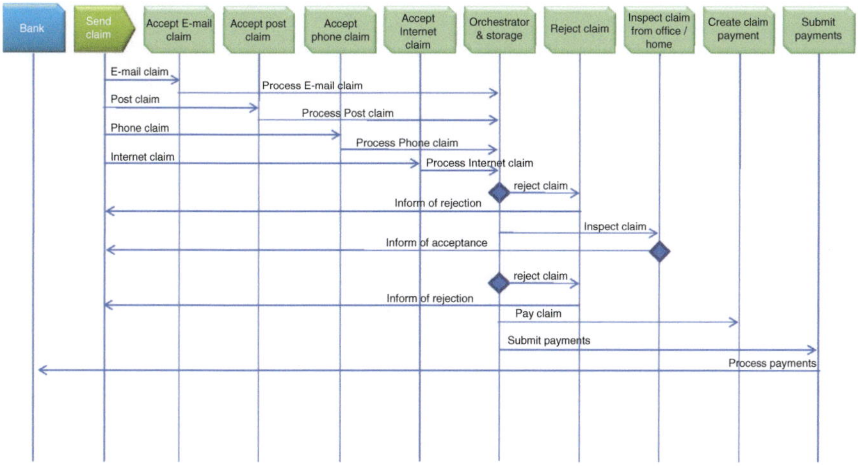

3.5.3 Information System Conceptual Views

3.5.3.1 Information System Service Security View and Non-functional Requirements View

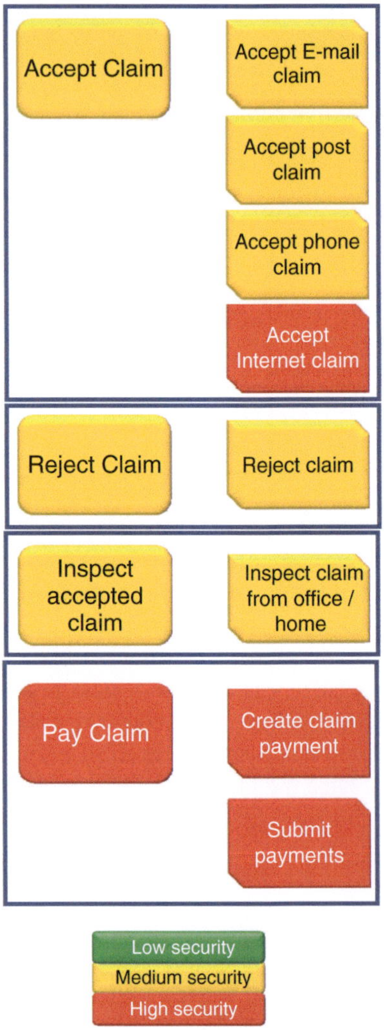

The most important views within IS conceptual are the security and non-functional requirements (governance) views. Because there is a potential one-to-many relationship between business information services and IS services, which involves a derivation of IS service attributes, you should check the defined attributes to see if they are still in line with the business information services. The example shows that we have decided that we want high security for the accepting of internet claims to prevent fraud.

The same type of view can be created to validate other IS service attributes like mean time to repair, mean time between failures and response times.

3.5.3.2 Other Conceptual IS Architecture Views

Just as in other areas you can create views to visualize aspects of Conceptual IS artifacts. You can also create an information system service gap view as described in Sect. 3.3.3.3 to show the difference between baseline and target of the defined IS Services. Service time views can be used to validate if all IS services have the correct service times. As you can see, the views in the conceptual IS architecture are not that complex. The trick in this part of IAF is to combine business and IS knowledge to define the right IS services, and then derive the IS attributes from the business attributes.

3.5.4 Information System Logical Artifacts

3.5.4.1 Logical Information System Component

A Logical Information System Component is the basic element of an 'ideal' or 'to be' application structure created by the grouping of one or more IS services.

The grouping criteria of IS services into Logical Information System Components (LISC) is typically based on architecture principles.

In our example:

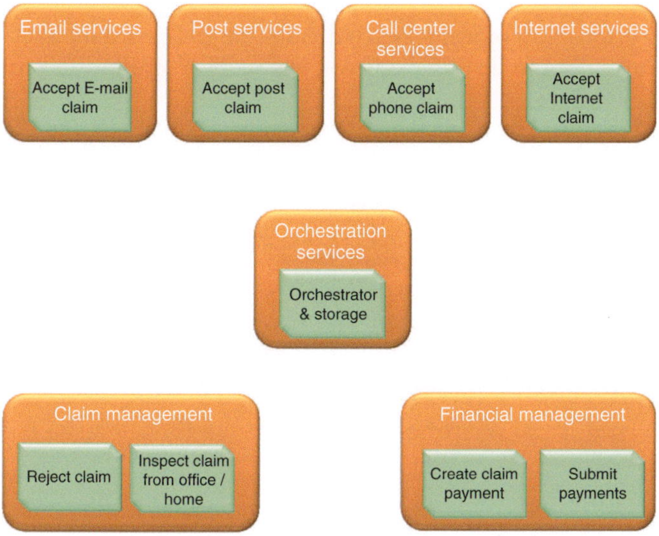

As you can see in the example we have kept most services separate. The only ones that have been grouped are the ones in claim management and financial management. The main reason behind this is that we want to buy as many components as possible. The components are grouped in such a way that they are in line with possible technology solutions we can buy. The insurance policy states the different ways a claim can be submitted. The customer can send an email to our company, ACME Insurances Ltd., requesting an email claims form. When an insurance policy is sent to the customer, a paper claims form is added, so they can mail their claim. The existing call center will be equipped to handle phone claims. ACME's internet portal will be amended to handle claims via a separate portlet.

Nowadays this is the most common way of constructing the logical information system components. Combine the architecture principles with package knowledge to construct LISCs that reflect what the business wants from a package that is to be selected later on in the physical level.

Another way of working can be done in a situation in which a package is being selected and the organization wants to change the processes to fit the package to avoid package customization. Then you have the option to re-engineer the LISCs and their IS services from the package documentation. Then you can also re-engineer the business services that the package needs to deliver. After a gap analysis between the existing business services and the ones the package can fulfill you know what to change in the business.

3.5.4.2 Logical Information System Component Interaction Model

The LISC interaction model is derived from the IS Service interaction model. Here you also need to investigate if you can merge collaboration contracts, as described in Sect. 3.3.4.2.

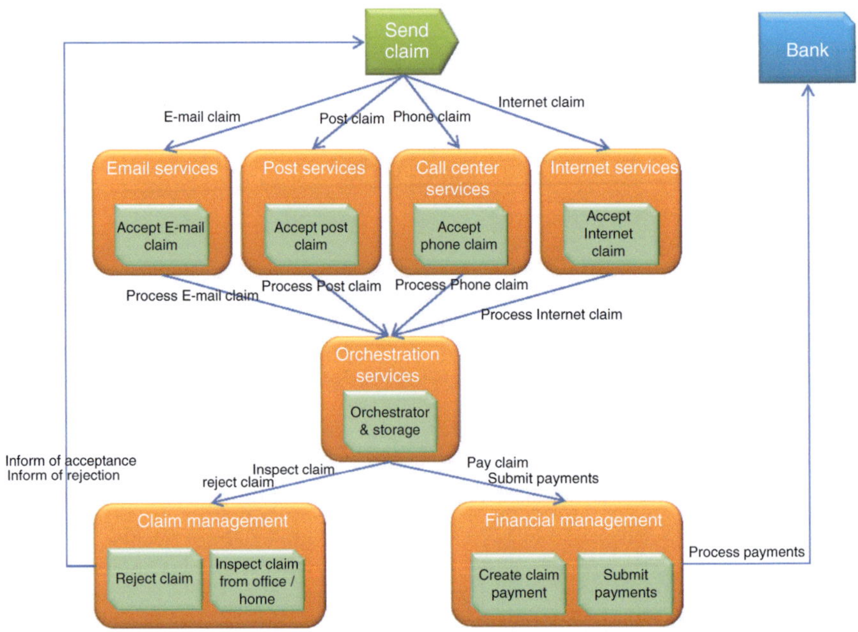

The example shows an alternate way to create the LISC interaction model. IAF does not prescribe how you create the models so you can fine tune this to your specific requirements. The drawback of this way of creating the model is that it invites to tightly link LISCs together. The other examples in this chapter invite you to think more in terms of loose coupling, enhancing the SOA mindset that IAF supports.

3.5.4.3 Logical Information System Component Collaboration Contract

The LISC collaboration contracts are derived from the IS Service collaboration contracts. When needed you can add attributes to the collaboration contract as shown in the example below. Remember, IAF is a framework, not a cookbook. You are encouraged to use what you need and also amend what you need (see the highlights attributes for examples).

Description	*Describe the collaboration contract*
Result	*Describe the outcome that is exposed to whom it concerns*
Error handling	*Describe how errors in the interaction need to be handled*
Contract input	*Describe input that is required by the receiving component*
Contract output	*Describe the outcome that will be exposed to whom it concerns*
Message format	*Describe the appropriate message formats*
Throughput	*Describe the average required throughput*
Throughput period	*Describes the throughput period.* <Second/ Minute/ Hour/ Day/ Week>
Growth	*Describe the expected growth in percentage.* %
Growth period	*Describes the growth period.* <Second/ Minute/ Hour/ Day/ Week/ Month/ Year>
Service window	*Or opening hours, describes when the service should be available*
Peak profile short term	*Describes the peak profile for the short term period.* <Standard office/ Morning peak/ Afternoon peak/ Flat>
Peak profile long term	*Describes the peak profile for the long period.* <Standard week/ Month end peak/ Month begin peak/ Mid month peak/ Flat/ Quarter end peak/ Year end peak/ something else>
Characteristics	*Describe the characteristics of the contract.* <Immediate response required/ Delayed response possible (within response limits)/ Transactional/ Batch/ Conversational>
Integration mechanism	*Describe the integration mechanism to be used.* <Synchronous / Async – PubSub / Async – Fire&forget / Async – Assured delivery / ...>
Response requirements	*Describes the normal time a service/component request should response.* <<1 Second/ >1 <5 Seconds/ > 5 seconds < 10 minutes/ >1 hour < 1 day/ < 1 week>
Quality of information required	*Describe the required quality of the information. Should the response be real time, info must not be older than 1 day or 1 week, etc.*
Contract control requirements	*Describe the control requirement of the contract.* <Control required every time the contract is activated/ Logging of contract activation & results insufficient/ No contract control requirements>
Result control requirements	*Describe the result requirement of the contract.* <No result control required/ Result control based on periodic checks/ Result control required every time the contract is supporting>
Importance	*Describe the importance of the contract.* <Failure allowed if only quality degrades/ Must complete within response times>

3.5.5 Information System Logical Views

3.5.5.1 Information System Solution Alternatives View

Grouping IS Services into LISCs can be done in different ways, with different consequences. Solution alternatives should be considered as a view in the logical information system architecture. The example below shows how different LISCs can be identified. If you were aiming at building the software yourself you could consider to put phone, email, and internet claims together. The internet portal could then be used by employees and clients to enter the claims.

The table shows how the different alternatives score in relation to the architecture principles. Based on the relative priority of the principles and the score for each alternative we can conclude that we were on the right path with our work. The 'Buy' alternative is the best one and we have proof of that fact, so we can tell people why this is the best solution when they ask.

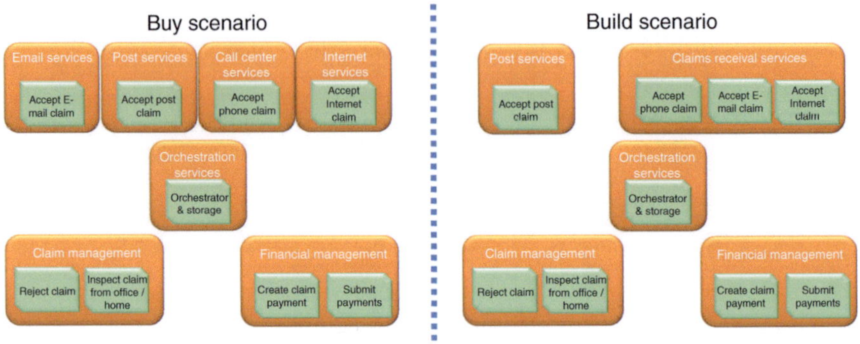

	principle + relative priority								
	Buy before build		Distribution channel flexibility		Good functional fit		Reuse where possible		
	3		2		2		1		
Alternative	Score	Result	Score	Result	Score	Result	Score	Result	Total result
Buy	3	9	3	6	2	4	0	0	19
Build	0	0	1	2	3	6	3	3	11

3.5.5.2 Integration View

This view can be constructed to validate and communicate which integration mechanisms are to be used to realize the communication between the LISCs. In the example the numbers in the arrows depict a specific collaboration contract between the LISCs.

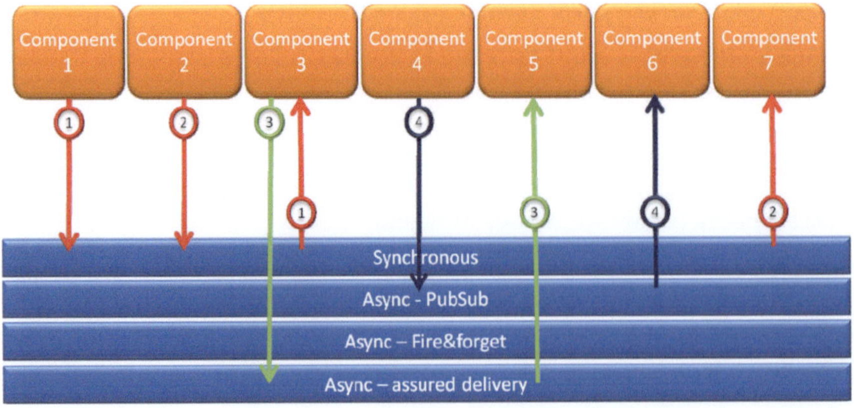

As you can imagine, this can become a complex view if it is done for all collaboration contracts between LISCs, so focus on the 'hot spots' or on the specific things you need to communicate to answer the concern the stakeholder has.

3.5.5.3 Distribution View

The logical location of LISCs can be of influence on the logical IS architecture. Of course the main influence is caused by non-functional requirements. We know of a situation in which a customer wanted to be able to access scanned letters of credit from Europe, the USA and Asia. Each scanned letter of credit was at least 50 Megabyte. They also wanted optimal response times. In the end we chose to create three databases and replicate the information between them to ensure the best possible response times. Hauling 50 MB files over wide area networks to three places in the world would not result in good response times, simply due to network limitations.

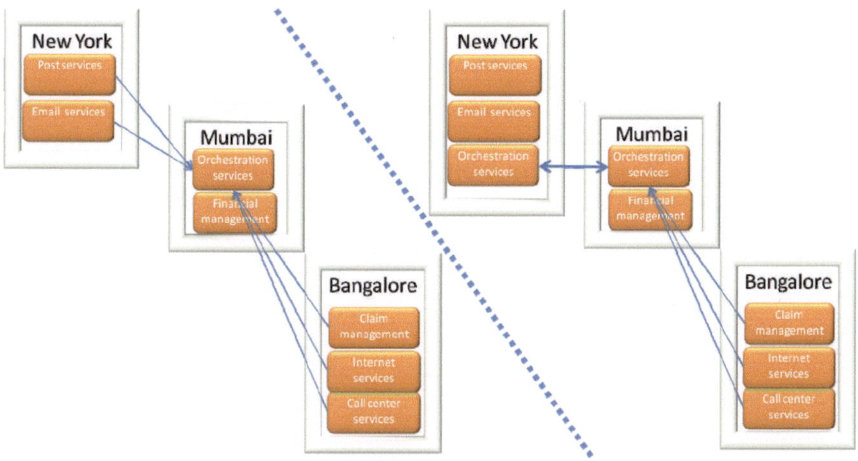

Our example shows the main data flows in two situations. In the first we only have one orchestration and data storage service in our Mumbai environment. This leads to data being accessed in Mumbai from New York, Mumbai and Bangalore. In the second situation we have duplicated the orchestration and storage service. We will replicate the data between Mumbai and New York. In that way we will be able to provide the people in the USA faster access. An additional benefit is that we also have an automatic backup of the data in New York.

You should consider this view if you are working in a geographically dispersed environment. In spite of all claims from technology vendors, performance is still an issue and you need to pay attention to it.

Of course, in this case this view is clearly reflecting the TI aspect area (network bandwidth) and, in many cases, views such as the distribution view will span both IS and TI aspects.

3.5.5.4 Migration View

There can be circumstances in which it is important to implement LISCs in a specific order. Reasons for this can be:

- One LISC is a prerequisite for another;
- If a certain LISC is created first, we can re-use a lot of things later;
- The business has stated they need something before the rest.

A migration view can be constructed to visualize the order in which LISCs need to be implemented.

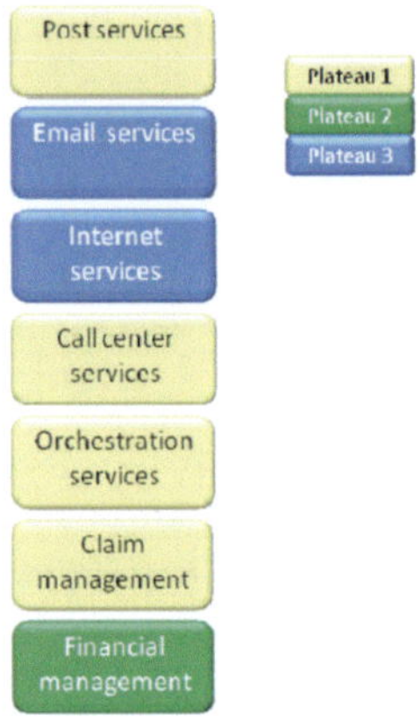

3.5.5.5 Information View

As Business information services do not have to have a one-to-one relationship with IS Services, the relationship between LISCs and logical information components (LICs) can be different from those between logical business information components and LICs. Relating the LISCs to the LICs they need can lead to the necessity to refine the LISC structure. The Information view can be constructed to show which LISCs use which LICs and determine if changes to the architecture are needed.

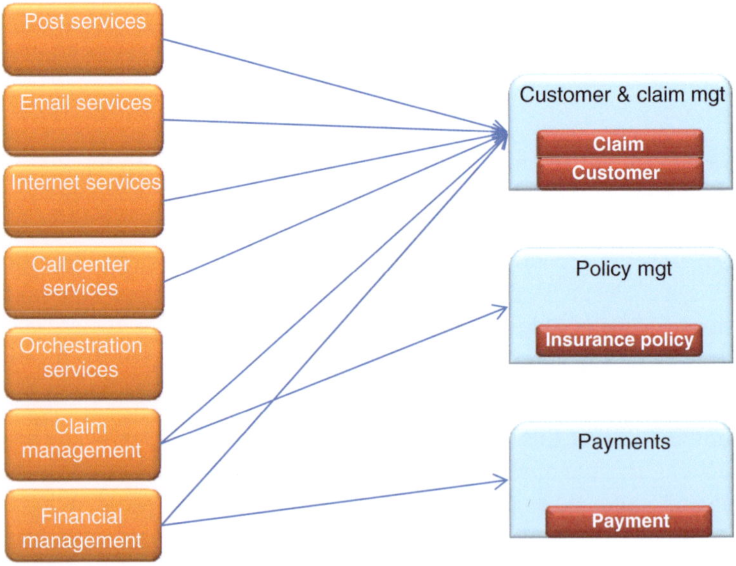

This view can be of particular use when you need to set up a master data management structure. It helps you understand which components need which data.

3.5.5.6 Logical Information System Component Landscape

This view is one that makes part of just about any architecture. It shows how the LISCs fit into the overall systems landscape.

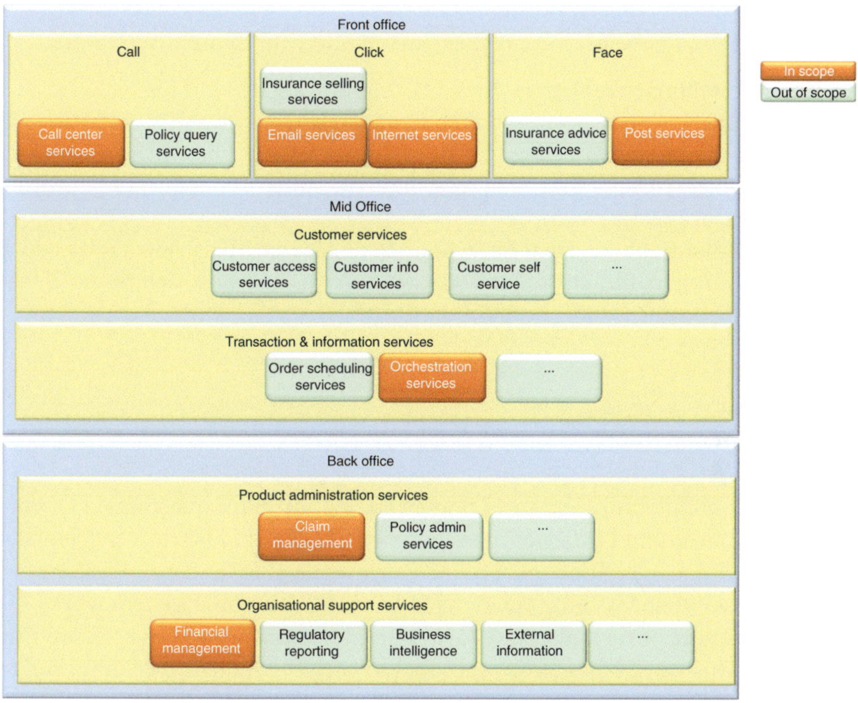

The pitfall in creating this view is that you want to be as complete as possible. This leads to drowning yourself and your audience in detail. Focus on what is important. Show you have left out less relevant parts to manage expectations.

3.5.5.7 Other Logical IS views

Views that have been explained in earlier parts of this chapter, and which can also be used here are:

- **Logical Information System Component view** to show a relevant subset of Logical Information System Component's attributes;
- **Logical Information System Gap view** to show gaps between baseline and target architecture;

- **Logical Information System Component Security view** to check if the security attributes of the IS services in the LISCs are in line with each other. This view should always be considered;
- **Logical Information System Component Governance (NFR) view** to check if the non-functional requirement attributes of the IS services in the LISCs are in line with each other. This view should always be considered;
- **Information System Design Decisions** can be documented in terms of architecture principles to help the architecture implementers understand WHY things are the way they are.

Other views that have been created as part of a logical IS architecture are:

- **Logical Information System Security Monitoring view.** This view shows which LISCs have been specifically designed to monitor security. In addition it can also show which security monitoring LISCs monitor which other LISCs. The view can help to judge if security monitoring is set up properly;
- **Logical Information System Encryption Services view.** This view shows which collaboration contracts require encryption. It helps to determine if the encryption services have been set up properly.

3.5.6 Information System Physical Artifacts

Physical IS architecture focuses on answering four main questions: (1) what do I buy, (2) what do I build, (3) how long will it take, and (4) how much will it cost. So package selection is part of the work we need to do here. We also need to identify what needs to be customized to make the whole system work. We need to estimate costs and effort for the implementation of the architecture. As a lot of this work has a close relationship with the same things that need to be done in the physical technology infrastructure architecture, we work together most of the time.

If package selection is part of your architecture work, you can use the same technique as solution alternative selection as described in Sect. 3.3.5.1. Define selection criteria, give them a relative priority, and score the packages against each criterion. Be aware that full blown package selection exercises can take many months. This due to the time it takes to (1) get the criteria agreed, (2) collect information via RFIs from the vendors, (3) analyze the information and score the packages, and finally (4) get the decision formalized in the organization. Depending on the level of available insights on whether and how to integrate with the existing environment, package selection RfI/RfP processes can also be initiated based on logical architecture descriptions, e.g. the Logical Components and their contracts.

3.5.6.1 Physical Information System Component

Once you have allocated the logical IS components to physical, real life things you can buy or build, you have created the physical IS components. In our case we were able find a package based solution for all of our Logical IS components. EmailIt from MEAC Inc. provides functionality to automatically process email requests and return claims forms to the customer. The company Pro-Duck-Tive Ltd. provides a suite of modules that cover the functionality required by the paper mail, call center and Internet services, as well as a business process management module called BpmPro. ErpItAll GMBH has modules for claims management and finance.

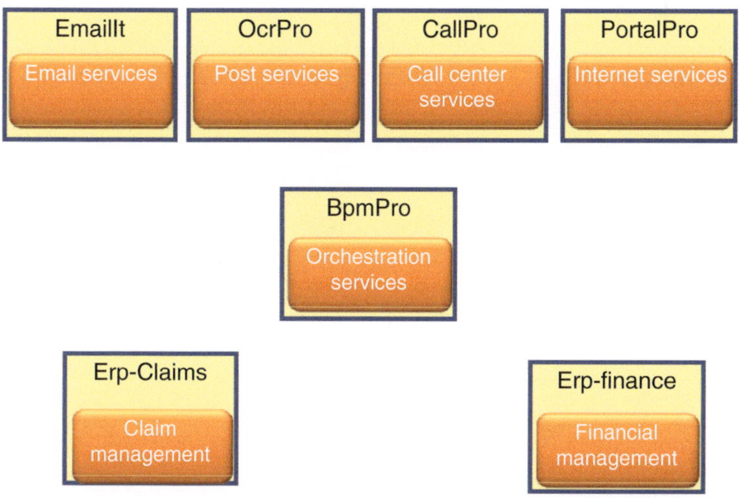

The techniques required to create the Physical IS components are not complex. The complex part here is managing the process. Many of the stakeholders have personal preferences and use whatever they can to influence the process. Most of the time the architect has to stay impartial because he/she is an advisor to the organization, not a decision maker. So stay objective and unbiased during the process.

3.5.6.2 Physical Information System Component Interaction Model

The Physical Information System Component Interaction Model gives insight into how these components are interacting. There are two common techniques to create this model. The first is to base it on the Logical IS component interaction model and add the physical choices made.

The second technique is to completely substitute the logical components with physical ones and create a model as shown in the second figure below.

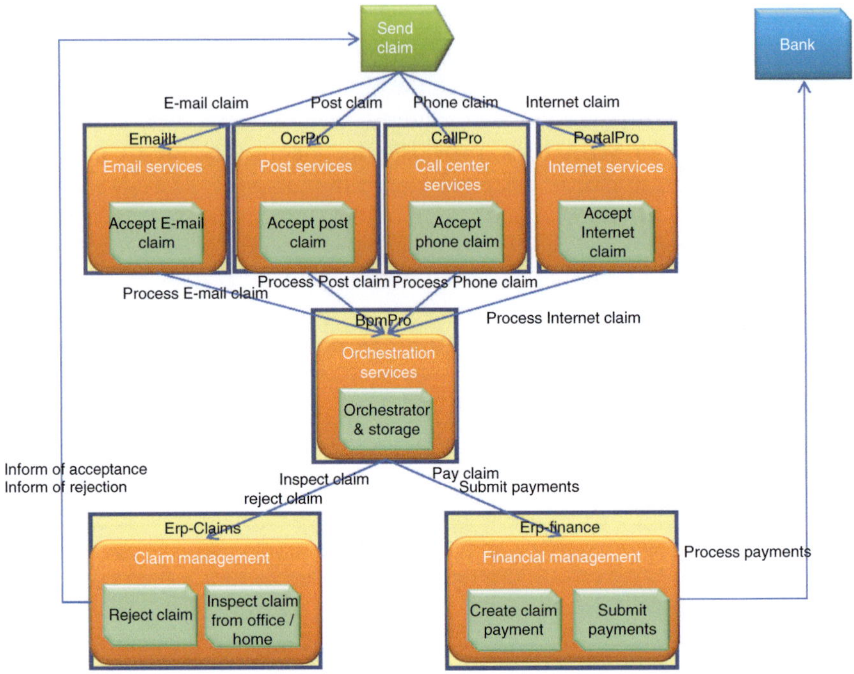
Send claim
Bank
E-mail claim
Post claim
Phone claim
Internet claim
EmailIt
Email services
Accept E-mail claim
OcrPro
Post services
Accept post claim
CallPro
Call center services
Accept phone claim
PortalPro
Internet services
Accept Internet claim
Process E-mail claim
Process Post claim
Process Phone claim
Process Internet claim
BpmPro
Orchestration services
Orchestrator & storage
Inform of acceptance
Inform of rejection
Inspect claim
reject claim
Pay claim
Submit payments
Erp-Claims
Claim management
Reject claim
Inspect claim from office / home
Erp-finance
Financial management
Create claim payment
Submit payments
Process payments

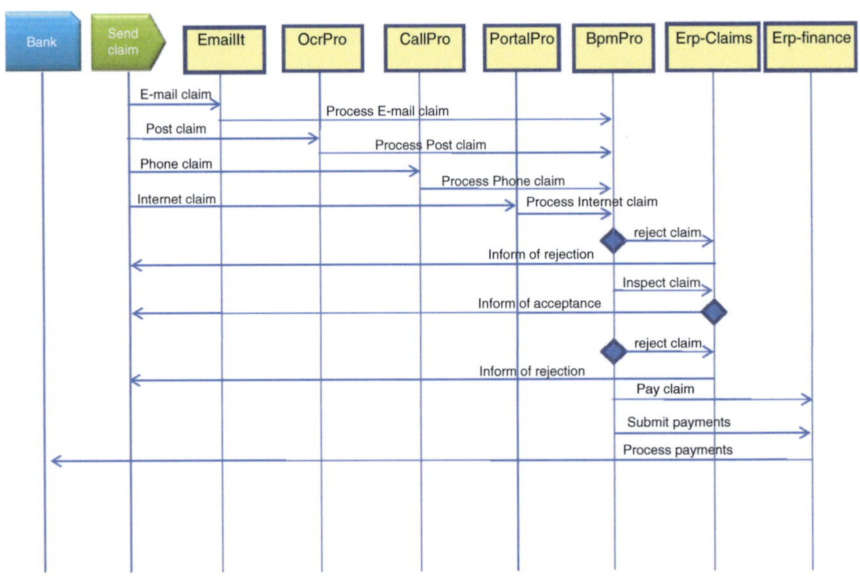
Bank
Send claim
EmailIt
OcrPro
CallPro
PortalPro
BpmPro
Erp-Claims
Erp-finance
E-mail claim
Process E-mail claim
Post claim
Process Post claim
Phone claim
Process Phone claim
Internet claim
Process Internet claim
reject claim
Inform of rejection
Inspect claim
Inform of acceptance
reject claim
Inform of rejection
Pay claim
Submit payments
Process payments

3.5.6.3 Physical Information System Component Collaboration Contract

The interaction between two Physical Information System Components is documented in the Physical Information System Component Collaboration Contract. Attributes are derived from the logical IS component collaboration contract. If needed you can add any attributes you require, just as described in the logical level.

3.5.6.4 Information System Standards, Rules and Guidelines

This key artifact in the IS architecture is the 'law' for anybody that will be using or implementing the architecture. It can – and often will – refer to generic SRGs that have been created for IS architecture. On top of that you should define which SRGs are specific to the implementation and usage of this IS architecture. Topics that can be part of the IS SRGs are:

- Message formats that are to be used;
- Interfacing standards;
- De-coupling layer prescriptions and standards e.g. how strict are specific de-coupling layers to be adhered to;
- Package implementation guidelines;
- Package versioning standards e.g. which version of packages are allowed;
- Software development standards.

It can also be helpful to promote architecture principles to SRGs to formalize the enforcement of those principles. Simple architecture principles like 'Errors are corrected at the source' can have large consequences for the projects that will be implementing the architecture, and might deserve a formal SRG status.

3.5.6.5 Information Migration Specifications

Just as in business and information architecture, there will be circumstances in which you want to pass on instructions regarding the information systems architecture to the implementers, without turning them into SRGs. They can address the same topics as will be mentioned within the SRGs, but will be less formal. Typical examples of migration specifications are related to (1) the order in which different information system components objects need to be migrated to ensure overall transaction integrity, (2) the rollback possibilities and implications, and (3) the deployment steps.

3.5.7 Information System Physical Views

3.5.7.1 Information System Cost View

The cost view answers one of the main questions the key stakeholders always have: 'what will it cost'. Depending on the architecture objective you might be able to calculate costs with relative accuracy, as shown in the example. In other cases, often when working on business unit or enterprise level it is not possible to estimate costs accurately. Best practice in estimating in such circumstances is to classify the different changes (small, medium, large) and assume –together with your stakeholders – how much a type of change will cost.

Cost group	Cost element	Price per unit	# units	Period 1	Period 2	Period 3	Period 4	Period 5	Period 6	Period 7	Period 8	Total costs
Information systems												
	Package licence costs	5000	1	5000								**5.000**
	Package maintenance costs: 15-20% of listprice per annum	1000	7		1000	1000	1000	1000	1000	1000	1000	**7.000**
	Package customisation costs	4000	4									
	Package implementation costs											
	Testing											
	Interface creation											
	Shadow production											
	ETC											
Totals				5000	1000	1000	1000	1000	1000	1000	1000	**12.000**

3.5.7.2 Information System Interfaces View

This view can be derived from collaboration contracts. It can be used to precisely specify how an interface has to work. This is only done at solution architecture level. Use the template below as a checklist and tune it to your specific needs.

Interface specification			
Interface	Meaningful name of interface	Reference number (Version number)	
Source PISC		*Author*	Person who wrote this specification
Destination PISC		*Approved*	Person who approved this specification
		Date created	
		Date approved	
		Change request	Reference no. of change request that has been raised against this form

Source	**Destination**

General information		
Description	Description of system that is the source of a message	Description of system that is the destination for a message
Information source	The source of information about the source system	The source of information about the destination system
Owner	The representative who is responsible for the system	Ditto; for the destination
Platform	Description of the platform hosting the source system (OS)	Ditto; for the destination
Notes	Any additional information that is relevant	Ditto; for the destination

Functionality		
Application	Description of the system application	Ditto; for the destination
Presentation	Description of the user presentation interface,	Ditto; for the destination
Data storage	Description of how data is stored in the system	Ditto; for the destination
Data format	Description of format in which data is stored	Ditto; for the destination
Dependencies	Description of any other interfaces or processes that this system interface is dependent on	Ditto; for the destination
Invocation	Description of how interface is to be invoked	Ditto; for the destination
Error handling	Description of how events that cannot be transmitted over the interface are to be handled	Ditto; for the destination
Interface failure	Description of emergency procedures, manual or automatic, to be invoked when the interface fails	Ditto; for the destination
Notes	Any additional information that is relevant	Ditto; for the destination

Transformation		
Current technology	Current applications or functions that transform data for sending to the destination system	Current applications or functions that transform data sent from the source system
Data type	Legal and illegal data-types	Ditto; for the destination
Translation	Data translation requirements	Ditto; for the destination
Explosion	Rules for exploding a unit of data into multiple units	Ditto; for the destination
Implosion	Rules for imploding multiple units down to a single unit of data	Ditto; for the destination
Validation	Rules for valid data e.g. ensuring what you get the other end is correct at the bit level and information level	Ditto; for the destination
Cleaning	Rules for cleaning dirty data, e.g. data that is not Y2K compliant	Ditto; for the destination
Transformation errors	Description of how Transformation Errors are to be handled	
Notes	Any additional information that is relevant	Ditto; for the destination

Monitoring & Management		
Current technology	Products, systems or processes used to monitor and manage the interface	Ditto; for the destination
General requirements	The requirements for monitoring and managing the data sent from the source	Ditto; for the destination
Notes	Any additional information that is relevant	Ditto; for the destination

Security		
Current technology	Products, systems or processes used to assure security	Ditto; for the destination
Authentication	Required level of authentication	Ditto; for the destination
Authorization	Required level of authorization	Ditto; for the destination
Audit	Required level of audit	Ditto; for the destination
Encryption	Encryption requirement	Ditto; for the destination
Notes	Any additional information that is relevant	Ditto; for the destination

Transport access		
Networking interface	Network interface supported at source	Network interface supported at destination
Protocol constraints	Protocol constraints at source	Protocol constraints at destination
Notes	Any additional information that is relevant	Ditto; for the destination

Communication		
Medium	The form in which the data is packaged for communication over the interface	
Routing	Routing protocols, requirements and rules	
Availability	The level of availability of the communication layer of the interface	
Resilience	Resilience requirements of the communication layer of the interface	
Data loss	Methods of mitigating data loss over the communication layer of the interface	
Recovery	Procedures for recovering the communication layer of the interface	
Load balancing	Methods of balancing the load on the communication layer of the interface	
Volumes	Expected volumes of data on the communication layer of the interface, including average loads and peak loads	
Frequency	Frequency patterns of data on the communication layer of the interface	
Performance targets	Required performance targets of the communication layer of the interface	
Dependencies	Current dependencies of the communication layer of the interface	
Notes	Any additional information that is relevant	

Syntax and semantics		
Syntax		
Semantics		

3.5.7.3 Physical Information System Component Landscape

The physical IS component landscape has the same objective as the logical IS component landscape. It shows how the physical components fit into the overall landscape. If relevant, the interfaces between components can be added to the view.

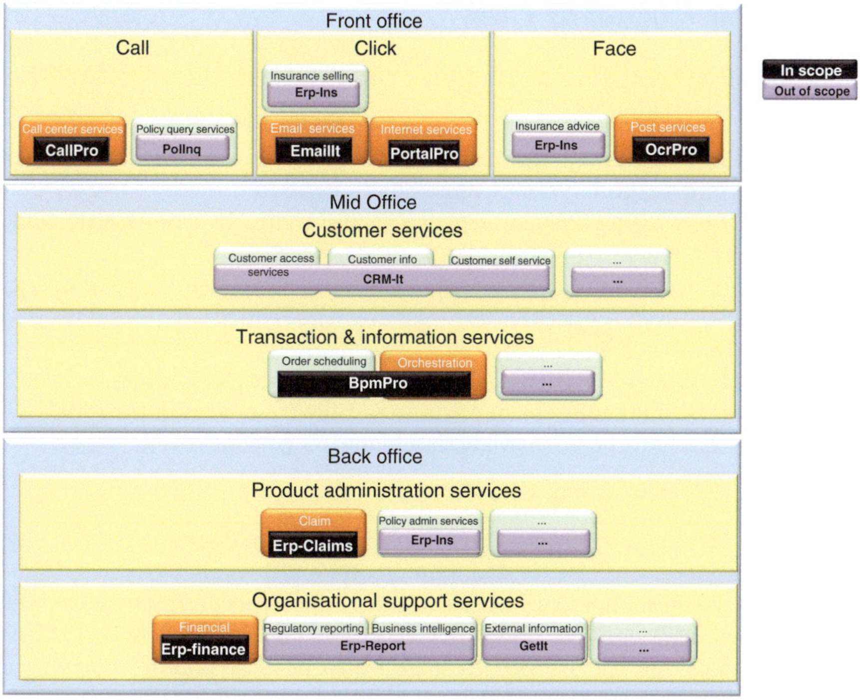
Front office
Call
Click
Face
Insurance selling
Erp-Ins
Call center services
CallPro
Policy query services
PolInq
Email services
EmailIt
Internet services
PortalPro
Insurance advice
Erp-Ins
Post services
OcrPro
In scope
Out of scope
Mid Office
Customer services
Customer access services
Customer info
Customer self service
CRM-It
...
...
Transaction & information services
Order scheduling
Orchestration
BpmPro
...
...
Back office
Product administration services
Claim
Erp-Claims
Policy admin services
Erp-Ins
...
...
Organisational support services
Financial
Erp-finance
Regulatory reporting
Business intelligence
Erp-Report
External information
GetIt
...
...

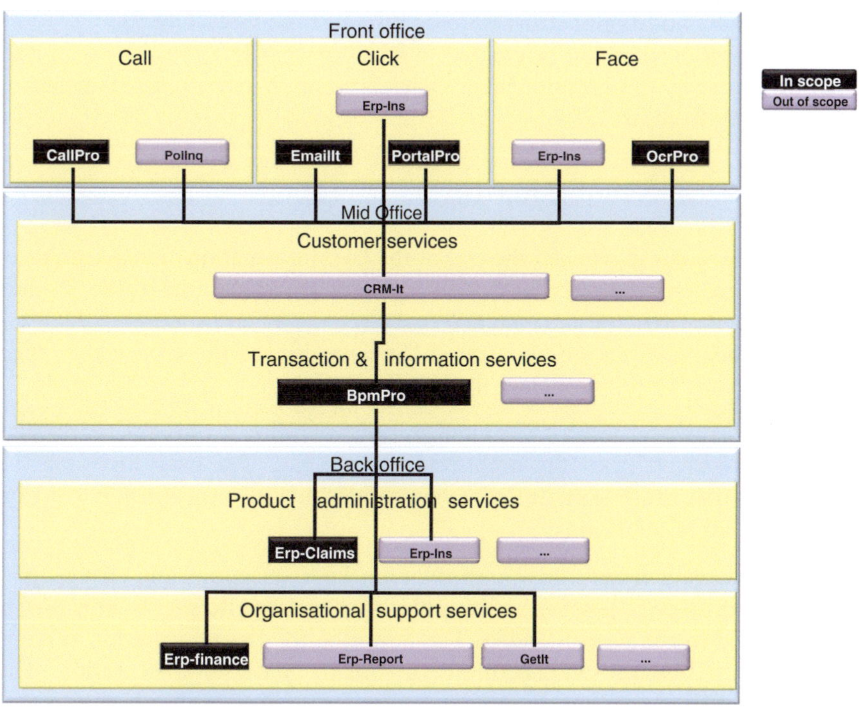
Front office
Call
Click
Face
Erp-Ins
CallPro
PolInq
EmailIt
PortalPro
Erp-Ins
OcrPro
In scope
Out of scope
Mid Office
Customer services
CRM-It
...
Transaction & information services
BpmPro
...
Back office
Product administration services
Erp-Claims
Erp-Ins
...
Organisational support services
Erp-finance
Erp-Report
GetIt
...

3.5.8 Other Physical IS Views

Views that have been explained in earlier parts of this chapter, and which can also be used here are:

- **Physical Information System Component view** to show a relevant subset of **Physical** Information System Component's attributes;
- **Physical Information System Gap view** to show gaps between baseline and target architecture;
- **Physical Information System Component Security view** to check if the security attributes of the IS services in the PISCs are in line with each other. This view should always be considered;
- **Physical Information System Component Governance (NFR) view** to check if the nonfunctional requirement attributes of the IS services in the PISCs are in line with each other. This view should always be considered.

Additional views that can be considered are:

- **Physical Information System Reuse/Buy/Build view** which shows which physical components will be re-used, bought and built;
- **The Development view** can be used to show which components will be built with which development tools;
- **The Product view** can be used to show which physical components will be delivered through a specific product. Additionally you can add the amount of customization required for the different products so people can understand where additional effort is needed to meet the requirements;
- **An Integration view** can be created to focus on specific aspects of the interfaces between the components, such as communication mechanisms or messaging formats.

3.5.9 IS Architecture Wrap-Up

At this point we have reached the end of the IAF information systems architecture. We have determined the level of automated support required by the business information services and documented that in terms of information system services and their collaboration contracts. We have derived the service and collaboration contract attributes from the business information service attributes.

We have created our logical IS architecture by defining grouping criteria that have been derived from the architecture principles. We have analyzed the logical IS architecture from different viewpoints and we have refined it to create the best possible solution.

Finally we have worked our way through package selections and cost estimations to end up with a set of deliverables that will ensure the architecture is implemented in the way intended. The next step for the information systems architect is to use the architecture as a tool to guide implementation. The technology infrastructure architect will use a lot of the IS architecture products to understand which infrastructure is needed to support the information systems. Let's have a look at how that works in the next chapter.

3.6 Technology Infrastructure Architecture

3.6.1 Overview

The Technology Infrastructure Aspect Area focuses on defining which infrastructure is needed to support the information systems architecture. Questions that always pops up when we talk about this subject is: 'What is infrastructure actually?' and 'What is the difference between IS architecture and TI architecture?' Well, there are two things that help in understanding the difference. The first is governance. The second is the presence or absence of business logic in the service. Let's elaborate on these two topics.

There are services that are used generically throughout the organization. It is hard to define one owner who can govern the service. Often services like that are managed centrally, typically by some form of IT department. Examples of generic services are: e-mail, instant messaging, video conferencing, and office automation. We position services like this in the technology infrastructure architecture area, as they can be seen as a form of infrastructure that is there for everyone. Services with a specific owner are positioned in the IS architecture area.

Another characteristic of infrastructure is that it is usable by everybody that needs it. It does not even know which different types of users are using it. To be a bit more specific: it does not contain any business logic. If it did, it would become specific to the business and belong to a specific area. In this line of thinking word processing software itself would be generic and belong in the TI architecture. The templates containing the company brand and look and feel would be specific and belong in the IS architecture. The same goes for data base management systems. The DBMS itself is generic and therefore infrastructure. The stored procedures contain business logic and belong in the IS architecture.

We normally distinguish the following types of infrastructure:

- **(User) interface services** which can vary greatly in size and shape. They can vary from a normal desktop system through a barcode scanner to and RFID scanner or a sensor in a machine.
- **Communications services** provide the connection between the interface services and the shared services described below. They can vary from proprietary interfaces in a machine to the internet.
- **Shared computing services** are the computing services that can be used by multiple users or departments within the organization, for different purposes and applications.
- **Shared storage services** provide means for storing data that needs to be shared between users.

- **Systems software and management services** consist of operating systems and systems management and maintenance software.
- **Generic application services** are the applications that are provided to everybody, like e-mail and word processing.

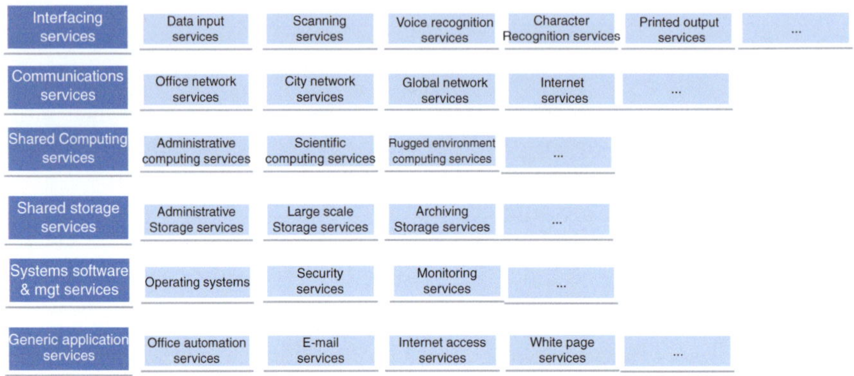

The first step in the TI architecture area is to define which TI services are needed to support the IS services or Logical IS components, which ever we choose to use as a basis. So for example we would have a look at our accept e-mail claims service and determine which TI services are needed to support it. We will need some form of desktop computer to be able to read and analyze the claim, so we do need an interface service. Let's call it 'Data processing service'.

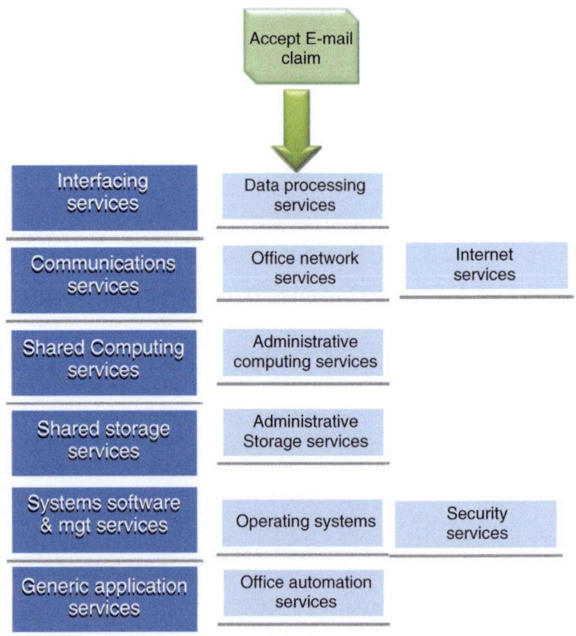

We would also need to connect the data processing service to the generic e-mail environment, so we'll need an 'Office network service'. To be able to receive e-mails from the outside world we will also need some form of internet service to communicate with our customers. This would go on until we have defined all services required to support the IS service.

Creating TI architectures this way ensures you have a very good link between the IS and TI services. It also is the most exact and time consuming way. Nowadays many companies create 'infrastructure catalogs' in which they define available sets of infrastructure that deliver a predefined Quality of service. They enable you to select what you can use and only architect the parts that are not available. The figure provides an example of an infrastructure catalog.

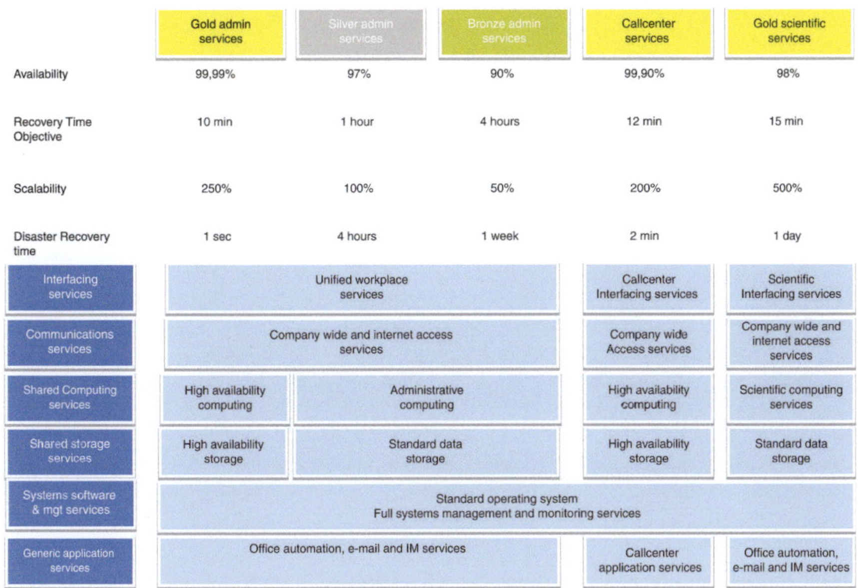

3.6.2 Technology Infrastructure Conceptual Artifacts

3.6.2.1 Technology Infrastructure Service

Technology infrastructure services are commonly derived from IS services or logical IS components. This does not mean that you always have to create an IS architecture before you can create the TI architecture. You can derive TI services from Business services if you need to. You will only have to assume more about the IS support that will be required. We do not advise to create a TI architecture without looking at the business at all. There is one exception. That is when you are basing the business on new infrastructure that is being created. An example in that area would be the creation of GPS navigation systems. The business idea was to create GPS navigation systems that were accessible to the general public. The infrastructure to create those devices can be defined without looking at the business, because you know you need a user interface, a GPS receiver, a map storage device etc. to make that piece of infrastructure work.

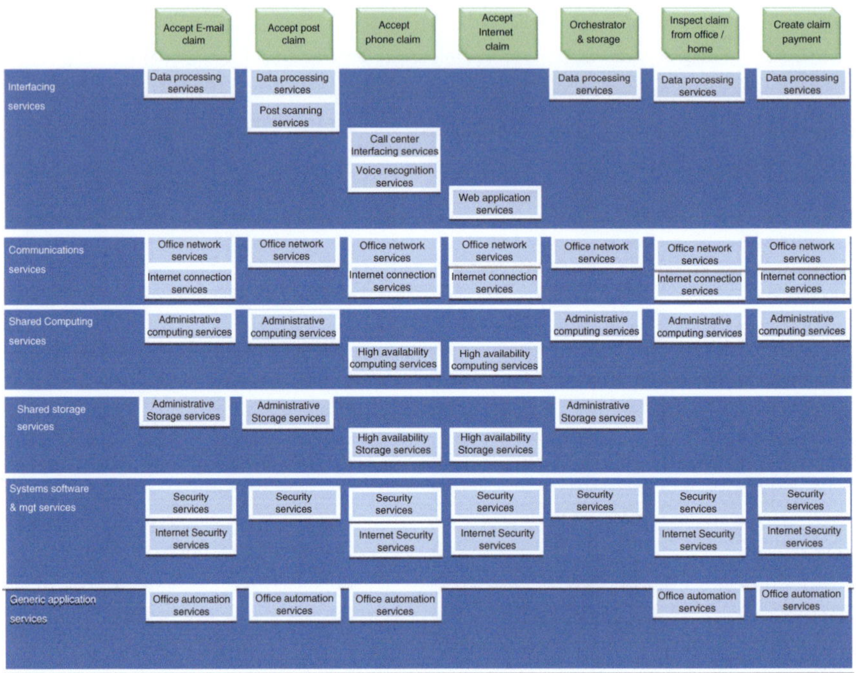

3.6.2.2 Technology Infrastructure Service Interaction Model

The Technology Infrastructure Service Interaction Model illustrates the Technology Infrastructure Services and their Interaction. These models can be created in the same way all other interaction models are. It is important to focus on the relevant interactions. The fact that there will be interaction between the TI service 'administrative computing services' and 'administrative storage services' might not always be relevant. On the other hand, it might be very relevant to show that customers can submit their claims through the internet connection service.

3.6.2.3 Technology Infrastructure Service Collaboration Contract

TI service collaboration contract attributes are derived from the IS service collaboration contracts. So if the IS service collaboration contract has defined that it has to be able to process 25 internet claims per day and it has to respond after maximum 2.5 seconds, then the TI service collaboration contracts could look like they are in the example. If the average network processing was 1.5 seconds, then the internal processing time would be maximum 1 second.

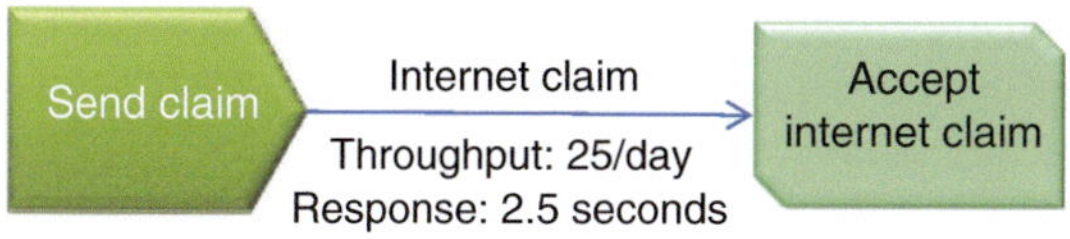

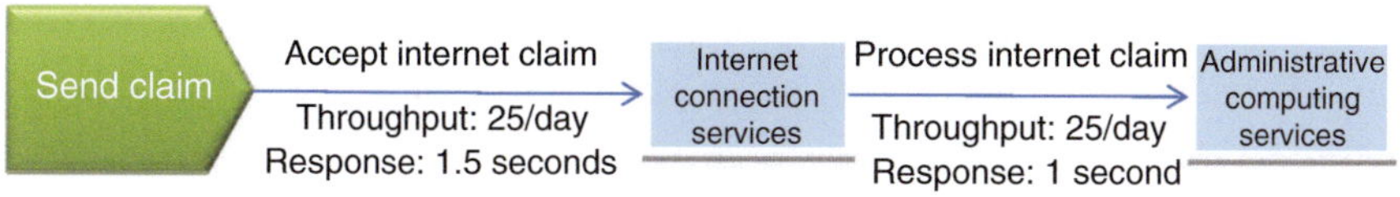

3.6.2.4 IS - TI Service Cross-Reference

The IS-TI Service cross-reference illustrates the 'uses this infrastructure'-link between the Information system service and the required Technology infrastructure services.

IS services / TI services	Accept e-mail claim	Accept Post claim	Accept phone claim	Accept Internet claim	Orchestrator & Storage	Reject claim	Inspect claim from office / home	Create claim payment	Submit payments
Data processing services	X	X			X	X	X	X	X
Post scanning services		X							
Callcenter interfacing services			X						
Voice recognition services			X						
Web application services				X					
Office network services	X	X	X	X	X	X	X	X	X
Internet connection services	X		X	X		X	X		X
Administrative computing services	X	X			X	X	X	X	X
High availability computing services			X	X					
Administrative storage services	X	X			X		X	X	
High availability storage services			X	X					
Security services	X	X	X	X	X	X	X	X	X
Internet security services	X		X	X		X	X		X
Office automation services	X	X	X			X			X

3.6.2.5 Technology Infrastructure Domain

Just like the other domains, the TI domains are used to communicate the TI services that have been defined. Very often they are copies of the IS domains, so they can show which TI services support the IS services within that domain. Other options are (1) to use the infrastructure types as described in Sect. 3.6.1 as domains and (2) base the domains on the sets of TI services that are present in the infrastructure catalog like in the example below.

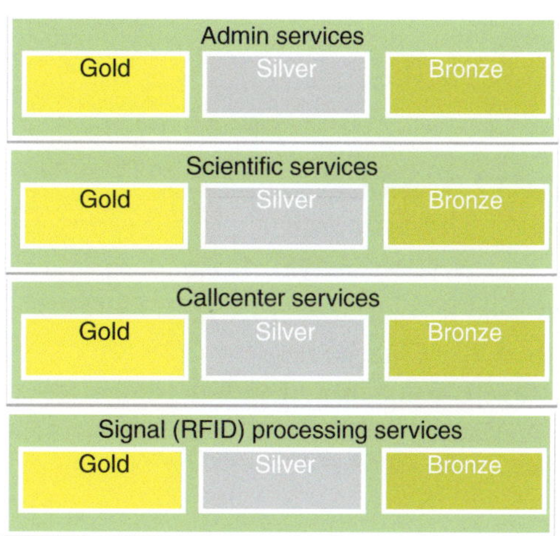

An additional approach to TI domain definition is to define domains based on the way they are governed. Typical domains in this approach are 'datacenter', 'network', 'workplace' and 'storage'.

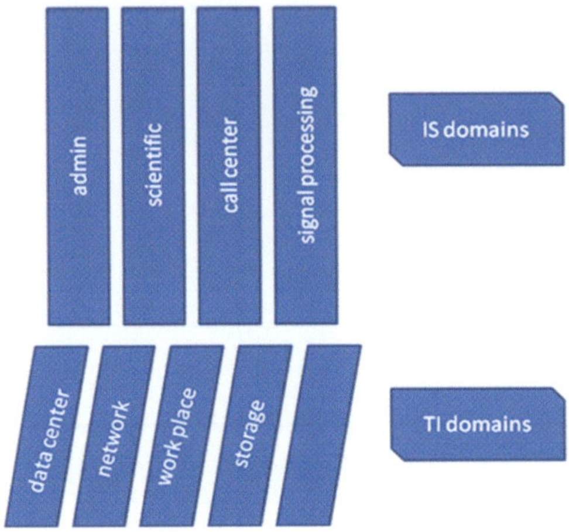

3.6.3 Technology Infrastructure Conceptual Views

3.6.3.1 Logical Information System and Technology Infrastructure Services View

This view's purpose is to show specific relationships between LISCs and TI services. Most of the time this view is used to validate that the correct TI services have been defined for a specific LISC. The example zooms in to the post and internet services.

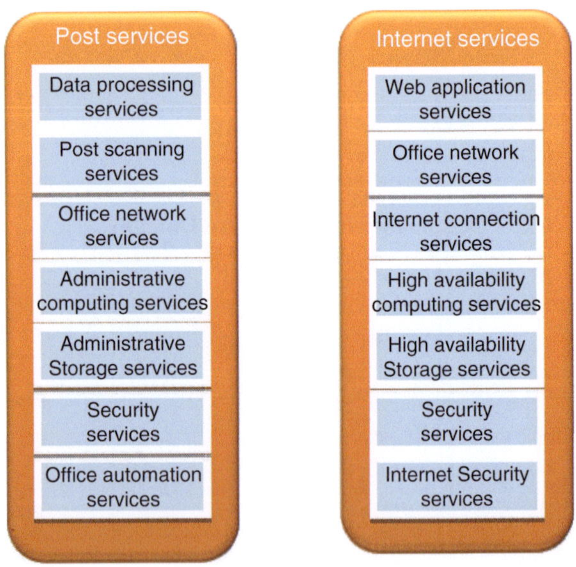

3.6.3.2 Technology Infrastructure Services Gaps

It can be necessary to show the technology infrastructure gaps at service level. This tends to be the fact when significant changes to the services are required, for example when availability requirements need to be increased like in the example.

Target → architecture Baseline ↓ architecture	Data processing services	Office network services	Internet connection services	Post scanning services	Eliminated services ↓
Data processing services	*Upgrade: current services are end of life.*				
Office network services		*Keep as is*			
Internet connection services			*Re-design: need higher availability*		
New →				New service: needs physical selection	

A second way of documenting and communicating gaps is to put them in a table like below.

Service	Description	Gap	Gap Impact	Effort to close the gap	Other remarks
Data processing services	Computers used by end users to access the applications	Services is end of life-cyce. Needs to be replaced	Creation of a new data processing service, and its implementation throughout the organisation	Out of pocket: €250K Implementation effort: 5 FTE for 3 months	-
Internet connection service	Service that enables end users to access the systems through the internet	Insufficient availability	Needs complete re-design due to defined availability requirements.	Out of pocket: €100K Implementation effort: 5 FTE for 4 months	

Although the technical infrastructure services gap view is one to consider, most of the time gaps are defined and communicated at the logical and physical level.

3.6.3.3 Technology Infrastructure Services Security View

Stakeholders looking for information about the different security classifications of the Conceptual Technology Infrastructure (TI) Services fulfilling the security requirements will find this information in the Technology Infrastructure Services Security View. This View shows the security classification for each of the TI Services of the TI architecture.

3.6.3.4 Technology Infrastructure Non-functional Requirements View

This view has the same objective and approach as all the other non-functional requirements views. It visualizes selected non functional requirements of the services and their collaboration contracts to ensure the correct attribute values have been derived from the IS service attributes.

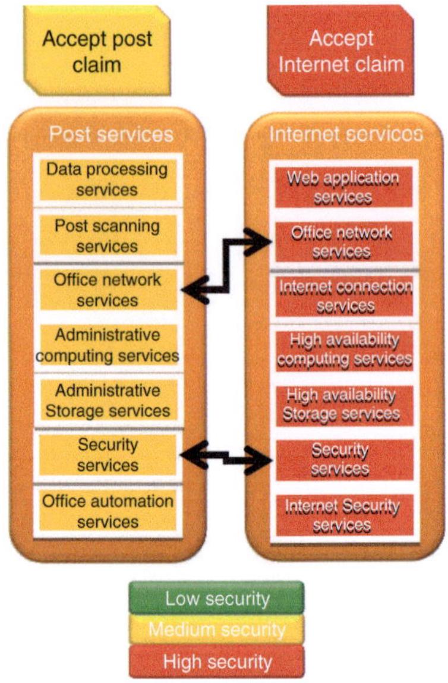

3.6.4 *Technology Infrastructure Logical Artifacts*

3.6.4.1 Logical Technology Infrastructure Component

Logical technology infrastructure components are created using the same technique as all other component types. Services are grouped into components based on criteria that have been derived from the architecture principles. Most of the time the defined technology infrastructure components are communicated as shown in the example. All components, and the most important connections between components are visualized using logical forms. This keeps people away from thinking physical, and getting confused as a result.

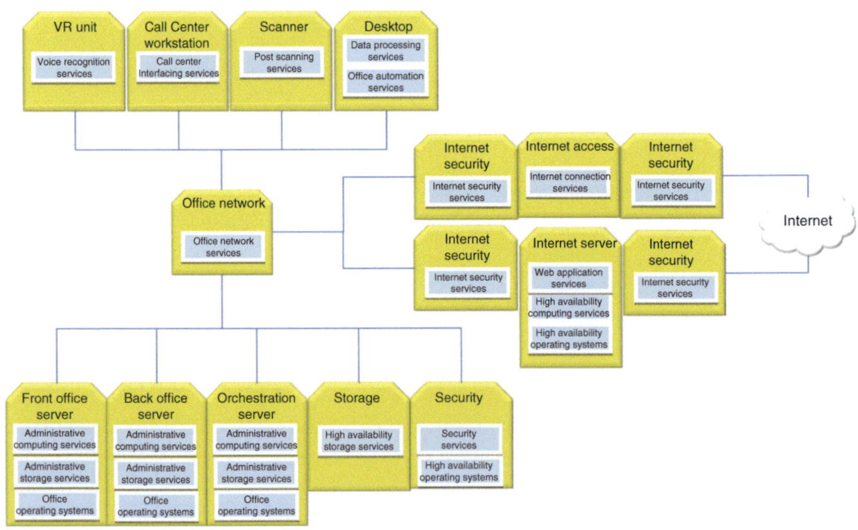

A second example from real life is shown in the figures below. Its advantage is that it uses standardized symbols for routers, switches, firewalls etc., which makes communication with technologists simpler. The drawback is that it tends to confuse less technical adept readers.

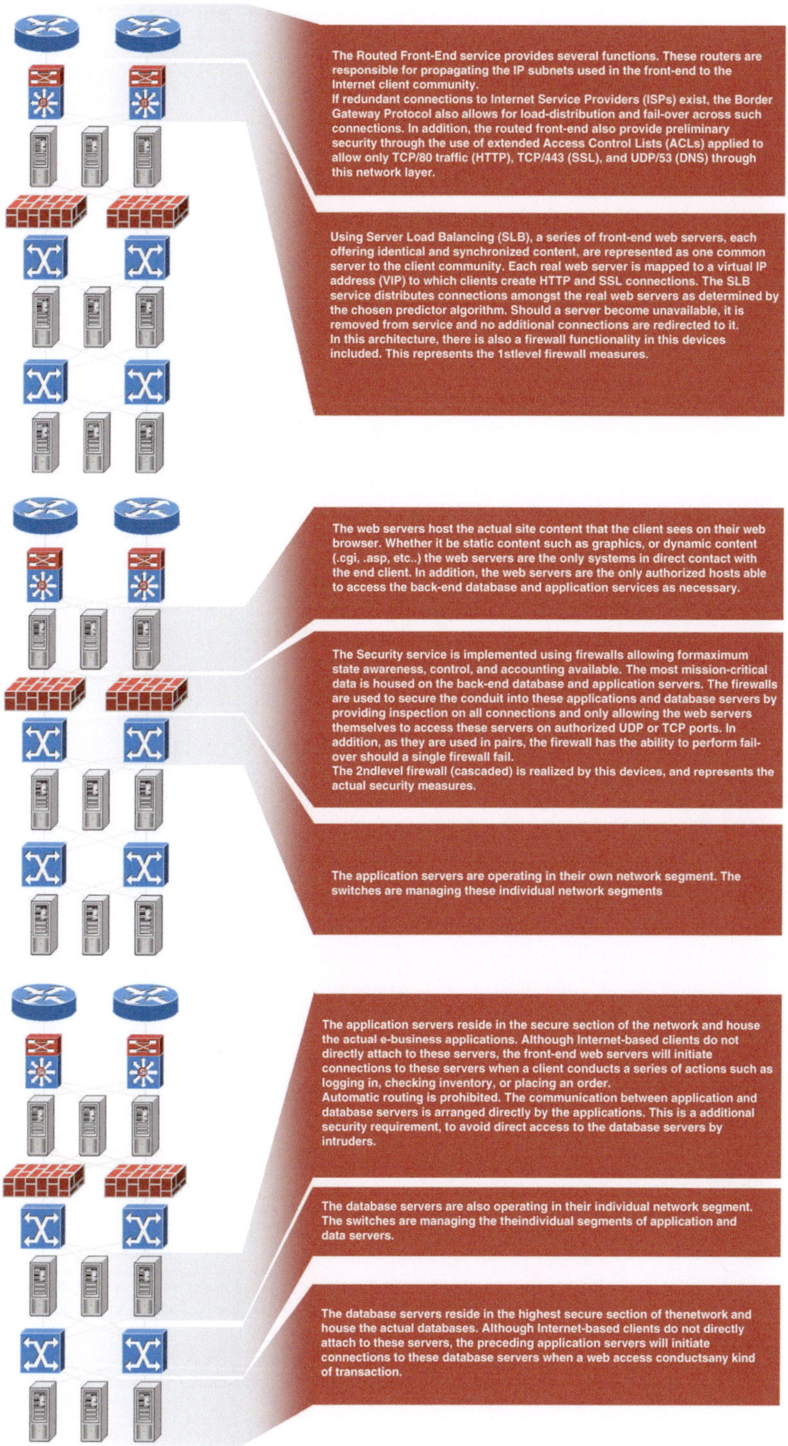
The Routed Front-End service provides several functions. These routers are responsible for propagating the IP subnets used in the front-end to the Internet client community.
If redundant connections to Internet Service Providers (ISPs) exist, the Border Gateway Protocol also allows for load-distribution and fail-over across such connections. In addition, the routed front-end also provide preliminary security through the use of extended Access Control Lists (ACLs) applied to allow only TCP/80 traffic (HTTP), TCP/443 (SSL), and UDP/53 (DNS) through this network layer.
Using Server Load Balancing (SLB), a series of front-end web servers, each offering identical and synchronized content, are represented as one common server to the client community. Each real web server is mapped to a virtual IP address (VIP) to which clients create HTTP and SSL connections. The SLB service distributes connections amongst the real web servers as determined by the chosen predictor algorithm. Should a server become unavailable, it is removed from service and no additional connections are redirected to it.
In this architecture, there is also a firewall functionality in this devices included. This represents the 1stlevel firewall measures.
The web servers host the actual site content that the client sees on their web browser. Whether it be static content such as graphics, or dynamic content (.cgi, .asp, etc..) the web servers are the only systems in direct contact with the end client. In addition, the web servers are the only authorized hosts able to access the back-end database and application services as necessary.
The Security service is implemented using firewalls allowing formaximum state awareness, control, and accounting available. The most mission-critical data is housed on the back-end database and application servers. The firewalls are used to secure the conduit into these applications and database servers by providing inspection on all connections and only allowing the web servers themselves to access these servers on authorized UDP or TCP ports. In addition, as they are used in pairs, the firewall has the ability to perform fail-over should a single firewall fail.
The 2ndlevel firewall (cascaded) is realized by this devices, and represents the actual security measures.
The application servers are operating in their own network segment. The switches are managing these individual network segments
The application servers reside in the secure section of the network and house the actual e-business applications. Although Internet-based clients do not directly attach to these servers, the front-end web servers will initiate connections to these servers when a client conducts a series of actions such as logging in, checking inventory, or placing an order.
Automatic routing is prohibited. The communication between application and database servers is arranged directly by the applications. This is a additional security requirement, to avoid direct access to the database servers by intruders.
The database servers are also operating in their individual network segment. The switches are managing the theindividual segments of application and data servers.
The database servers reside in the highest secure section of thenetwork and house the actual databases. Although Internet-based clients do not directly attach to these servers, the preceding application servers will initiate connections to these database servers when a web access conductsany kind of transaction.

3.6.4.2 Logical Technology Infrastructure Component Interaction Model

Very often we use the technology infrastructure component model as the basis for the interaction model. We superimpose the relevant interactions on the model and add a legend to explain the different interactions.

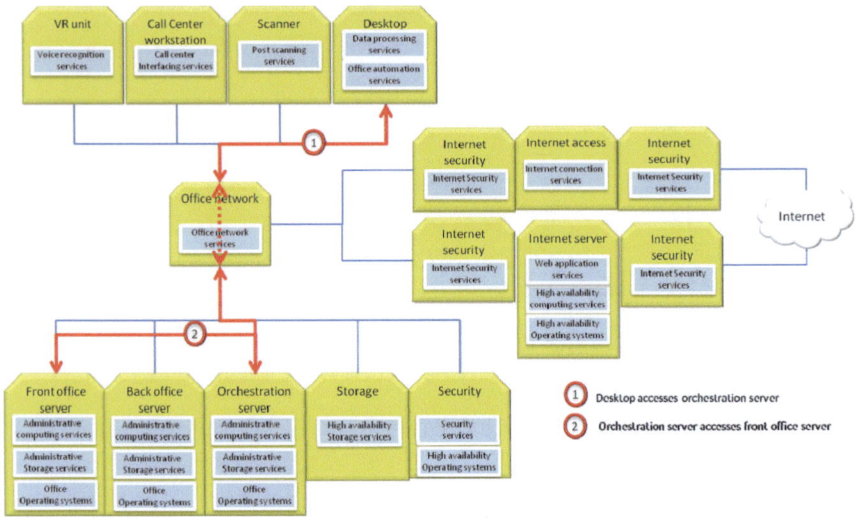

3.6.4.3 Logical Technology Infrastructure Component Collaboration Contract

Most of the attributes that are defined in the standard collaboration contract are also relevant for technology infrastructure collaboration contracts. Some might be less relevant and can be removed (see the strikethrough attributes for examples).

Description	*Describe the collaboration contract*
Result	*Describe the result that gets passed back to the caller*
Error handling	*Describe how errors in the interaction need to be handled*
Contract input	*Describe input that is required by the receiving component*
Contract output	*Describe the output that is delivered as result*
Throughput	*Describe the average required throughput*
Throughput period	*Describes the throughput period.* <Second/ Minute/ Hour/ Day/ Week>
Growth	*Describe the expected growth in percentage.* %
Growth period	*Describes the growth period.* <Second/ Minute/ Hour/ Day/ Week/ Month/ Year>
Service window	*Or opening hours, describes when the service should be available*
Peak profile short term	*Describes the peak profile for the short term period.* <Standard office/ Morning peak/ Afternoon peak/ Flat>
Peak profile long term	*Describes the peak profile for the long period.* <Standard week/ Month end peak/ Month begin peak/ Mid month peak/ Flat/ Quarter end peak/ Year end peak/ something else>
Characteristics	*Describe the characteristics of the contract.* <Immediate response required/ Delayed response possible (within response limits)/ Transactional/ Batch/ Conversational>

Integration mechanism	*Describe the integration mechanism to be used.* <Synchronous / Async – PubSub / Async – Fire&forget / Async – Assured delivery / ...>
Response requirements	*Describes the normal time a service/component request should response.* <<1 Second/ >1 <5 Seconds/ > 5 seconds < 10 minutes/ >1 hour < 1 day/ < 1 week>
Contract control requirements	*Describe the control requirement of the contract.* <Control required every time the contract is activated/ Logging of contract activation & results insufficient/ No contract control requirements>
Result control requirements	*Describe the result requirement of the contract.* <No result control required/ Result control based on periodic checks/ Result control required every time the contract is supporting>
Importance	*Describe the importance of the contract.* <Failure allowed if only quality degrades/ Must complete within response times>
Other attributes	*Any other attributes you need to achieve your architecture objectives*

3.6.5 Technology Infrastructure Logical Views

3.6.5.1 Technology Infrastructure Solution Alternatives View

This is a very common view in the logical technology infrastructure architecture. Very often the real technology choices are made and analyzed at this point in time. The example shows that the shared components scenario is slightly better that the dedicated components scenario. If cost efficiency had been one of the principles, the shared components scenario would have been even better.

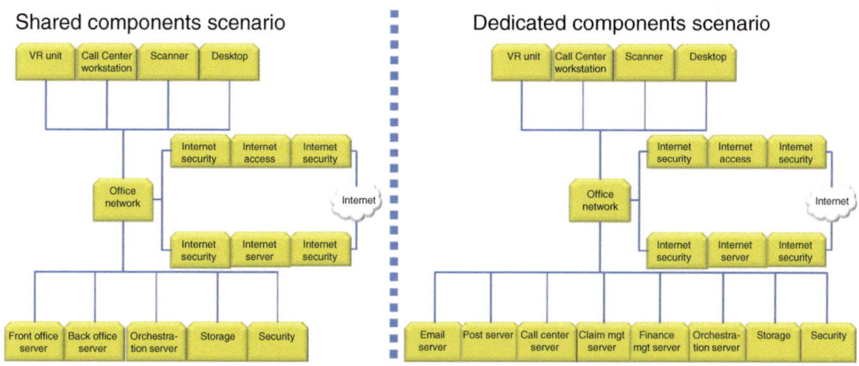

Scenario	principle + relative priority: Buy before build (3)		Distribution channel flexibility (2)		Good functional fit (2)		Reuse where possible (1)		Total result
	Score	Result	Score	Result	Score	Result	Score	Result	
Dedicated components	3	9	0	0	3	6	0	0	15
Shared components	3	9	0	0	2	4	3	3	16

3.6.5.2 Logical IS-TI mapping

A second popular view in the logical technology infrastructure architecture is the logical IS-TI mapping. This view shows the relevant relationships between the logical IS and TI components. Of course the mapping could be done in a simple cross-reference table. Most of the time we prefer to superimpose the logical IS components on top of the logical TI components as shown in the example. The main benefit is that it tends to be much easier to spot potential errors in the architecture. A second benefit is that many stakeholders like to hang this view on their wall so they can discuss technology topics using the view.

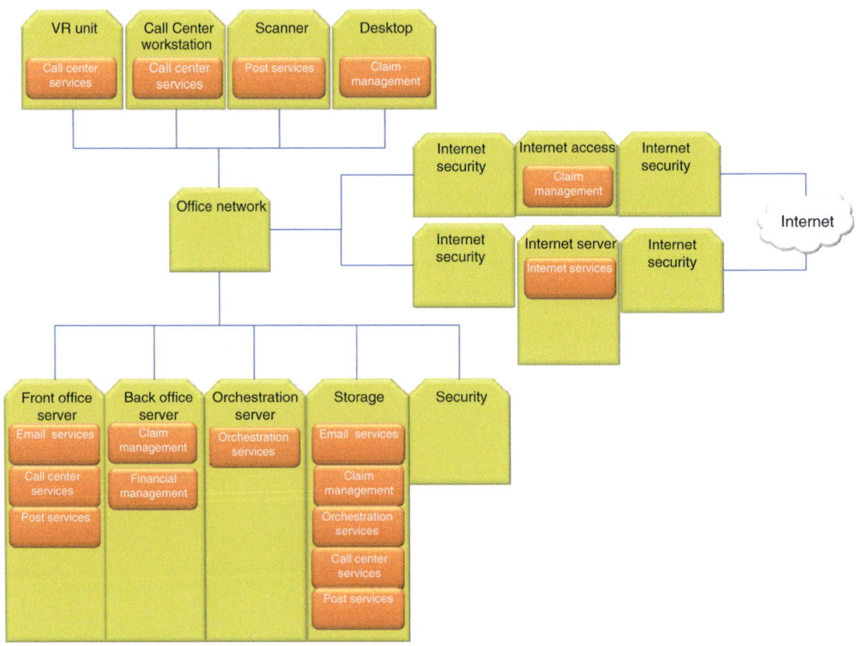

3.6.5.3 Other Logical Technology Infrastructure Views

Views that have been described in earlier chapters and can be considered here are:

- **Logical Technology Infrastructure Component Gap View** to show gaps between baseline and target architecture.
- **Logical Technology Infrastructure Component Security View** to check if the security attributes of the TI services in the Logical TI components are in line with each other. *This view should always be considered.*
- **Logical Technology Infrastructure Component Governance (NFR) View** to check if the non-functional requirement attributes of the TI services in the

Logical TI components are in line with each other. *This view should always be considered.*

- **Technology Infrastructure Design Decisions** can be documented in terms of architecture principles to help the architecture implementers understand WHY things are the way they are.
- **Logical Technology Infrastructure Migration View** to pass on instructions regarding the logical Technology Infrastructure architecture to the implementers.

Other views that can be considered are:

- **Logical Technology Infrastructure Disaster Recovery View**. This view zooms into disaster recovery and highlights how it has been addressed in the TI architecture. Very often the logical TI component model is used as the basis for this view. Annotations and comments are added to show how disaster recovery has been addressed. The rest of the views in this list can be constructed in the same way as described here. They highlight the topic in the view's name.
- **Logical Technology Infrastructure Logging and Monitoring View.** This view shows which mechanisms have been selected for the control of activities performed (logging) and the control of availability of the system (monitoring).
- **Logical Technology Infrastructure Backup and Archive View.** Here we zoom in on the components we have defined for backup and archive of data. Besides showing the components, we often highlight specific aspects like frequency of backup/archive, capacity of the components and duration of the activities.
- **Logical Acceptance Environment,** showing the specific components that are to be used for acceptance of new/changed IS components.
- **Logical Test Environment,** showing the components used for testing.
- **Logical Development Environment,** showing the components used for development of IS components.

3.6.6 Technology Infrastructure Physical Artifacts

Physical TI architecture focuses on answering three main questions: (1) what do I buy, (2) how long will it take, and (3) how much will it cost. Technology usually is acquired, either as boxes or through services. This implies that product selection is a very common activity in physical TI architecture. It can be approached as described in Sect. 3.5.6.

3.6.6.1 Physical Technology Infrastructure Component

Products or technologies chosen to realize a Logical Technology Infrastructure Components are called Physical Technology Infrastructure Components. Possible examples could be HP UX, Oracle, Cisco's network appliances or Microsoft's Office Suite. Their specifications can be documented using the component attributes. Very often they are visualized using pictures from real life.

3.6.6.2 Physical Technology Infrastructure Component Interaction Model

This model is constructed in the same way as in the logical architecture. The relevant interactions are superimposed on top of the model of the physical components. As stated earlier, focus on the relevant interactions, and not on all interactions. This model would turn into an 'interaction blur' if all interactions would be plotted on the model.

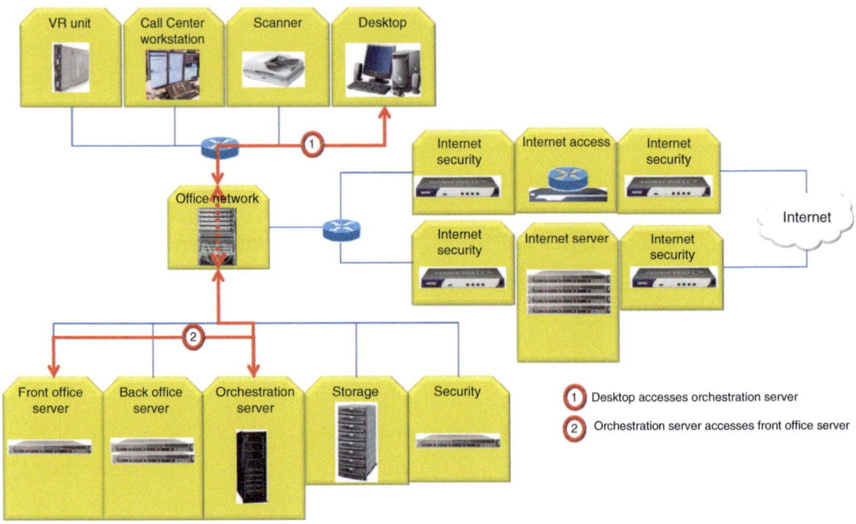

3.6.6.3 Physical Technology Infrastructure Component Collaboration Contract

These are derived from the logical TI component collaboration contracts. They commonly have the same attributes.

3.6.6.4 Technology Infrastructure Standards, Rules and Guidelines

Just as in the IS architecture, this is a key artifact in the TI architecture. It is defined for the same purpose, it is the 'law' for anybody that will be using or implementing the architecture. It can – and often will – refer to generic SRGs that have been created. On top of that you should define which SRGs are specific to the implementation and usage of this TI architecture. Topics that can be part of the TI SRGs are:

- Hardware that is to be used
- Systems software that is allowed
- Network device standards
- Communications protocols to be used
- Disaster recovery
- Logging and monitoring

Just as in the IS architecture it can be helpful to promote TI oriented architecture principles to SRGs to formalize the enforcement of those principles.

3.6.6.5 Technology Infrastructure Migration Specifications

Just as in all the other aspect areas, there will be circumstances in which you want to pass on instructions regarding the TI architecture to the implementers, without turning them into SRGs. They can address the same topics as will be mentioned within the SRGs, but will be less formal. Typical examples of migration specifications are related to (1) the order in which different technology infrastructure components objects need to be migrated to ensure overall transaction integrity, (2) the rollback possibilities and implications, and (3) the deployment steps.

3.6.7 Technology Infrastructure Physical Views

3.6.7.1 Technology Infrastructure Cost View

This gives insight in the costs related to the technology infrastructure architecture aspects.

Cost group	Cost element	Price per unit	# units	Period 1	Period 2	Period 3	Period 4	Period 5	Period 6	Period 7	Period 8	Total costs
Information systems												
	Package licence costs	5000	1	5000								**5.000**
	Package maintenance costs: 15-20% of listprice per annum	1000	7		1000	1000	1000	1000	1000	1000	1000	**7.000**
	Package customisation costs	4000	4									
	Package implementation costs											
	Testing											
	Interface creation											
	Shadow production											
	ETC											
Totals				5000	1000	1000	1000	1000	1000	1000	1000	**12.000**

Purchasing, implementation and testing costs are just part of the costs that have to be taken into account in the TI architecture. Maintenance costs commonly are 20% of the purchase price per year, and thus a significant part of the total cost. HVAC (Heating, ventilation and air conditioning) can also be a significant cost element. Ensure that this topic is addressed. We have encountered situations in which the utilities company could not deliver sufficient power to the datacenter to run all the machines and the HVAC needed. TI costing can be a detailed exercise, especially if the total cost of ownership (TCO) has to be compared for multiple scenarios. There are models available on the internet to assist in defining TCO.

3.6.7.2 Physical IS - TI mapping

This is a popular view in the physical TI architecture, sometimes even more popular than the logical IS-TI mapping. It serves the same goals as the logical IS-TI mapping, and is created just as the logical view is created. The physical IS components are superimposed on top of the physical TI components.

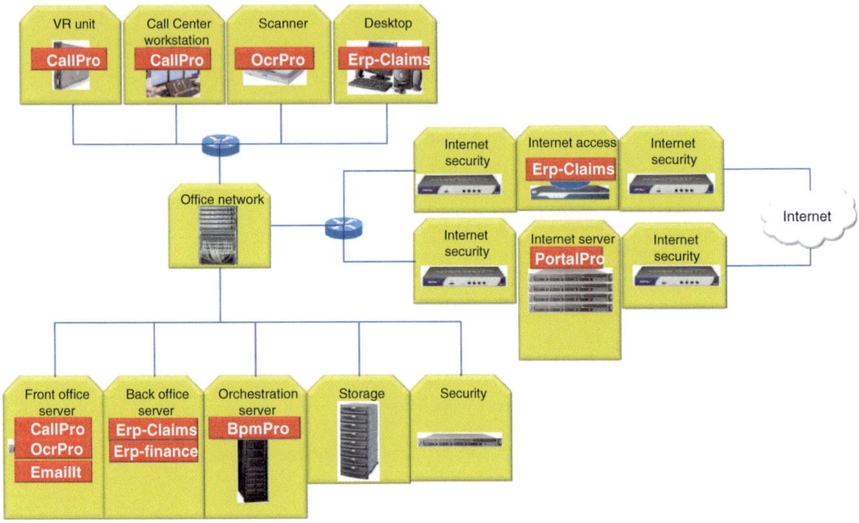

3.6.7.3 Physical Technology Infrastructure Transaction View

If you suspect that the number of transactions per second might be critical for certain components in the architecture you can create the Physical TI transaction view. The view is created by analyzing the physical IS components, and by determining the different transactions that will result from the usage of the service. After that you can determine which physical TI components will be involved in processing the transactions. The transaction characteristics will enable you to determine average and peak transaction volumes per component. Benchmark data regarding transaction load that machines can handle can be found at www.tpc.org.

		Characteristics						Technology Component				
Transaction	ID	# Trans / period	Period type	Transaction class	Usage period	Peak period	Characteristics verified?	Front office server	Back office server	Orchestration server	Internet server	VR unit
Call center claim	Clm01	100	Day	Light	Office hrs	Standard	Y		•	•		•
Email claim	Clm02	100	Day	Medium	Office hrs	Standard	Y	•	•	•		
Internet claim	Clm03	500	Day	Heavy	24hrs	20.00	Y	•	•	•	•	
Paper claim	Clm04	500	Day	Light	DayEnd	DayEnd	Y	•	•	•		

This view needs knowledge from the IS as well as the TI area. It is commonly created as a joint view for both areas.

3.6.7.4 Physical Technology Infrastructure Dataflow View

If network bandwidth usage needs to be analyzed, you can create the dataflow view. Characteristics to be gathered here are: # flows per period, size of the messages sent through the network and peak characteristics. If you map all the flows to the physical (network) components they flow through, you can determine average and peak bandwidth requirements per component. Take network protocol overhead into account when determining bandwidth. TCP/IP overhead can be as much as 50%.

3.6.7.5 Physical Technology Infrastructure Data Storage View

The size of the required data storage for a specific component can be determined in the same way as the physical technology infrastructure transaction view. The characteristics to be collected here are the size of the records to be stored and the duration that they need to be stored.

3.6.7.6 Other Physical Technology Infrastructure Views

- **Physical Technology Infrastructure Component Security View** to check if the security attributes of the TI services in the physical TI components are in line with each other. *This view should always be considered.*
- **Logical Technology Infrastructure Component Governance (NFR) View** to check if the non-functional requirement attributes of the TI services in the physical TI components are in line with each other. *This view should always be considered.*
- **The Physical Technology Infrastructure Service Levels View** focuses on showing average and maximum levels of service the components can deliver. If so desired this information can be complemented with information from the transaction, data flow and data storage views to show which service level is demanded by the IS components.

Other views that zoom into specific aspects of the physical TI architecture are:

- Physical Technology Infrastructure Disaster Recovery View
- Physical Technology Infrastructure Logging and Monitoring View
- Physical Technology Infrastructure Backup and Archive View
- Physical Acceptance Environment
- Physical Test Environment
- Physical Development Environment
- Physical Technology Infrastructure Component Gap View
- Physical Technology Infrastructure Migration View

3.6.8 TI Architecture Wrap-Up

Now we have reached the end of the technology infrastructure architecture as defined in IAF. The information system components defined in the IS architecture can now run on the required infrastructure. We also have defined which generic applications are needed to support the business. We have defined and analyzed the required interfaces between the infrastructure components. We have also analyzed different solution alternatives, at logical and physical level.

We are not finished with the architecture work. Security and governance, which are quality aspects, have had a lot of attention in the architecture work so far. However, we still need to address them from another angle. The next chapter shows what that angle is.

3.7 The Quality Aspect of Architecture

3.7.1 Introduction

The degree as to which an architecture fulfils the objectives is a constant field of tension that an architect must deal with. There usually is a prime motive that a client and his associated stakeholders have with the outcome of the architecture, being an operational system in some form. Associating quality factors with elements of the architecture helps to determine which combination of elements is core in achieving the objectives. These factors are expressed in terms of quality needs, also referred to 'non-functional requirements' (NFR's), 'quality attributes', 'service quality' or 'quality of service requirements'. Quality factors are applicable throughout the entire architecture design, for which several approaches have been developed as a common practice.

3.7.2 Quality

For the scope of architecture we will simply regard 'quality' as the set of characteristics of a system that give that system the ability to satisfy expressed and implicit needs. In that sense, quality expressions are always in the context of something. Qualities can relate to execution, such as security and usability, which are observable while the system is operating. Another group of qualities relate to the ability of the system to evolve, such as agility, testability, maintainability, extensibility and scalability. These are embodied in the structure of the system.

The quality parameters are quite diverse, which is the reason that the industry has developed classification schemes and taxonomies that present them in a useful structure. One of these schemes is ISO 9126[4], which deals

[4] ISO/IEC 9126, information available via Wikipedia. Http://en.wikipedia.org. Accessed April 2009

with software quality, although the factors are applicable to IT-related architectures in general; it identifies important factors to determine the shape of an architecture: factors like performance, availability, throughput. These factors have become mainstream elements of dealing with requirements in architecture.

ISO 9126 is an international standard for the evaluation of software quality. It contains a quality model that classifies software quality in a structured set of characteristics and sub-characteristics. The key characteristics are:

- *Functionality* – A set of attributes that bear on the existence of a set of functions and their specified properties. The functions are those that satisfy stated or implied needs.
- *Reliability* – A set of attributes that bear on the capability of software to maintain its level of performance under stated conditions for a stated period of time.
- *Usability* – A set of attributes that bear on the effort needed for use, and on the individual assessment of such use, by a stated or implied set of users.
- *Efficiency* – A set of attributes that bear on the relationship between the level of performance of the software and the amount of resources used, under stated conditions.
- *Maintainability* – A set of attributes that bear on the effort needed to make specified modifications.
- *Portability* – A set of attributes that bear on the ability of software to be transferred from one environment to another.

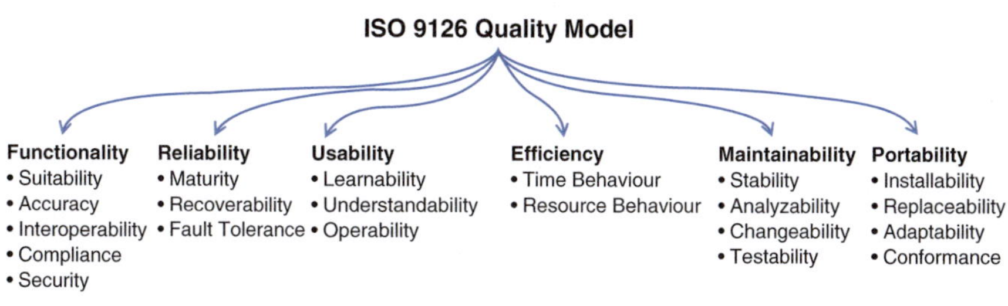

Another such classification scheme is ISO 7498-2 for security services and related mechanisms.

3.7.2.1 Evolution of Quality Needs

There is a set of basic non-functional requirements that express the conditions that the system must meet, in terms of throughput, response time, availability. These factors are usually included in the standard approaches of requirements management and expressed in metrics such as transactions per unit of time, office hours system availability, seconds per transaction. Throughout the evolution of IAF, different areas of quality factors have generated increased attention, fueled by specific trends, events or developments[5] that underlined the need to better control particular conditions, e.g.:

- Early 1990s: with distributed computing models, the increased complexity of the technology landscape made **manageability** generate requirements that must be part of the overall design; here the focus is on a continuous and continued service provisioning and monitoring the agreed service level; over time, manageability has expanded into the much broader area of **IT governance**, which is the set of mechanisms that control the decision making on business-aligned IT-related changes;
- Mid-1990s: with the emerging Internet, a new breed of **security** issues had to be dealt with; for example, controlling access to systems in an open network environment generated a new range of security mechanisms and appliances that provide standardized solutions;
- Around 2000: fraud cases and malpractices in the financial world led to a call for better transparency of the way these institutions do their business, leading to more stringent **compliance** and **corporate governance** regulations in virtually all sectors and industries; since the financial crisis of 2008 and a possible revision of the financial world ahead, we can expect new regulations and new types of control frameworks in this area;
- After 2005: an increasing attention for all things environmental, not in the least generated from the possible effects of global warming, made the IT industry rethink their contribution to energy usage and spill, leading to **green IT** initiatives.

This list is in no way complete, and each area covers subjects that may overlap with another. For example, 'availability' can be treated both as a security theme and as a IT service operations theme. It is the architect's task to guard the scope and purpose of the architecture by addressing such different notions of 'availability' in a balanced way.

As time and maturity in working with architecture progresses, we can expect new areas to emerge that generate specific additional quality requirements that must be covered in the architecture.

---

[5] It should be noted that several of these quality models may not have been altogether new and might have emerged long before; we only try to indicate the point in time where these areas actually entered the 'holistic' Business/IT architecture arena, and required the architect to develop skills in them.

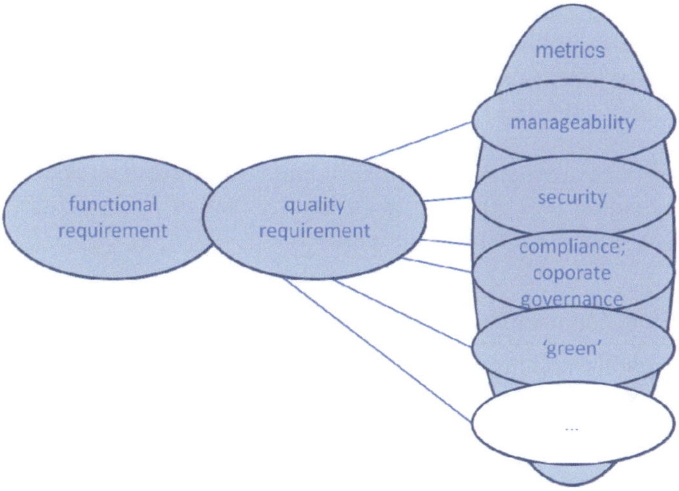

The architect must be equipped with a framework that deals with these diverse areas where quality is in the core of the subject at hand. In IAF we see these notions of quality affect all aspect areas, and as such we say they form a separate layer 'behind' the framework, touching all – or many – cells and artifacts in the IAF matrix; hence we speak of the 'third dimension' of the framework. It enables both general and specialized business/IT architects to work along the same line of thinking (one of the principles behind IAF being 'architects hunt in packs'). In the current IAF v4 a provision was made to address quality aspects in line with the core aspects' artifacts through additional quality attributes.

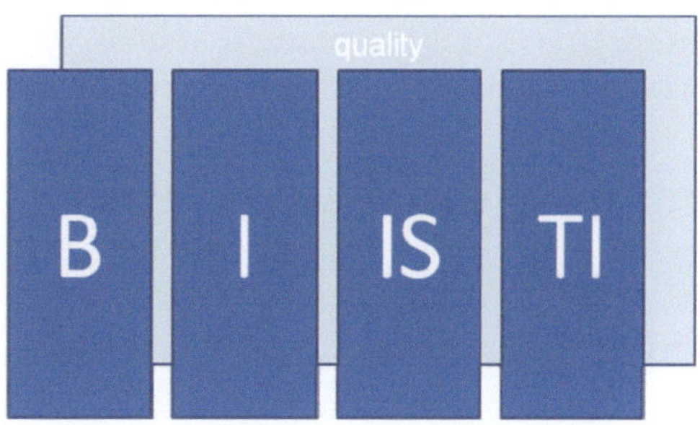

In the following sections we will address topics that are of additional relevance for the architecture when dealing with these dedicated quality areas.

3.7.2.2 Quality of What?

The pursuit of a certain level of quality always serves a purpose, which implies that quality is an aspect that can be attributed to all artifacts the architect primarily works with. In IAF we will see no additional quality artifacts; but we can expect new occurrences of existing artifact types to emerge as a result of an architecture design that meets each quality requirement; for example, the manageability quality requirements may require new business services to be identified that deal with IT service operations; and in order to make them work effectively, additional monitoring components may be needed to measure the actual IT service provisioning. Or there could be a business service 'monitoring security breaches' – you usually don't identify that as a core activity, but it is derived from security quality requirements.

3.7.2.3 What Approach to Address Quality?

In developing the architecture, quality is pursued at all times, although in some cases we see some emphasis on the demand from a particular quality viewpoint. In general there are some different approaches to meet this demand:

- Management of non-functional requirements (NFR's) in line with the core objectives of the architecture; these NFRs are attributes of the artifacts that were identified there to fulfill the prime objectives of the architecture; for example, an order entry service has a quality requirement for a given throughput during peak times;
- Identification of additional artifacts that incorporate the quality management, for example, if transparency is important, monitoring services in IS and TI automate the production of information at a quality level that meets the demands from the business; and if important enough, we can even identify new actors (e.g. a compliance officer) or business services (auditing, reporting);
- Since the aspect areas of IAF can be tailored to meet any scope, specific quality domains such as security, the IT services organization, or risk management can be architected using IAF as if it is a business in itself. See below for an IAF diagram that was populated for Service Management, using the ITIL templates.

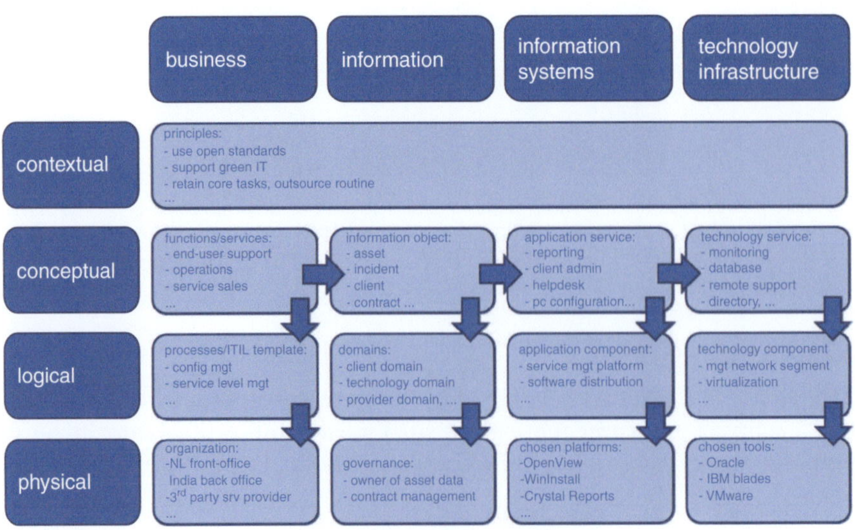

IAF applied to service provisioning

3.7.3 *Contextual*

3.7.3.1 Principles

While expressing the general purpose and ideas behind the architecture, the architecture principles typically also address the need to fulfill certain quality needs, e.g. in IT service provisioning, security or compliance. These principles can originate from the organization's vision and corporate values (e.g. 'information must be available on a need-to-know basis'), or from sources that impose their compliance regulations ('solutions must adhere to the data protection act', 'all financial transactions of over €25.000,- must be reported to the financial supervisory authority', or 'company websites must adhere to the W3C Web Accessibility Initiative guidelines'). It is up to the business vision and strategy to determine the style with which the business will adhere to these regulations; the chosen style will then be reflected in some architecture principles.

Especially for security, compliance and governance a good place to find related principles is in the company policies. Many organizations will have a compliance policy or security policy.

Since principles drive the assessment of alternatives within the architecture, we can expect these quality-related principles to have a notable influence on the overall architecture, as we will see below; it is therefore important that the set of quality-related principles is balanced, consistent and complete given the scope of the architecture.

Depending on the type of architecture (enterprise or solution level) the quality related principles might be quite high level or detailed. At enterprise level the architecture principles might be expressed as 'business agility through a short time-to-market for implementing legislative changes', or 'operational excellence through maximizing straight through processing of customer orders'. For solution level architecture the quality requirements need to be more precise and detailed than at enterprise level. Typical examples would be 'the system must be capable of processing 10,000 orders per day, each within 2 seconds', 'every user must be authenticated through a combination of knowledge and biometrics' or 'multi-language support for at least English, French and Spanish'.

3.7.4 *Conceptual*

3.7.4.1 Quality of Service

The conceptual phase typically is the place where requirements are gathered and organized so that the architect can demonstrate he actually understood the context, scope and depth of the problem area. As discussed before, quality pertains always to something, it is the quality of something. At the conceptual level the architect should look at the non-functional requirements that a given service should be able to fulfill. In other words: what are the quality characteristics of a service, or in short what is the Quality of Service (QoS)?

Quality has an impact on all aspect areas. The architect needs to define the quality of all types of service: the quality of business service, the quality of business information service, quality of information system service and the quality of technology infrastructure service. The focus of the quality attributes can be different for each of the service types. Confidentiality is typically a quality aspect that will be most applicable for the quality of information, whereas useability is likely to be emphasized in the information systems. Some other quality aspects are important to all aspect areas, performance being a prime example.

3.7.4.2 Classifications of Quality Requirements

There may be a broad continuum of quality aspects, all of which tend to express their requirements to specific services – here is the danger of drowning in detail.

In order to create a manageable solution and have the architecture express the essentials of the real objective, it is important that these quality requirements are classified in some form, e.g. service categories expressed as Bronze, Silver and Gold; or confidentiality categories ranging from Public via Restricted to Top Secret.

In several sectors and disciplines these categories have been standardized, and it is the architect's task to assess the architecture's level of alignment with those. The classification schemes will typically vary from one industry to another and from one organization to another.

Many organizations treat security (confidentiality, integrity and availability) as the most critical non-functional requirement and classify it as such. The remaining non-functional requirements dimensions are also considered important but treated as secondary when compared to confidentiality, integrity and availability. An example of a security classification for confidentiality, integrity and availability is given below.

Confidentiality	**Integrity**	**Availability**
Top secret	Vital	Always on (24 * 7)
Restricted	Important	Extended office hours (07.00–20.00, weekdays)
Company confidential	Non vital	Office hours (08.00–18.00, weekdays)
Public	Unimportant	Best effort

In order to keep such a classification scheme manageable, the architect should keep the number of possible classifications down to a reasonable number.

3.7.4.3 Services

While architecting, you will discover new services which have a strong relationship with quality: you will need services to ensure the desired quality. Basically the process to discover those quality related services is exactly the same of the process for all other services. You could start by defining a goal like 'ensure quality' or 'ensure compliance' or by identifying a role such as 'security officer'.

In many quality areas, best practice frameworks have been developed; these enable the architect to anticipate the need for additional quality-related conceptual services and actors in an early stage. Beware that a large number of best practice quality frameworks tend to be activity oriented. Example for systems management: from the ITIL best practices we can anticipate a configuration data service, as shown the diagram below, arrow 1.

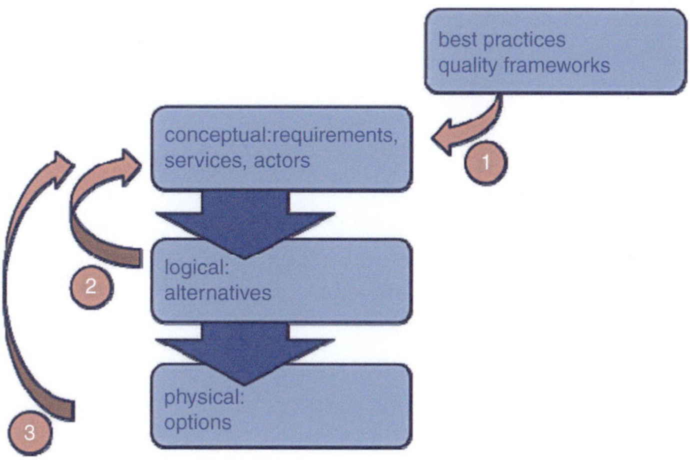

Early or deferred discovery of quality-related conceptual services or actors

In other cases, where best practices are not available or the requirements are to a level conflicting, the assessment of alternatives and options may lead to the deferred identification of additional conceptual services in the logical or physical stage (diagram above, arrows 2 and 3). An example of the latter case is, an initially identified service called 'investigate case' where expected transaction volume and confidentiality level may induce the architect to split the service into a 'high-volume/low confidentiality' service and a 'low-volume/high confidentiality' service, in order to make the overall solution cost-effective; otherwise the confidentiality requirement of a low volume would dictate the overall 'high-water mark' confidentiality level for the generic service to be needlessly high.

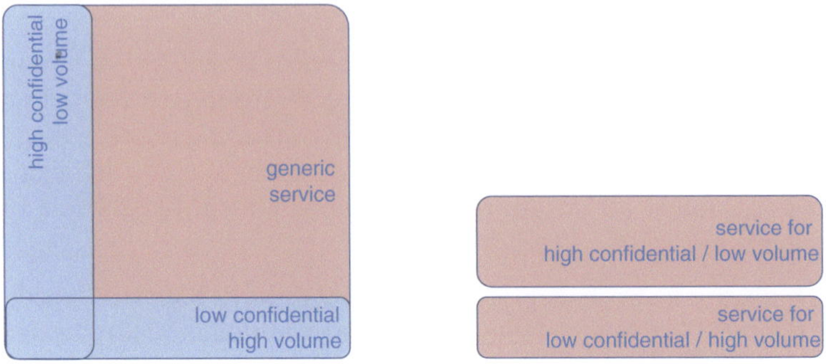

Alternatives – one generic service or two more specific services

3.7.4.4 Contracts

Services interact with each other. These interactions and their nature are described in service collaboration contracts. Within the contracts the Quality of Service requirements are formalized. The contracts form the basis for negotiating service level agreements.

3.7.4.5 Roles

You might want to introduce new roles from a quality perspective. Examples of new roles that can be introduced are: compliance officer, security officer, quality manager and IT operations manager. Whether these roles are introduced in the architecture will depend on a number of factors:

- Scope and objective of the architecture.
- Importance of one or more quality aspects for the organization. The more important, the more likely it is that you will need to define specific roles.
- Level of maturity of the organization with respect to quality. In more mature organizations specific roles will already be identified or can be more easily introduced.

Remember that each of the roles that are introduced should be associated with at least one business goal and business activity, and should lead to the introduction of new business services – otherwise the objective of having such a newly identified role would remain unclear of implicit.

3.7.5 Logical

As an architect you will have to find an integrated solution with the right attention for the quality requirements. This means designing a logical architecture across all aspect areas in scope balancing the principles and quality requirements. As the focus switches toward quality, the architect will need to find solutions that meet the expressed quality requirements for the services (QoS).

The quality related principles and QoS will have a strong impact on the design of the logical architecture. Some logical alternatives will not be feasible because of constraints imposed from a quality perspective. Or you will find that you are not able to design an architecture that meets the high quality requirements and the 'low cost' principle.

Typically you would group the services with the same QoS characteristics and find a solution for meeting those quality requirements. In finding those solutions you might benefit from best practices and patterns. A solution for meeting the quality requirements often calls for a new service, in case the original service cannot provide for the desired level of quality.

It could also result in splitting of one service into multiple services. As an example a business service which has high availability/low security and medium availability/high security requirements. In this case you might decide it is better to split this service into two services than to find one solution that will support both requirements.

The quality principles might lead to a different or more detailed clustering of components as opposed to the clustering without paying attention to quality, based on other principles. This is natural. You could end up with different components based on the segregation of governed and governing or IT operations being separate from those using IT. Or: a component in which secret information is processed is separated from a component in which information up to company confidential information is handled.

3.7.5.1 Logical Components

Some logical components have their main reason of existence justified in governance or security reasons. This holds true for all IAF aspect areas. This could take the form of an actor such as 'security officer', 'compliance officer' or the business component 'IT operations'. On the information side it could be the CMDB (Configuration Management DataBase) or the set of compliance rules. In other cases these type of components have over time become elements of the technology infrastructure. Examples of these common security technology components are: directory server, virus checker, access manager, firewall, etc..

3.7.5.2 Controls

Especially in the field of security and compliance the word 'control' is often used. A control is a means of managing the risk of a required level of quality being compromised. Within IAF v1 and v2 we have used the word 'mechanism', but that was abandoned in later versions. The term 'control' is also used as a synonym for a safeguard, security measure, countermeasure or mitigation.

Controls take different forms, depending on function and nature.

- *Preventive controls* can be selected to prevent undesirable outcomes before they happen.
- *Detective controls* are installed to identify the undesirable outcomes when they occur.
- *Corrective controls* are put into place to make sure that corrective action is taken to reverse undesirable outcomes or to see to it that they do not recur.

As an example to explain the differences between these types of controls: a smoke detector is a detective control and a fire extinguisher is a corrective control.

Controls can be found in all aspect areas of IAF and even outside IAF. Some controls are applicable to the business aspect area, as can be seen from examples such as segregation of duties, staff screening, authorization, and monitoring, logging and auditing business services. For the information aspect an organization might consider classification of information, encrypting information or keeping copies of information. Technology – wise it could be automated intrusion detection, redundant equipment, smartcards to store authorizations and identities, and so on. True physical controls should also be considered.

All of these types of controls should function in concert to ensure that the objectives and principles will be met. A system of controls reduce business risk, which is the probability that certain exposures will impact the required level of quality of the business system.

The selection of controls and the integrated design of the system of controls will be founded and justified in the architecture principles.

3.7.5.3 Best Practices and Patterns

As an architect you can benefit from best practices and patterns. Especially in this area you should look for them. They might come in the form of best practices, such as:

- The original BS7799[6] 'Code of Practice for Information Security Management', providing guidance on best practices in information security management. BS7799 has now evolved into the international best practice information security management standard, defining and guiding Information Security Management System (ISMS) development (ISO 27001:2005[7]).
- COBIT providing good practices across a domain and process framework and presents activities in a manageable and logical structure. COBIT can be

[6] BS 7799, information available via Wikipedia. Http://en.wikipedia.org. Accessed April 2009

[7] ISO/IEC 27001, information available via Wikipedia. Http://en.wikipedia.org. Accessed April 2009

used at the highest level of IT governance and helps organizations in meeting their conformance and performance requirements.
- ITIL: The Information Technology Infrastructure Library is a set of concepts and policies for managing information technology infrastructure, development and operations.

Others come in the form of industry patterns, mainly focused on IT. If you for example need to architect a high available computing facility, we advise you to do some research. Patterns do exist for this. If you decide to use biometrics as a means for authenticating users, you will find that you will not only need technology components for reading, validating and storing biometric data. Business services will also be needed for initially capturing biometric data, issuing the smartcards on which the data will be stored, etc..

It is crucial to understand that these best practices and patterns are not designed as silos. They bring solutions for meeting specific quality objectives and cover more than one aspect area.

3.7.6 Logical Quality Views

Many of the views described in the previous paragraphs can be used to express the quality aspects of the logical architecture. In real life projects we have found that especially views focusing on the security, compliance and/or governance aspect are most commonly produced. Some typical example are:

- A view in which risks and all measures to ensure quality (security, compliancy) are depicted, showing the type of measure (preventive, detective, corrective) and the component to which they have been allocated;
- A view in which the owners and stewards of the business/information/ information system/ technology infrastructure components can be seen;
- The areas or components in which sensitive information is held and processed;
- The information flows that hold information with respect to monitoring the quality.

As for the 'green' aspect we could expect a view on for example the carbon footprint of the datacenters.

3.7.7 Physical

3.7.7.1 Physical Components

For the quality aspect in the physical phase we follow the usual architecture practice. Physical components are allocated to the logical components. If we find that the physical components cannot completely fulfill the specifications of the logical components, we have encountered a gap. From a quality perspective, the architect will try to define other measures or controls that will compensate for the gap. If this is not feasible, make sure the organization understands the reason for gap and accepts the risk and impact associated with it.

At physical level you have to realize that you seldom work in a greenfield, without any existing quality control. Normally there is a baseline of existing quality controls. By performing a gap analysis between required quality level and baseline you find out which additional controls have to be detailed at physical level.

3.7.7.2 Quality Standards, Rules and Guidelines

The architect specifies additional standards, rules and guidelines to ensure that the required level of quality is guaranteed. These SRGs can take the form of specific (quality, security, governance, ...) standards, rules or guidelines, or they can be added to the SRGs specified for the aspect areas.

With respect to security and compliance SRGs the architect is advised to discuss these with the security or compliance officer. It is likely that there will be a strong relationship with security or compliance policies. A security policy might give rules on passwords length, allowable characters and frequency of change.

3.7.7.3 Service Level Agreement

A Service Level Agreement (SLA) is as a physical contract between two parties, in which one party agrees to deliver services to another with a guaranteed level of service. The quality of the services needed are defined in the logical contracts. The actual level of service that is agreed upon in the SLA might differ for reasons of feasibility, cost, etc.

Chapter 4
IAF in Perspective with Other Frameworks and Methods

4.1 Introduction

Previous chapters provided a sound explanation of philosophy, structure and background of IAF itself. Now it is a necessity to take the next step: applying IAF. After all, that's what it's all about. This chapter elaborates on the different ways IAF can be used in projects, in combination with other tools, methods and frameworks. All information on these tools, methods and frameworks originates from public resources and own experience; for detailed information we advise to contact the respective organisatins.

More specific, this chapter addresses IAF in combination with:

- Other architecture frameworks and methods like TOGAF, DYA or Zachman;
- Business transformation approaches commonly used;
- Analysis, design or development methods like RUP, SEMBA or Linear development;
- Industry process frameworks like ITIL, COBIT or CMMI;
- Project management methods like Prince2 or MSP;
- Architecture tooling like System Architect and CaseWise;
- Modeling languages like ArchiMate;
- Modeling techniques like UML or IDEF;
- TechnoVision, Capgemini's comprehensive perspective on the evolution of technologies.

The goal of these paragraphs is to show how we as architects can use IAF in collaboration with a wide range of available topics we come across in our daily work. Although each paragraph provides a short description of the specific topic dealt with in that paragraph, you should use other sources to learn and understand that topic more extensively.

Before continuing, realize that we have to take into account which type of architecture is required. We distinguish four major types:

- *Enterprise architecture*, which supports planning purposes. Enterprise architecture engagements are often executed at enterprise level, spanning business units;

J. van 't Wout et al., *The Integrated Architecture Framework Explained*,
DOI 10.1007/978-3-642-11518-9_4,

- *Domain architecture,* which also supports planning purposes, but now within a business unit;
- *Solution architecture*, which supports design and shaping of solutions. Solution architecture engagements realize changed business (processes) and their supporting applications running on changed infrastructure. The term project architecture is also often used in this context;
- *Software architecture*, which is aimed at guiding the development of software, ensuring that the right software patterns, style guides etc. are used.

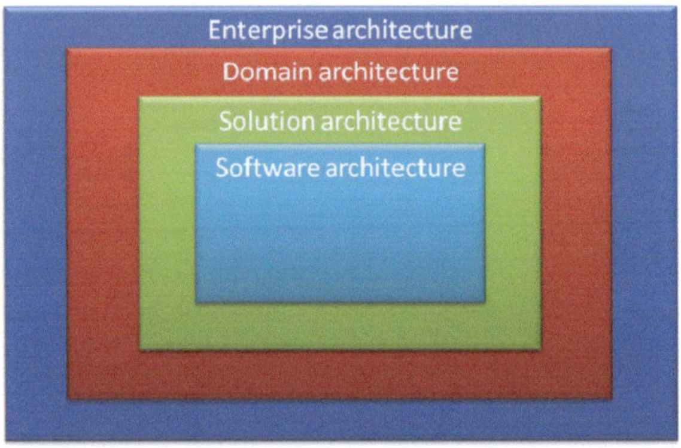

Architecture types: decreasing scope and increasing level of detail

Depending on the type of engagement we were in, the following types of architecture engagements have been recognized and realized using IAF:

- *Transformation architecture*; Enterprise type architecture aimed at supporting major business change – new business models, new product/market combinations, etc.;
- *Rationalization architecture*; Uses lifecycle management mindset at enterprise level to support business and IT rationalization after mergers & acquisitions;
- *Integration architecture*; Complex architectural engagement at solution level, aimed at guiding large integration projects, like linking a new CRM system to 200 other systems;
- *Optimization architecture*; Solution and software type architectures that are aimed at reducing IT time to market. Provides structure, standards, rules and guidelines to analysts and engineers.

4.2 IAF and Other Architecture Frameworks

Multiple types of architecture frameworks exist. John Wu[1] in 2006 organized the wide range of architecture frameworks by distinguishing different kinds of frameworks: artifact frameworks, reference frameworks, design

[1] http://it.toolbox.com/blogs/lea-blog/frameworks-and-models-the-myth-10999.

frameworks, governance frameworks, and others. IAF typically is an artifact framework.

This section describes IAF in relationship with other architecture frameworks.

4.2.1 IAF and TOGAF 8

4.2.1.1 Characteristics of TOGAF 8

TOGAF 8[2] is organized into three sections, all of which provide guidance on what the outputs of TOGAF architecture should be and how they should be structured:

1. The architecture development method (ADM);
2. The enterprise continuum;
3. The resource base.

The *ADM* explains how to derive an organization-specific enterprise architecture that addresses business requirements. It provides a reliable, proven way of developing an architecture. The Enterprise Continuum provides a model for structuring an architecture repository, based on architectures and solutions being stored at various levels of abstraction.

- Architecture Building Blocks reside within the Enterprise Continuum;
- The Enterprise Continuum also contains the TOGAF Technology Reference Model, a foundational architecture template for defining the capabilities of technology components.

The *TOGAF Resource Base* provides reference materials on various tools and techniques to be used to support architecture activity.

The Architecture Development Method (ADM) is the major component of TOGAF 8 and provides guidance for architects on a number of levels:

- It provides a number of architectural phases (e.g. Business Architecture, Information Systems Architecture, Technology Architecture) in a cycle, as well as an overall process template for architectural activity.
- It provides a narrative of each architecture phase, describing the phase in terms of objectives, approach, inputs, steps and outputs. The inputs and outputs sections provide an informal definition of the architecture content structure and deliverables.
- It provides cross-phase summaries on requirements management and phase input and phase output descriptions for deliverables.
- It includes the concept of Architecture Building Blocks, which allow the enterprise to be segmented into re-usable components, described by architectures and then re-combined to construct new architectures. For example, the

[2] Source: TOGAF ADM Card.

creation of a web application building block that could be used to support architecture definition for many specific web applications.

4.2.1.2 Combining IAF and TOGAF 8

ADM can be used in combination with IAF; it is essentially an IAF roadmap.

- TOGAF Preliminary phase defines architecture principles and phase A focuses on requiring information on scope, constraints and creating a first architecture vision. Phase A defines stakeholders and validates business context. IAF contextual and the 0.1 version of the overall architecture are positioned in these phases;
- TOGAF phase B develops Business Architecture: the Baseline ('As is') and Target ('To be') architecture and analyzes gaps. This is where IAF Business conceptual, logical and physical architectures are positioned;
- TOGAF phase C develops Information Systems Architecture: the Baseline ('As is') and Target ('To be') architecture and analyzes gaps. This is where IAF Information and IAF IS conceptual and logical architectures are positioned;
- TOGAF phase D develops Technology Architectures: the Baseline ('As is') and Target ('To be') architecture and analyses gaps. This is where IAF TI conceptual and logical architectures are positioned;
- TOGAF phase E evaluates and selects among the implementation options identified in the target architectures. This is where IAF Information, IS and TI physical is positioned;
- TOGAF phase F, G and H address migration planning, implementation governance and architecture change management. These parts of the ADM are used if the engagement objectives require them. No specific parts of IAF are positioned in these phases.

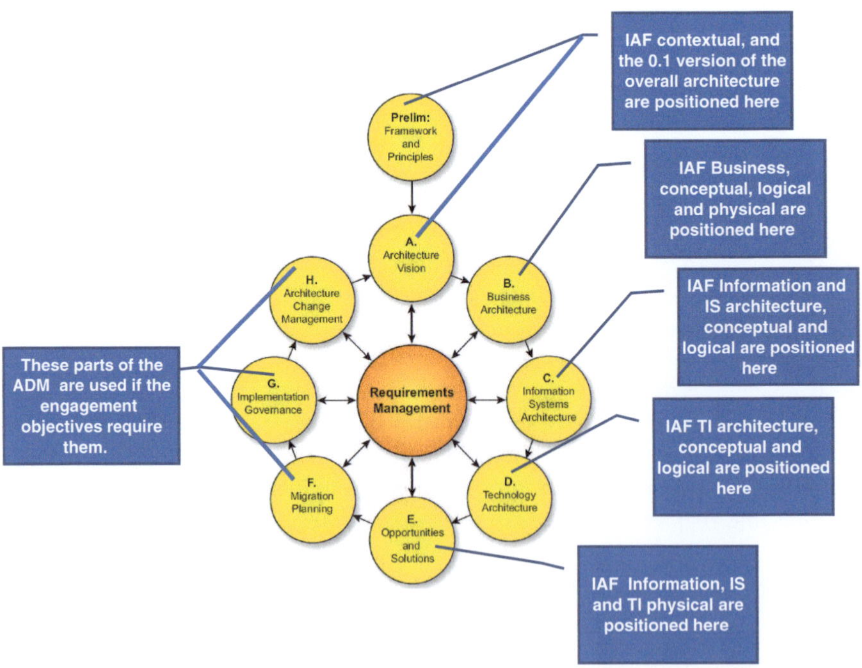

Furthermore, the IAF structure can be used to position assets within the enterprise continuum. Finally, the Resource base can be used as reference material during the creation of the architecture.

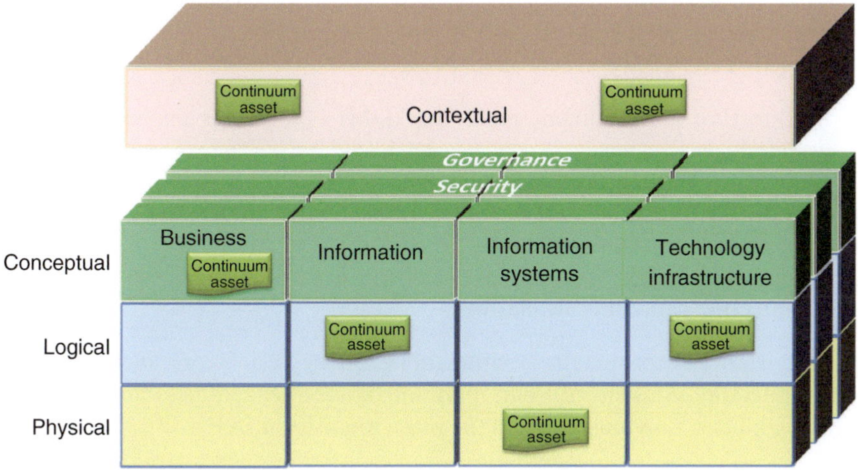

A set of features that show the differences between IAF and TOGAF 8 are shown in the table below.

Topics	TOGAF	IAF	Explanation/Rationale
Framework for Enterprise IT architecture	+	+	
Architecture Processes	+	-	TOGAF ADM helps in formalizing the processes (usable as IAF roadmaps)
Guidelines and techniquess management	+	-	TOGAF has formalized this in the resource base
Views	+	=	TOGAF and IAF use this mechanism. TOGAF uses it more formally. IAF 4.0 Identifies views, but does not provide detailed guidance. IAF 4.5 does provide guidance on views
Business Process description	=	-	TOGAF proposes some artifacts to describe business processes
Architecture repository management	+	-	The enterprise continuum and TOGAF's emphasis on requirements management are present to address this topic. IAF does not address this.
Linking business and IT within the architecture	-	+	TOGAF identifies this. IAF specifies how to do it.
Specific area for Information architecture	-	+	IAF proposes a way to describe the information used by Business
Distinction between Information and Data	-	+	IAF makes a distinction between non-automated and automated information
Description of Collaboration contracts - behavior of the system	=	+	In IAF, the contracts and their dependency clearly describe the behaviors
Governance of the Architecture	+	-	TOGAF is designed to manage reference architectures
Ensuring QoS in the solution	-	+	IAF specifically addresses this in the governance architecture area.
Derivation rules between architecture artifacts	=	+	In TOGAF there are no real derivation rules between areas and/or levels
Definition of Business Services	=	+	The Business Services in IAF is very well defined and shows the link with business objectives
Alignment of Aspect Areas	=	+	The alignment between areas (B&I and IS&TI) is key
Traceability of design and decisions	-	+	IAF has been designed to support traceability
Decision process based on principles	=	+	Architecture is about decision making

4.2.2 *IAF and TOGAF 9*

The Open Group published TOGAF 9 in February 2009, as successor to TOGAF 8. Although large parts of TOGAF 8 are included in TOGAF 9 without change, there are some important changes. The structure of TOGAF 9 changed. TOGAF 9 consists of six parts:

1. Architecture Development method (ADM) – basically unchanged from version 8;
2. ADM guidelines and techniques;
3. Architecture content framework;
4. Enterprise continuum and tools;
5. Reference models;
6. Architecture capability framework.

An important new part is the Architecture Content Framework, defining what an architecture consists of. This part introduces deliverables, artifacts and building blocks. Obviously, that's the place to position IAF.

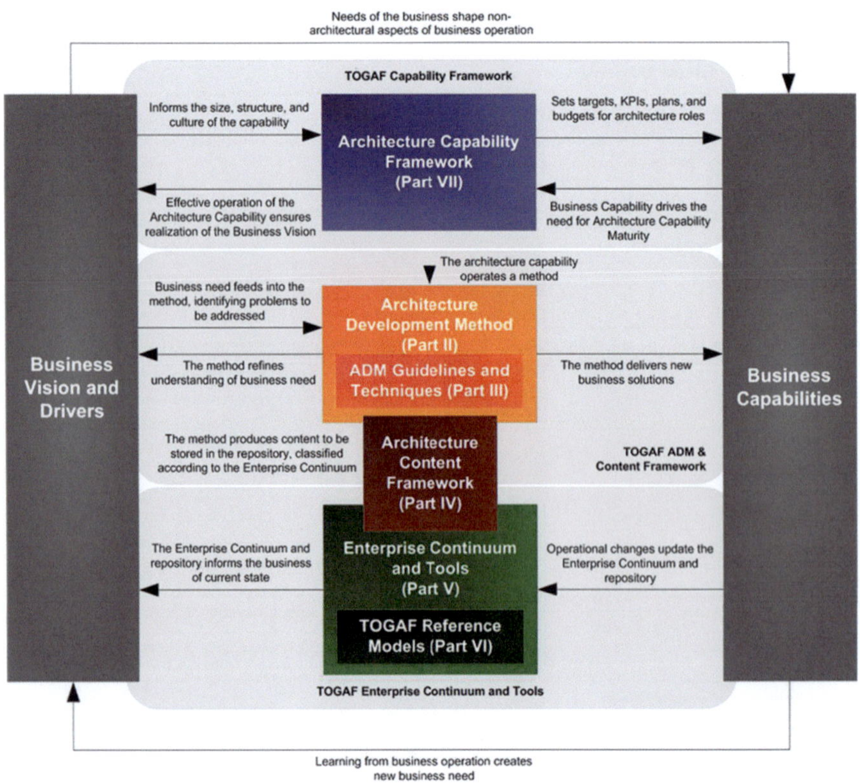

As a member of the Open Group, Capgemini contributed in defining TOGAF 9. One way of contributing was providing IAF 4.0 as input for the definition of the architecture content framework, so it is no surprise that many of the artifacts and attributes defined in TOGAF 9 are similar to IAF 4.0.

Despite that, there are some differences. Business architecture is approached differently, since Business services provide one or more functions. In IAF this would be positioned as a logical business component.

The TOGAF 9 architecture content framework contains some attributes that IAF does not identify. The IAF artifact attributes can be extended if desired. Examples are:

- Standards class;
- Standards creation date;
- Retire date;
- Next standard review date;
- Credibility characteristics.

4.2.2.1 Combining IAF and TOGAF 9

Combining IAF and TOGAF 9 can be done the same way as combining IAF and TOGAF 8: using the TOGAF ADM as architecture roadmap and IAF as the content framework. TOGAF 9 explicitly states that it is a viable option to combine the ADM with a different content framework.

4.2.3 IAF and DYA

DYA is an approach to enterprise architecture from Sogeti – Netherlands. DYA stands for DYnamic Architecture and places an emphasis on the process of architecting in general, and more specifically on the development and improvement of the architecture function. DYA is based on 10 principles. In summary:

1. Architecture is not an end in itself, but should support the goals an organization want to achieve.
2. Architecture can be developed piece by piece. It should evolve in line the organization.
3. Deviations from the architecture can sometimes be necessary.

The DYA model is the core of DYA. The DYA model consists of four processes covering all phases between strategy and realization. DYA is complimented by a architecture framework, although with less detail and emphasis. Focus is on the architecture model.

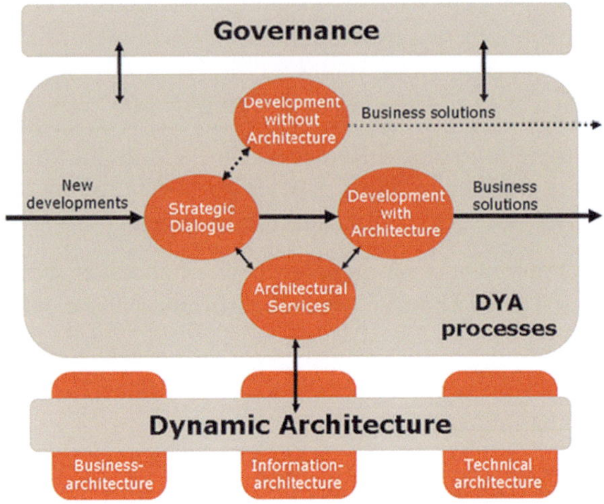

DYA model recognizes processes and architecture types

The four DYA processes are:

1. *Strategic dialogue*. Business goals are determined and via business cases transformed to project proposals. Key is alignment and cooperation between Business and IT.
2. *Architectural services*. Architectures are produced to support both strategic dialogue and development. Reference architectures provide the overall frame to operate in.
3. *Development with architecture*, based on project start architectures and realizing business solutions.
4. *Development without architecture*. In urgent circumstances development of temporary solutions without architecture is allowed. In these situations explicit agreements must be made how the temporary solutions will be transformed to business solutions developed with architecture.

Furthermore, DYA recognizes three architecture types:

- Business architecture, in which products/services, processes and organization are positioned.
- Information architecture, in which data and application are positioned.
- Technical architecture, in which middleware, platform and network are positioned.

DYA recognizes the creation of enterprise and domain (business unit level) architectures. They are the basis for the creation of project start architectures,

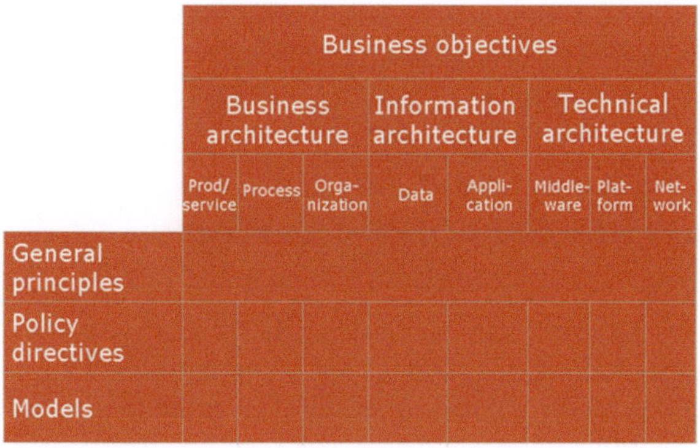

which provide projects with architectural objectives and constraints. A project start architecture contains a context model, scoping of the proposed IT solution (both logical and technological), design criteria and standards and guidelines.

4.2.3.1 Combining IAF and DYA

IAF and DYA have been used together. DYA describes how to embed architecture within an organization and offers descriptions of processes, architectures, architecture team and governance of architecture. DYA does not describe how to architect and does not describe which steps with respect to content have to be taken to produce a good architecture. That's where IAF comes into place. So, the DYA processes are used as architecture roadmaps which create IAF based architecture content.

4.2.4 IAF and EAF

During 2006 The Open Group accepted the SAP company as a member of The Open Group. SAP wanted a certified methodology with their product and Franck Lopez, SAP Global lead for Enterprise Architecture, began looking for a partner with qualified architectural skills to help them. SAP chose to work with Capgemini.

Early 2007, a program was set-up to realize a new methodology based upon SAAF, TOGAF and IAF from Capgemini. A team of 15 consultants and architects from SAP and Capgemini worked on this methodology, to be launched as SAP EAF (Enterprise Architecture Framework).

At The Open Group conference in Paris and at SAPPHIRE in Vienna in June 2007 the EAF initiative between SAP and Capgemini has been shown by SAP and EAF is now being rolled out within SAP (mainly in the US at first)

EAF is an architecture framework that specifies how an organization can architecturally define and govern their IT landscape. It is based on open standards and was created by leveraging Capgemini Experience and SAP Accelerators:

- TOGAF provides the basis for EAF's process and repository structure.
- IAF provides the basis for EAF's content metamodel.
- SAP provides content tools (e.g. solution manager, solution composer, product availability matrix and enterprise services repository) and landscape tools.
- SAP provides architecture definition tools (e.g. roadmap composer), methods (e.g. ASAP) and Reference Models (e.g. Business maps).

EAF offers a practical process framework for developing and governing architecture at all levels or the organization. Overview of the EAF process framework:

- EAF is intended to support architecture processes at different levels within an Enterprise.
- The EAF process is iterative and tailored to suit package scenarios.
- EAF shows how to relate architecture content between levels and execute architecture governance for an organization.
- Process objectives, breadth and depth will be different at different levels of the Enterprise.
- Enterprise Architecture has a focus on taxonomy, standards, best practice and change roadmaps.
- Enterprise Solution Architecture has a focus on rationale, scope, scale and context of strategic change initiatives.
- Solution Architecture has a focus on completeness, depth and ability to realize.

4.2.4.1 Combining IAF and EAF

EAF content framework uses language from TOGAF and structure from IAF. EAF has matched the IAF meta-model to TOGAF terminology and then merged in bits of TOGAF missing from IAF and bits of IAF from TOGAF.

Overview of the EAF content framework:

- EAF uses a structured meta-model to identify architecture content, relationships between content and architecture deliverables.
- Using a structured meta-model allows architects to demonstrate traceability and assess impacts. The meta-model can be implemented in specialist EA tools, or can be used to structure Office style deliverables.

- The EAF meta-model is derived as much as possible from TOGAF terminology, but uses Capgemini IAF as a basis for structure.
- EAF also defines a set of catalogues, matrices and views that show how architecture can be represented and presented to stakeholders.

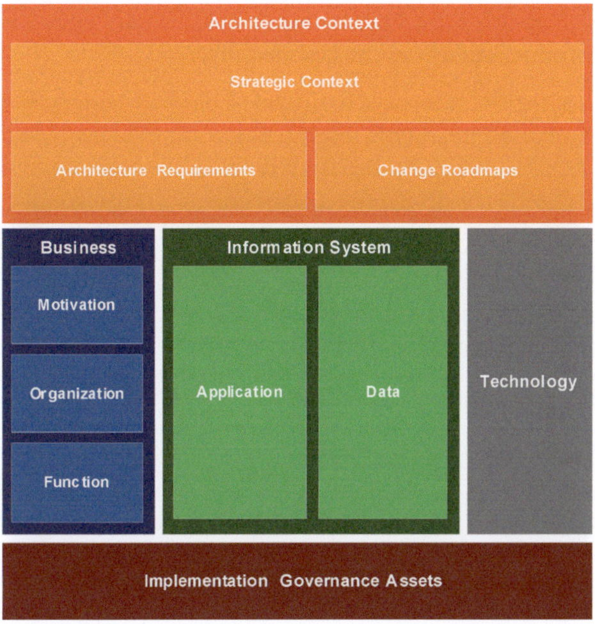

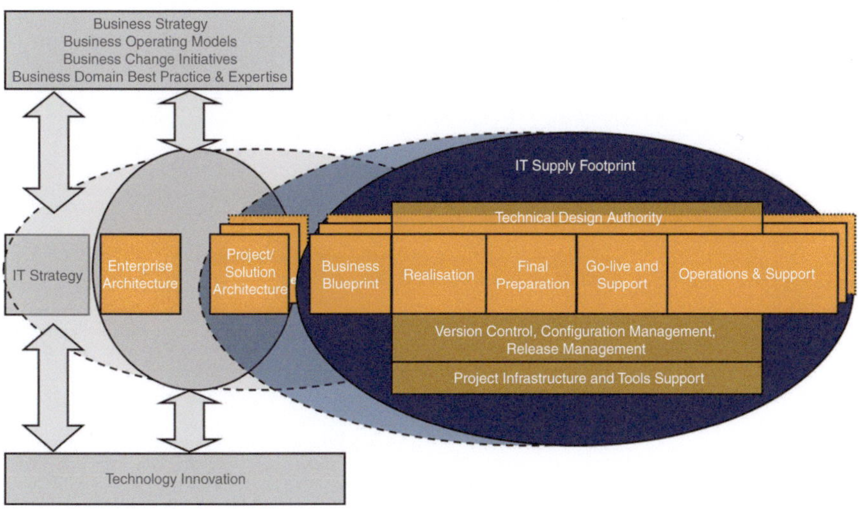

4.2.5 IAF and Zachman

The Zachman[3] Framework is a widely used approach for developing and/or documenting an enterprise-wide Information Systems Architecture. Zachman based his framework on practices in traditional architecture and engineering. This resulted in an approach which on the vertical axis provides multiple perspectives of the overall architecture, and on the horizontal axis a classification of the various artifacts of the architecture.

The purpose of the Framework is to provide a basic structure which supports the organization, access, integration, interpretation, development, management, and change of a set of architectural representations of the organization's information systems. Such objects or descriptions of architectural representations are usually referred to as artifacts.

The framework, then, can contain global plans as well as technical details, lists, and charts as well as natural language statements. Any appropriate approach, standard, role, method, technique, or tool may be placed in it. In fact, the Framework can be viewed as a tool to organize any form of metadata for the enterprise.

4.2.5.1 Relationship to IAF

The Zachman enterprise architecture framework combines a number of aspects with each other to create a matrix in which example models are positioned that result in the architecture:

1. Architecture topic, term and stakeholder. The combinations are:

Architecture Topic	Architecture Term	Stakeholder
Scope	Contextual	Planner
Enterprise model	Conceptual	Owner
System model	Logical	Designer
Technology model	Physical	Builder
Detailed representations	Out of context	Subcontractor

2. Architecture object, and answer it provides. The combinations are:

Architecture Object	Provides the
Data	what
Function	How
Network	Where
People	Who
Time	When
Motivation	Why

[3] The Zachman Institute for Framework Advancement (ZIFA) is at: www.zifa.org

Both Zachman and IAF are artifact frameworks. In effect many of the items identified within the cells of the Zachman framework can be seen as potential viewpoints for IAF.

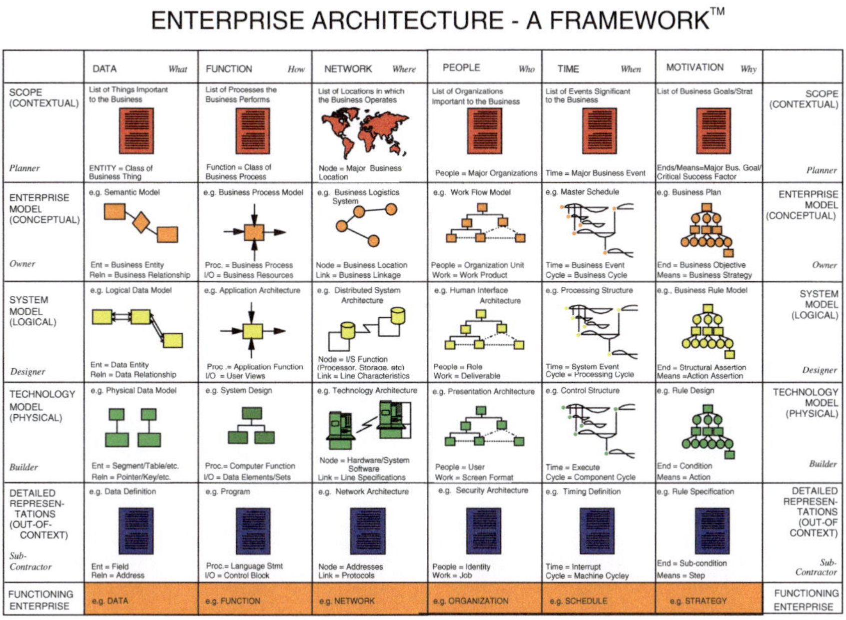

John A. Zachman, Zachman International (810) 231-0531

4.2.5.2 Relationship Between Zachman and TOGAF

The ADM mapping to the Zachman Framework supports a close correlation between the Zachman Framework and the TOGAF ADM.

The Zachman Framework provides a very comprehensive and well-established taxonomy of the various viewpoints, models, and other artifacts that an enterprise may want to consider developing as part of an enterprise architecture. (The recommendation of the Zachman Framework itself is that all the cells be covered.)

The current recommended set of viewpoints in TOGAF does not cover all 30 cells of the Zachman Framework. However, with TOGAF it is possible to develop viewpoints and views to cover other aspects of the Zachman Framework as necessary.

TOGAF recommends some viewpoints that are not included in the Zachman Framework; for example, the security and manageability viewpoints. The selection of viewpoints needs to be determined by the purpose of the architecture, and the TOGAF ADM defines a process for driving that selection.

The vertical axis of the Zachman Framework provides a source of potential viewpoints for the architect to consider. The horizontal axis could be regarded as providing a generic taxonomy of concerns.

The Zachman Framework says nothing about the processes for developing viewpoints or conformant views, or the order in which they should be developed. It does not provide a method such as TOGAF's ADM, or a Foundation Architecture (Technical Reference Model (TRM) and Standards Information Base (SIB)).

4.2.6 IAF and DEMO

DEMO, acronym for Design and Engineering Methodology for Organizations, is a method to describe business processes, whereby the acts of humans have a central position. The method focuses on creating an implementation independent description of an organization's products and processes. The resulting description is relatively stable because it describes the essence of the products and processes, without taking context into account. DEMO is focused on the Dutch marketplace.

DEMO is a method for designing, implementing and aligning organizations. In doing so, the communication actions have a central position: communication and communicating is essential for organization to survive. All kind of agreements between employees, customers and suppliers are the result of communication between the parties involved. The same is valid for accepting the results of these agreements.

DEMO is based upon a few basic principles:

- Essence of an organization is that the organization consists of people both responsible and accountable for their actions and negotiations.
- Modeling of business processes and information systems is a rational activity, leading to uniformity.
- Models have to be understandable by all people involved.
- Information systems have to fit on psychonomics of their users.

Basic assumption in DEMO is that an organization consists of three levels:

- Business level,
- Information level,
- Infrastructure level.

Business level is the essence of the organization, independent of the specific implementation that might be possible. Really understanding business level is the proper starting point when setting up an organization, among which is the action to set up the software to support the business processes.

Given this vision, DEMO distinguishes three levels of abstraction:

1. Essential, the business system (B-system)
2. Informational, the information system (I-system)
3. Documentary, the data system (D-system)

Each level of abstraction does have its own category of system that work at that level. So DEMO acknowledges B-systems (Organization and Business), I-systems (Informational and Information) and D-systems (Documentary and Data). Focal point in DEMO is at the Essential level; both other levels are described in much detail.

DEMO comprises five organizational models:

1. Interaction model
2. Process model
3. Action model
4. Facts model
5. Intersection model

Based on these models, DEMO defines a series of diagrams like the Communication diagram, the Process diagram, Transaction diagram, Facts diagram or Action diagram.

4.2.6.1 Aligning IAF and DEMO

Aligning IAF and DEMO starts by having a close look at the basic principles behind DEMO, stating that the essence of an organization is that it consists of people responsible and accountable for their actions and negotiations, thereby modeling business processes and information systems. These statements position DEMO mainly in the upper left of IAF, on conceptual and logical level of both Business and Information aspect area.

The use of DEMO organizational models does align with IAF best for the Interaction Model and the Process Model:

- DEMO Interaction Model is comparable with IAF Business Interaction Model. However, DEMO Interaction Model describes how business services interact, what and where responsibilities are to be positioned and what information is required. IAF Business Interaction Model just describes the interaction between business services; responsibilities are described in contracts and in the business services itself. Information required in business services is described in IAF Business Information services.
- DEMO Process Model is comparable with IAF Logical Process Component and the IAF Logical Business Component Interaction model. DEMO process steps can be positioned as the elementary business services of the

organization, where the processes are the most essential processes within the organization. The processes and process steps can be positioned as a reference model for the real life IAF architecture that is influenced by the context (business strategy, compliancy, etc.).

Especially the DEMO Interaction Model is found helpful in combination with IAF, since the Interaction Model helps to gain clear and quick insight in results and responsibilities in providing services. Terminology and schematics appeal to business managers, as they use their terminology as much as possible.

The use of the DEMO Action Model, Facts Model and Intersection Model is less widespread and more difficult to match upon IAF artifacts. However, the Facts Model could be positioned in Logical Information Component or Logical Information Component Structure Model.

4.2.7 IAF and ArchiMate

Many organizations feel the need to document their Enterprise Architecture and to maintain that documentation along the way. More and more organizations choose ArchiMate as modeling language as it is adopted by The Open Group.

When documenting architectures the main goal is to document the chosen architecture and solutions. ArchiMate is very well equipped to model and analyze architectures, including high level changes. Apart from documenting the solution the documentation of the rationale behind the solution and documentation of solution alternatives is equally important.

ArchiMate takes care of unambiguous registration of all parts of an architecture, with univocal meaning of terminology used and with a predefined structure of architecture elements. This is essential to achieve proper documentation to reproduce and trace why specific architectures and solutions were chosen.

4.2.7.1 Combining IAF and ArchiMate

IAF and ArchiMate supplement each other, where IAF provides a structured content framework with sufficient rationale, abstraction levels and solution alternatives and where ArchiMate provides the modeling language to document parts of the IAF content framework. The figure below demonstrates that both IAF and ArchiMate have similar terminology. However, despite that there are substantial differences in the architectural meaning of these terms and architecture mechanisms.

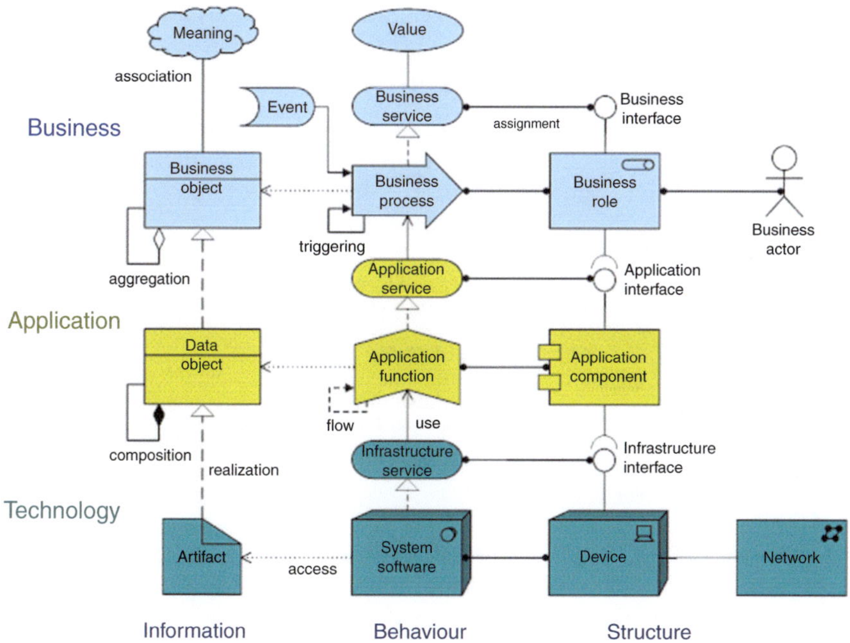

4.3 IAF and Business Transformation

4.3.1 Characteristics of Business Transformation

In general, characteristic of all approaches in business transformation is a phased approach as outlined in the following paragraphs. Business transformation approaches are used by strategy consultants, business or management consultants in order to develop a strategy or to develop a transformation design. Typical phases are Start, Design and Delivery.

During Phase 0, Start, the scene is set. Major deliverables are Vision and transformation ambition to set the goal and ambition. Next focus is on the initial transformation strategy, making clear what the case for action is and what that action has to be. Without alignment with and commitment of top-management a transformation can't be successful, so that's an explicit step. Final action of phase 0 is establishing a mobilized partnership between the consulting and customer organization.

During Phase 1, Design, the design for transformation is established. Major deliverables of this phase are As-is and To-be solution designs. Usually multiple To-be designs are made in order to show what will be changed in each iteration. The initial transformation strategy from the previous phase is revised and completed and the transformation design is finished as well. Important aspects as the Business Case behind the transformation at hand and impact on people and technology are addressed.

Finally, during Phase 2, Delivery, the transformation is actually delivered in timeboxes. Most important deliverables are obviously solutions and results in conformance with design, well managed entry and exit points of the transformation phases. Quality of service is established.

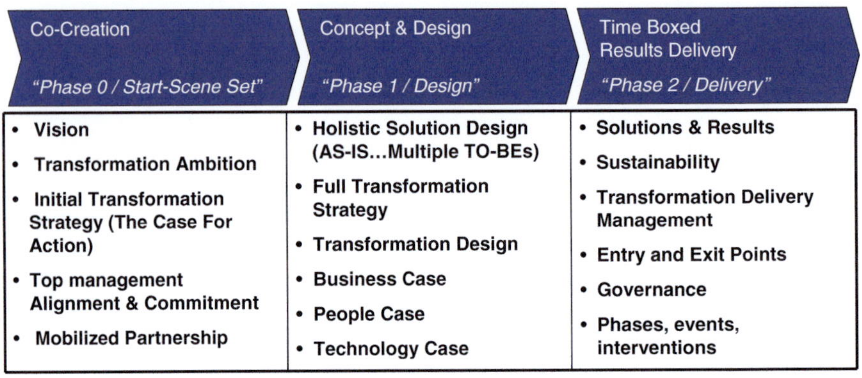

4.3.2 Combining IAF and Business Transformation

- Phase 0 resembles the contextual level of IAF. After all, phase 0 is pretty much about determining why transformation is needed. What is the case for action? Contextual information is collected during phase 0 and completed during phase 1.
- The transformation design in phase 1 is based on IAF for the parts that are in IAF: Business, information, IS, TI, security and governance.
- The architectures that have been created are during phase 2 are used as the basis for control of delivery. If necessary, transformation delivery management can be supported by implementing a design authority.
- In case of a Technology Push being (one of) the major reason(s) for this transformation, this can be presented as IS & TI services that help set ambition levels in phase 0.
- Other aspects addressed during these phases, like financials, communication or product/market combinations are addressed as separate topics outside IAF. Of course cost estimation for the business and technology changes are in scope of the architecture work.

Be aware of the fact that the architecture work in business transformation engagements is part of the change that the organization is undergoing. The importance of people-, and resistance management during the creation of the architecture should not be underestimated. Involve the key stakeholders by getting them to participate in architecture creation.

4.4 IAF and Analysis/Design/Development

4.4.1 IAF and RUP

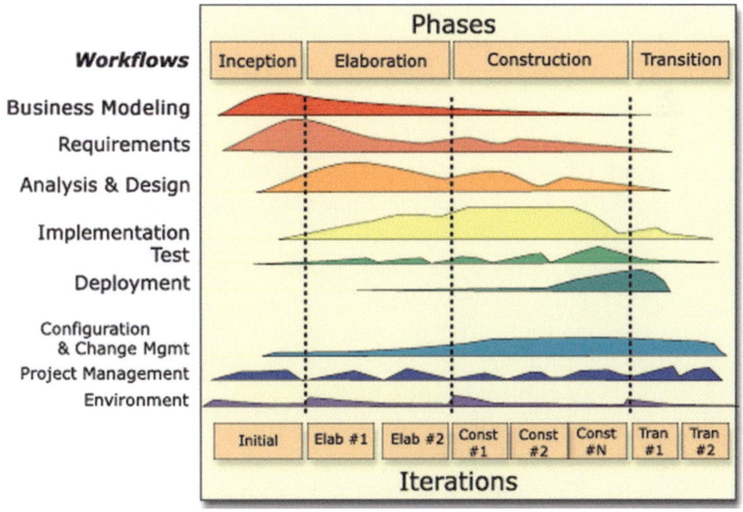

4.4.1.1 Characteristics of Rational Unified Process (RUP)

RUP[4] is a framework for the design, development and implementation of applications that unifies best practice from many disciplines and uses the Unified Modeling Language (UML) as a standard for many of the design deliverables. This approach was developed primarily to address the problems of iterative and component based development, for which the 'traditional' tools and approaches simply did not work. RUP has subsequently been extended to also address the issues of e-development, where the aggressive timescales and lack of clear requirements often 'break' traditional development approaches.

Over the years, UML and RUP have gained widespread acceptance within the industry as providing a common approach for development projects – and Rational have developed and acquired a comprehensive suite of development tools to support the process.

The RUP framework is build on Workflows and Phases (see picture).

---

[4] www.wikipedia.com: IBM Rational Unified Process.

RUP recognizes the following six engineering disciplines (a.k.a. workflows):

- *Business modeling discipline* explains how to describe a vision of the organization in which the system will be deployed and how to then use this vision as a basis to outline the process, roles and responsibilities. With core deliverables Business use cases and business object model.
- *Requirements discipline* explains how to elicit stakeholder requests and transform them into a set of requirements work products that scope the system to be built and provide detailed requirements for what the system must do.With core deliverables System use cases and the actors.
- *Analysis & design discipline*, where design results in a design model and analysis optionally in an analysis model. The design model consists of design classes structured into packages and subsystems with well-defined interfaces, representing what will become components in the implementation. The goal of analysis and design is to show how the system will be realized. With core deliverables analysis model, design model, data model.
- *Implementation discipline*. Systems are realized through implementation of components. The process describes how you reuse existing components, or implement new components with well defined responsibility, making the system easier to maintain, and increasing the possibilities to reuse. With core deliverable an implementation model.
- *Test discipline* RUP proposes an iterative approach, which means that you test throughout the project. Tests are carried out along four quality dimensions: reliability, functionality, application performance, and system performance. With core deliverable a test model.
- *Deployment discipline* The purpose of deployment is to successfully produce product releases, and deliver the software to its end users. Although deployment activities are mostly centered around the transition phase, many of the activities need to be included in earlier phases to prepare for deployment at the end of the construction phase.

Furthermore RUP recognizes three supporting engineering disciplines: Configuration and change management, Project management and Environment discipline.

RUP has determined a project lifecycle consisting of four phases. These phases allow the process to be presented at a high level in a similar way to how a 'waterfall'-styled project might be presented, although in essence the key to the process lies in the iterations of development that lie within all of the phases. Also, each phase has one key objective and milestone at the end that denotes the objective being accomplished. RUP recognizes following phases:

- *Inception*. The primary objective is to scope the system adequately as a basis for validating initial costing and budgets. In this phase the business case which includes business context, success factors (expected revenue, market recognition, etc.), and financial forecast is established. To complement the business case, a basic use case model, project plan, initial risk assessment and project description (the core project requirements, constraints and key features) are generated.

- *Elaboration*. The primary objective is to mitigate the key risk items identified by analysis up to the end of this phase. The elaboration phase is where the project starts to take shape. In this phase the problem domain analysis is made and the architecture of the project gets its basic form.
- *Construction*. The primary objective is to build the software system. In this phase, the main focus goes to the development of components and other features of the system being designed. This is the phase when the bulk of the coding takes place. In larger projects, several construction iterations may be developed in an effort to divide the use cases into manageable segments that produce demonstrable prototypes.
- *Transition*. The primary objective is to 'transition' the system from the development into production, making it available to and understood by the end user. The activities of this phase include training of the end users and maintainers and beta testing of the system to validate it against the end users' expectations. The product is also checked against the quality level set in the Inception phase.

4.4.1.2 Combining IAF and RUP

IAF Business architecture at conceptual level determines business services, based on business goals, business activities and business roles. This replaces RUP workflow business modeling. Therefore IAF is the main source of input for RUP workflow Requirements.

The information objects from IAF Information architecture at conceptual form the basis for the RUP analysis models. The information interaction model from IAF information conceptual forms the basis for RUP system use case realizations.

The Logical Information Component Structure Model from IAF Information logical level is the starting point for the components in the RUP Software component architecture.

From IAF IS the IS Services establish the RUP System Use cases and define the project scope in the RUP Requirement workflow. RUP requirements are established by IS services in combination with the IS service contracts.

Quality of Services are a basis for Iteration Planning in order to mitigate risks and for an indication of development costs and schedule (RUP project management workflow).

The Logical IS component Interaction Model is the basis for the Component View of the Software Architecture and IS Standards, IS Guidelines and IS specifications define RUP Requirements. An IAF Development View determines which components (partially) actually have to be developed and defines the scope.

From IAF TI architecture conceptual level, the TI Services determines candidate Mechanisms to be used in the RUP Software Architecture. TI Services determines the RUP Supplementary Requirements. Parts of TI conceptual will be described in the RUP Software Architecture Document.

RUP Software Architecture is provided with information from IAF TI logical and physical. From IAF TI architecture logical level, the Logical TI Interaction Model and different Views are part of the RUP Software Architecture. From IAF TI architecture physical level, the Physical TI Component Interaction and different Views are part of the Software Architecture

TI standards, TI Guidelines and TI Specifications are input for the Software development environment.

As a summary of aligning IAF and RUP:

- Overall, architecture provides requirements
- Business Services help you to validate the use-cases and check for coverage of business goals
- RUP Classes or Entities can be derived from the IAF Information Objects
- RUP Class Packages can be derived from the IAF Information Components
- Business Components help you derive service oriented software component boundaries
- IAF physical could contain a reference architecture for following engagements

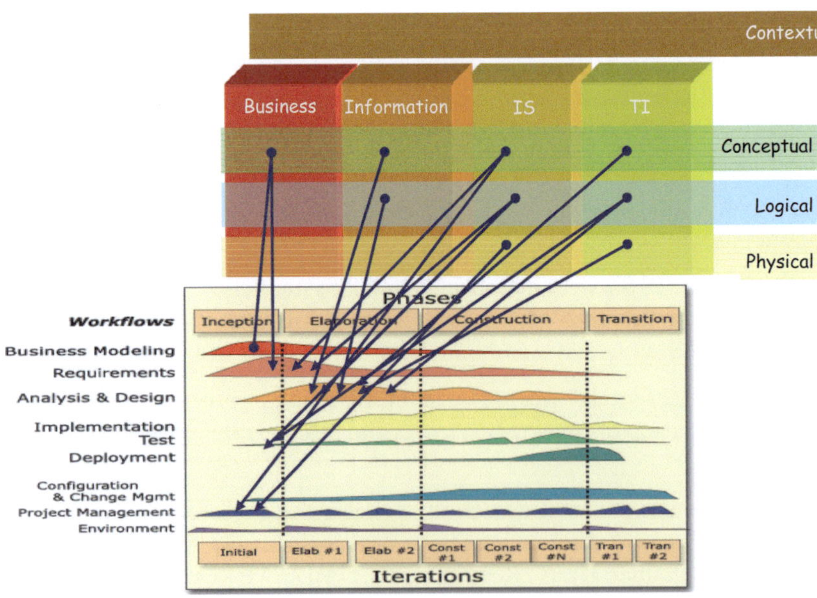

4.4.2 IAF and Linear Development

In general, most linear development methods have a common approach. There is an information planning phase, which is conducted outside the scope of projects. Most of the time it is executed once a year to determine which projects will be executed in the coming period.

The definition study is mainly aimed at determining the feasibility of the project. In effect it executes a first high level analysis and design, ending with input for the required go/no-go decision.

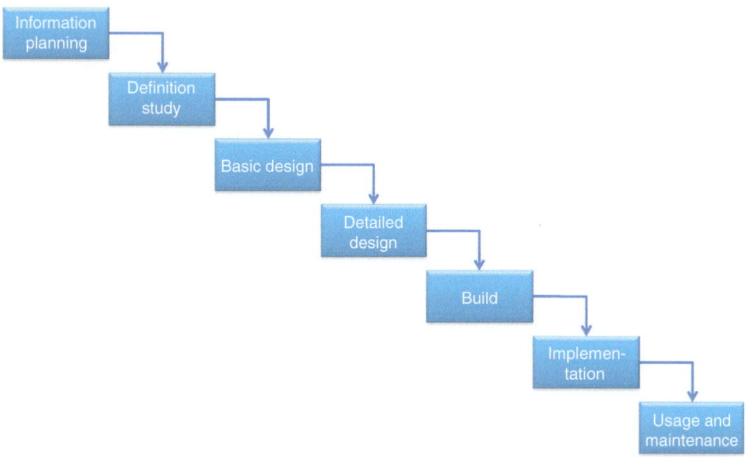

The basic design focuses on:

1. Defining a user oriented information system design
2. Determining the technical structure of the information system
3. Determining sub-projects
4. Creating project plans

The detailed design is a second iteration of the topics in the basic design, aimed at enabling the build phase. The build phase itself is aimed at building the required software, while Implementation is about implementing the system and migrating data from old systems to the new system. Usage and maintenance of the system can be part of the method, more often it is addressed separately.

IAF can be used in combination with linear development:

- The information planning phase can be supported by creating an IAF based reference architecture, which covers many of the topics in information planning. Of course the planning activities itself still need to come from the linear development method, as they are out of scope for IAF.

- The definition study can be supported by creating a solution architecture, which should be based on the reference architecture. The solution architecture will replace most of the content oriented deliverables of the definition study.
- The solution architecture should be used to guide the creation of the products in the consequent steps. It is also used to validate the architecture conformance of the products.

4.4.3 IAF and SEMBA

SEMBA – Structured Expert Method for Business Analysis – has been developed by Capgemini and put forward to the Open group as input for an open method for business analysis.

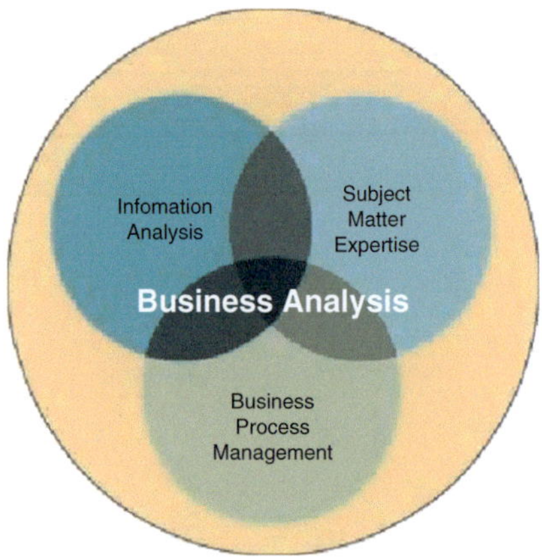

SEMBA touches the Integrated Architecture Framework (IAF), especially the B and I column. The difference however, is the lower level of detail the Business Analyst works out compared to the Architect.

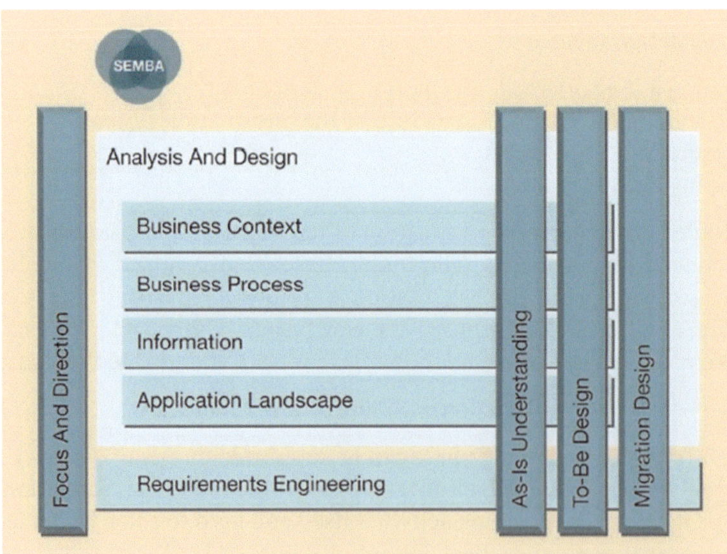

There is a focus difference between business architect and business analyst. The architect puts more focus on fitting 'the system' into its environment, while the analyst/engineer focuses on the internal structure of 'the system'. If both roles are executed by one person (which happens frequently), there is no real distinction between the architecture and the business analysis work.

4.4.4 IAF and IDF

4.4.4.1 Characteristics of Infrastructure Design Framework (IDF)

The IDF, the infrastructure design framework, has been developed by Capgemini infrastructure engineers. IDF covers the complete infrastructure lifecycle, whereas IAF focuses on the architecture part of infrastructure development.

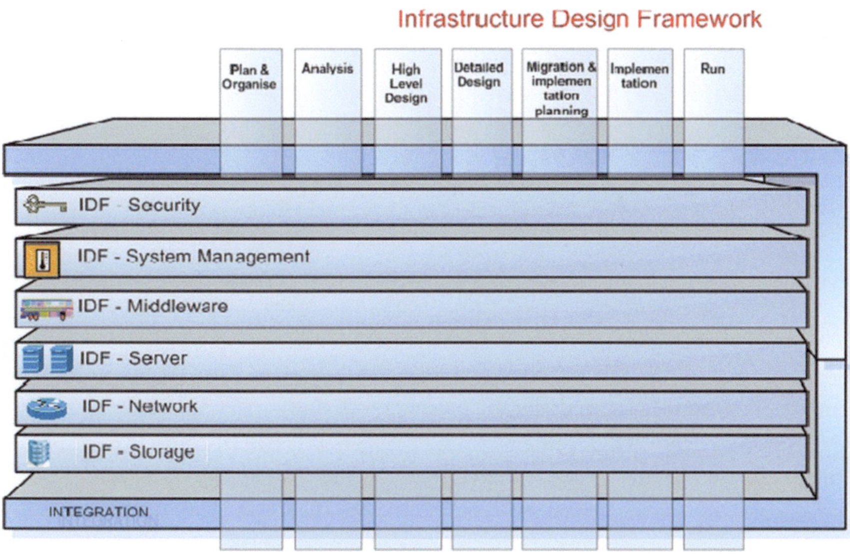

When combining IAF and IDF the project has to choose which approach is the best. Rule of thumb: When the engagement is about planning the change, then IAF is the best. If it is a major change to the infrastructure that has to be implemented, then IDF will provide more support.

IDF is used in Infrastructure Engineering (IE) projects and describes in details steps and deliverables. IDF contains seven phases and addresses different technology areas:

1. Integration
2. Network

3. Servers
4. Storage
5. Middleware
6. Security
7. Governance

A phase is made up of a number of stages. Each stage covers multiple activities each of which create a work product. A deliverable is the combination of Work Products that are the output of a phase.

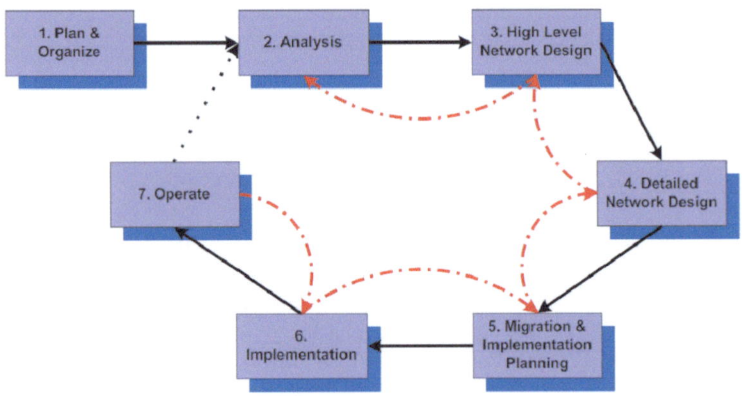

Working according IDF represents a structural approach to IE projects. IDF brings best practices from different projects together.

The goal is to deliver better IE projects to our customers and to ourselves.

4.4.4.2 Combining IAF and IDF

At first glance there might be a number of causes that makes combining IAF and IDF, combining architecture and infrastructure, a real challenge. The use of different terminology and languages might lead to insufficient mutual understanding or insufficient trust. Both frameworks might have different goals and timing, which makes it difficult to achieve sufficient co-operation and transfer of knowledge and deliverables.

Still, aligning IAF and IDF is necessary to mitigate risk, to prevent returning to the drawing board for delivery and increase delivery awareness by enhancing training courses.

When having a closer look at both, we note that IDF and IAF serve different purposes and are complementary to one another, as illustrated below.

IDF	IAF
Process driven	Framework model
Technology best practices	Content driven
Supports implementation	Supports decisions
Based on Technology Domains	Overall view, with B&I supporting Business and IS&TI supporting Technology Services.

It's not only that IDF and IAF serve different purposes, it is also that infrastructure engineers and architect have a different approach. An Infrastructure Engineer works bottom up, is solution driven with a strong technology focus and on detail. An architect on the other hand works top down, is advice driven with a strong focus on Business and IT, overview and relationships. Another reason why Infrastructure engineers and architects need each other.

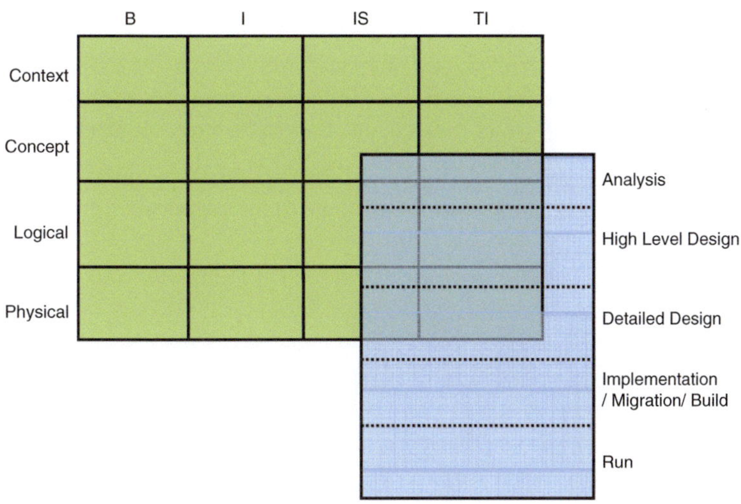

Process alignment of IAF and IDF

As illustrated above, IDF partially overlaps IAF, certainly for logical and physical TI. In IDF the Analysis is a drill down of the requirements for the project and the current situation within the domain of the project. Objectives of this phase are to have a clean set of requirements and to achieve a detailed understanding of the existing situation to be able to develop realistic transition scenarios from the existing to the new infrastructure. These activities overlap with the IAF activities to define IS&TI services and the accompanying contracts. The transition scenarios overlap with the activity to develop solution alternatives.

IDF High Level Design provides a high level indication of which solutions are needed and at what cost. Attention is given to both logical and physical design aspects, covering the standards, mechanisms and protocols used. These activities overlap with IAF activities to further develop and select solution alternatives, specify interaction models and specify the accompanying contracts.

During IDF Detailed Design the infrastructure engineer defines the level of detail for the various components for each segment, including the characteristics of the components. The level of detail is determined by the complexity, scope and intended audience. Impact for migration and implementation is checked, a test plan is developed. These activities overlap with IAF activities at physical level where physical components and contracts are specified, alongside with migration view, distribution view, security view, product view, etc.

IDF activities Implementation/Migration/Build and the activity Run have no counterpart in IAF.

Ideally, there is a gradual transfer from architect to infrastructure engineer during these activities.

4.4.4.3 Content Alignment of IAF and IDF

On the content side, there is no clear boundary between IAF and IDF; the boundary shifts depending on the circumstances. The shaded area in the picture below shows essential inputs to IDF which may include principles, reference models, patterns, etc.

As said, the boundary is not fixed and does depend on customer, project, scope, etc. and this will affect the content artifacts that flow between IAF and IDF.

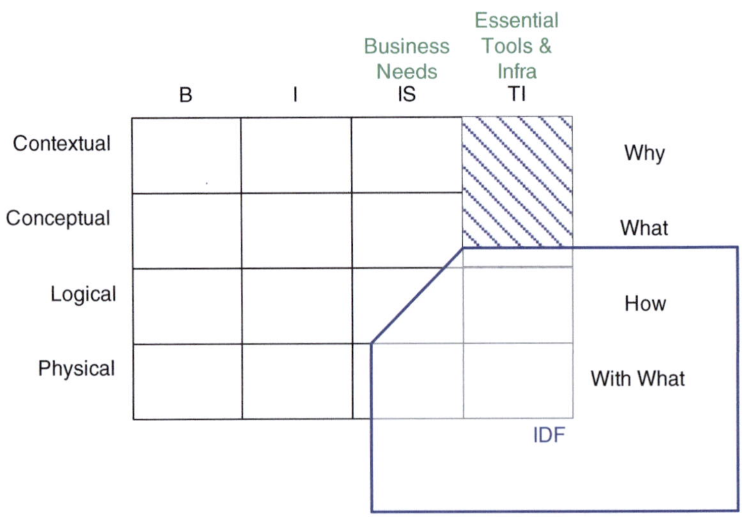

It's no surprise that information sharing is strongest in Physical TI-level, this content will be used in several phases within IDF. Information flows from IAF to IDF and vice versa.

The interaction between IDF and IAF varies with customer, scope and people involved. For instance, it is possible that IAF will not go into physical TI, because this responsibility may be devolved to the IDF implementation. However, it is also possible that architecture decisions within Physical TI will also exist, and these will also become inputs to the IDF.

The IAF Physical TI cell provides the logical service mappings for the High Level Design Phase in IDF (physical TI components and the Physical IS – TI cross-references). The IAF physical phase is usually shared by IS and TI areas, because the borderline between IS-components and TI-components is somewhat arbitrary. Somewhat depending on sector, many common package applications, like browsers, text processing tools, e-mail clients, system management tools, etc. are defined in the TI aspect area.

4.5 IAF and Industry Process Frameworks

4.5.1 IAF and ITIL

4.5.1.1 Characteristics of ITIL

The Information Technology Infrastructure Library (ITIL) is a set of concepts and policies for managing information technology (IT) infrastructure, development and operations.

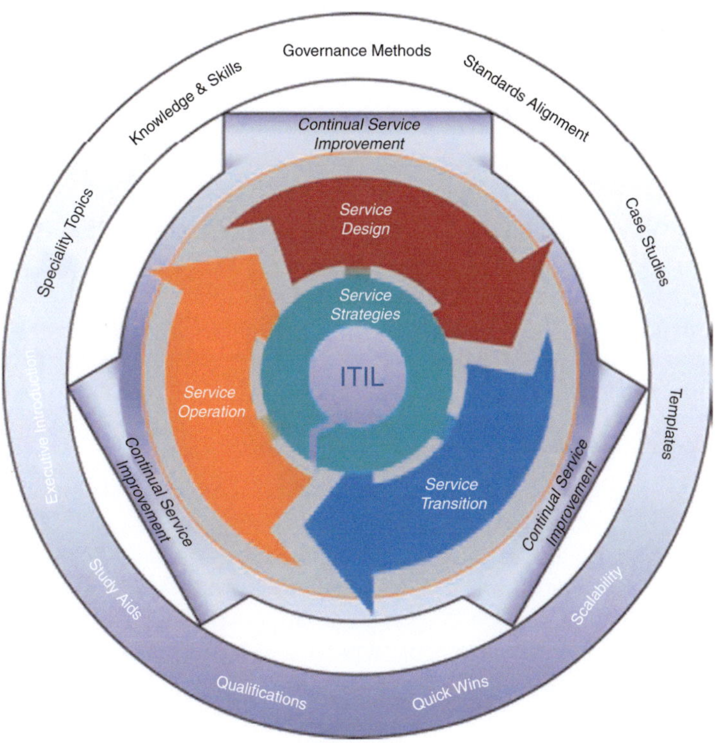

ITIL gives a detailed description of a number of important IT practices with comprehensive checklists, tasks and procedures that can be tailored to any IT organization.

ITIL v3, published in May 2007, comprises five key volumes:

1. Service Strategy
2. Service Design
3. Service Transition
4. Service Operation
5. Continual Service Improvement

These volumes cover all the stages of the service management lifecycle. Each lifecycle stage provides guidance through describing: purpose, principles, key processes and activities, key roles and responsibilities. The following paragraphs describe these key stages in more detail.

4.5.1.2 Service Strategy

Service strategy is shown at the core of the ITIL v3.1 lifecycle but cannot exist in isolation to the other parts of the IT structure. It encompasses a framework to build best practice in developing a long term service strategy. It covers many topics including: general strategy, competition and market space, service provider types, service management as a strategic asset, organization design and development, key process activities, financial management, service portfolio management, demand management, and key roles and responsibilities of staff engaging in service strategy.

4.5.1.3 Service Design

The design of IT services conforming to best practice, and including design of architecture, processes, policies, documentation, and allowing for future business requirements. This also encompasses topics such as Service Design Package (SDP), Service catalog management, Service Level management, designing for capacity management, IT service continuity, Information Security, supplier management, and key roles and responsibilities for staff engaging in service design.

4.5.1.4 Service Transition

Service transition relates to the delivery of services required by the business into live/operational use, and often encompasses the project side of IT rather than Business As Usual. This area also covers topics such as managing changes to the Business as Usual environment. Topics include Service Asset and Configuration Management, Transition Planning and Support, Release and deployment management, Change Management, Knowledge Management, as well as the key roles of staff engaging in Service Transition.

4.5.1.5 Service Operation

Best practice for achieving the delivery of agreed levels of services both to end-users and the customers (where 'customers' refer to those individuals who pay for the service and negotiate the SLAs). Service Operations is the part of the lifecycle where the services and value is actually directly delivered. Also the monitoring of problems and balance between service reliability and cost etc. are considered. Topics include balancing conflicting goals (e.g. reliability versus cost etc.), Event management, incident management, problem management, event fulfillment, asset management, service desk, technical and application management, as well as key roles and responsibilities for staff engaging in Service Operation.....

4.5.1.6 Continual Service Improvement (CSI)

Aligning and realigning IT services to changing business needs (because stand-still implies decline).

The goal of Continual Service Improvement is to align and realign IT Services to changing business needs by identifying and implementing improvements to the IT services that support the Business Processes. The perspective of CSI on improvement is the business perspective of service quality, even though CSI aims to improve process effectiveness, efficiency and cost effectiveness of the IT processes through the whole lifecycle. In order to manage improvement, CSI should clearly define what should be controlled and measured.

CSI needs to be treated just like any other service practice. There needs to be upfront planning, training and awareness, ongoing scheduling, roles created, ownership assigned, and activities identified in order to be successful. CSI must be planned and scheduled as process with defined activities, inputs, outputs, roles and reporting.

Some example processes identified in ITIL:

Access Management	Availability Management
Capacity Management	Change Management
Demand Management	Evaluation
Event Management	Financial Management
Incident Management	Information Security Management
IT Service Continuity Management	Knowledge Management
Problem Management	Release and Deployment Management
Request Fulfilment	Service Asset and Configuration Mgmt
Service Catalogue Management	Service Level Management
Service Measurement	Service Portfolio Management
Service Reporting	Service Validation and Testing
Strategy Generation Transition Planning and Support	Supplier Management

4.5.1.7 Combining IAF and ITIL

As we see above, ITIL describes the business processes required for Service Management. In an IAF engagement we can use ITIL for the design of the service management organization. In fact, ITIL is a pattern or a reference model for IT governance, describing how the business processes required for Service Management should be structured. That would place ITIL as a Business Reference Model in aspect area Business at logical abstraction layer, as part of IT Governance Business architecture.

The ITIL Technical Service Catalog of an organization can be matched with IAF as well. All relationships between ITIL technical services and the supporting services and logical components are described in this catalog. The items described in the catalog provide a significant overlap with the items described in IAF Logical TI Components and Logical TI Contracts.

However, we should realize that ITIL does not provide complete coverage for a governance architecture (which will also include business governance, information governance). Neither does ITIL provide in depth implementation details. Equally, ITIL does not provide specific linkage for why a specific organization will want to do specific elements of governance or how important this capability is to the business. All of these gaps are where IAF would be expected to add the value around ITIL – by providing a complete view of governance in the context of the business and by ensuring that the capabilities needed by the business were implemented.

4.5.2 IAF and COBIT

Control Objectives for Information and related Technology (COBIT®) is a registered trademark of the Information Systems Audit and Control Association (ISACA) and the IT Governance Institute (ITGI). COBIT provides good practices across a domain and process framework and presents activities in a manageable and logical structure. COBIT can be used at the highest level of IT governance and helps organizations in meeting their conformance and performance requirements. COBIT can easily be combined with other best practices frameworks and standards.

COBIT identifies four domains in which processes, activities, controls, goals, metrics, roles and responsibilities are defined. These four domains are:

1. Plan and Organize, with 10 defined processes
2. Acquire and Implement, with 7 defined processes
3. Deliver and Support, with 13 defined processes
4. Monitor and Evaluate, with 4 defined processes

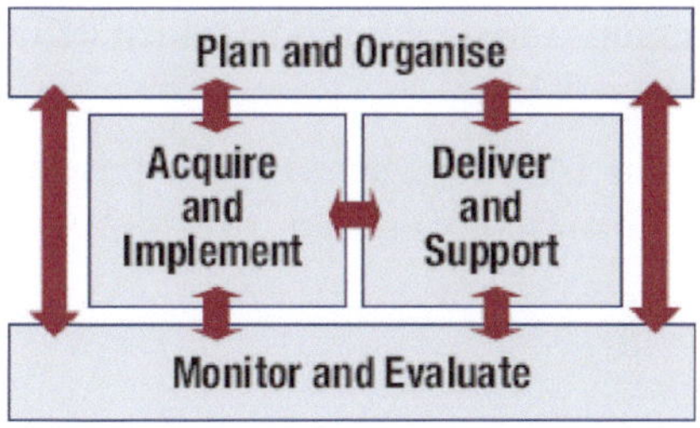

The following picture (which is Figure 23 in COBIT 4.1) shows the overall COBIT framework, with these four domains and their defined processes.

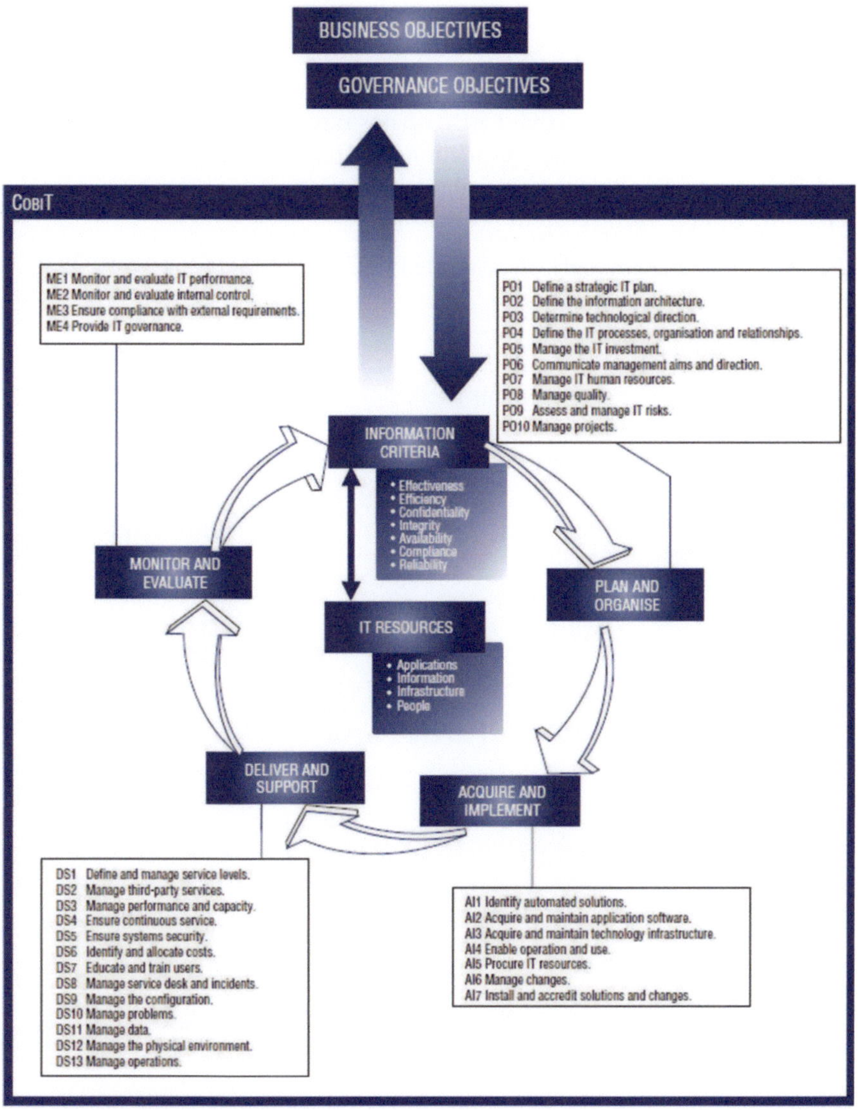

Besides this COBIT contains a maturity model which defines when a specific process is at a certain maturity level.

COBIT can be used in an IAF engagement as a business reference model for the design of IT Governance in an organization (logical business architecture).

4.5.3 IAF and CMMI

Capability Maturity Model® Integration (CMMI, Software Engineering Institute of Carnegie Mellon University) is a process improvement approach that provides organizations with the essential elements of effective processes. It can be used to guide process improvement across a project, a division, or an entire organization. CMMI helps integrate traditionally separate organizational functions, set process improvement goals and priorities, provide guidance for quality processes, and provide a point of reference for appraising current processes.

CMMI has different models, all generated from the CMMI framework, that are grouped into constellations.

The constellations are:

1. CMMI-DEV – for development processes
2. CMMI-SVC – for delivering services
3. CMMI-ACQ – for acquisition leadership

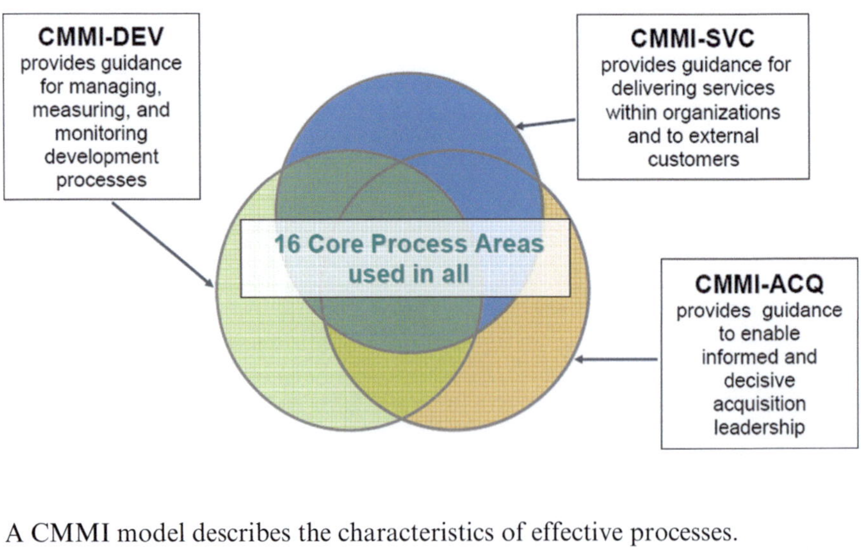

A CMMI model describes the characteristics of effective processes.

CMMI can be used as a business reference model if the architecture contains development processes, service delivery or acquisition (logical business architecture).

4.6 IAF and Project Management Methods

4.6.1 IAF and Prince2

4.6.1.1 Characteristics of Prince2

PRojects IN Controlled Environments (Prince2) is a project management method designed to provide a framework covering the wide variety of disciplines and activities required within a project.

The focus throughout PRINCE2 is on the Business Case, which describes the rationale and business justification for the project. The Business Case drives all the project management processes, from initial project set-up through to the finish of the project.

Prince2 consists of the following processes:

- *Directing a Project* describes the project board's decision making activities.
- *Starting up a Project* delivers a project brief and an initial business case.
- *Initiating a Project* delivers a project initiation document, and a refined business case.
- *Controlling a Stage* is aimed at ensuring the different stages that have been defined deliver their products within the plan.
- *Managing Product Delivery*.

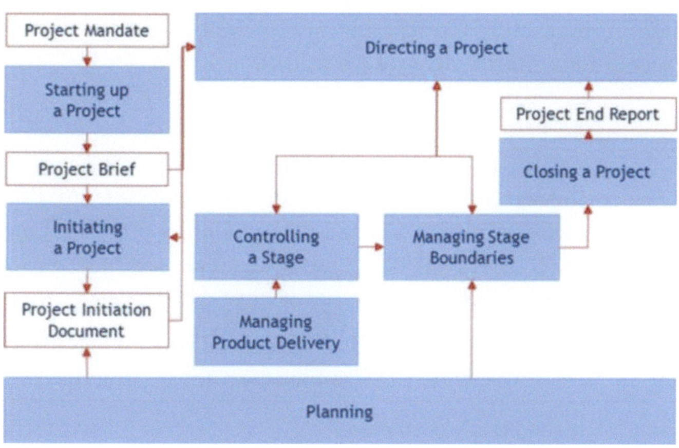

- *Managing Stage Boundaries* is aimed at ensuring the different stages of a project link sufficiently. End stage reports, exception reports, next stage plans and refined business cases are the core products here.
- *Planning*
- *Closing a Project*

Important products and deliverables throughout these processes are:

- Business Case
- Project Initiation Document (PID)
- Product Breakdown Structure
- Product Flow Diagram
- Product Description
- Work Breakdown Structure

4.6.1.2 Combining IAF and Prince2

IAF and Prince2 can be combined in multiple ways:

1. Using IAF to create the solution within a Prince2 managed project
2. Using Prince2 to manage an IAF engagement

Using IAF in a Prince2 Managed Project Given a project managed by Prince2, IAF can be used to create the solution architecture which accompanies the Business Case. Its initial version is created during 'Starting Up a project'. The solution architecture should be relatively complete at the end of 'Initiating a project' if the project wants the first 'Managing Product Delivery' stage to be designed. Otherwise the solution architecture and a refined business case can be delivered as one of the first 'Managing Product Delivery' stages of the project.

The solution architecture should be sufficiently complete to provide guidance to the consequent stages of the project. It should contain the (physical) components, with their interaction models that are to be delivered, along with principles, design decisions, standards and guidelines.

4.6.2 IAF and MSP

Managing Successful Programs (MSP) is a project management approach by the British Office of Government Commerce, originally published in 1999 and revised in 2004 and 2007. MSP is public domain and all organizations are free to use the method, although the method itself is copyrighted.

MSP is a program management method, developed to realize changes in an organization in an effective way. MSP is based on seven principles:

- Stay in line with the business strategy
- Leadership during the change

- Visualization and communication of the better future
- Focus on benefits and risks regarding the benefits
- Value creation
- Design, develop and deliver coherent capabilities
- Learn from experience

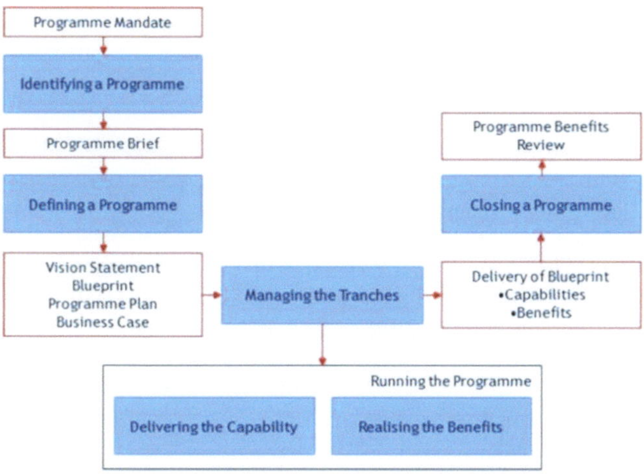

MSP provides a set of processes and governance themes.

These processes are:

- *Identifying a Programme*, triggered by a Programme Mandate and resulting in a Programme Brief.
- *Defining a Programme*, resulting in a Vision Statement, a Blueprint, a Programme Plan and a Business Case.
- *Managing the Tranches* manages and controls the running of the tranches of the programme.
- *Delivering the Capability* and *Realizing the Benefits* together form Running the programme.
- *Closing a Programme* runs when the programme ends.

The MSP governance themes support these MSP processes. Governance themes are:

- Organization.
- Vision, which provides a good vision of the goal. A Vision is easy to communicate and can be verified to be the future state.
- Leadership and Stakeholder Management.
- Benefits Realization Management.

- Blueprint Design and Delivery, which complements the Vision. The Blueprint is an accurate description of the future state in terms of business models, organizational structures, processes, information flows and technology. The Blueprint is designed at the start of the program and maintained during the program.
- Planning and Control.
- Business Case.

4.6.2.1 Combining IAF and MSP

IAF can be used to create both Vision and the Blueprint that form the enterprise architecture, which accompanies the business case. These deliverables are created during 'Defining a programme'.

The enterprise architecture should be sufficiently complete to provide guidance to the consequent tranches of the program. Very often it contains contextual, conceptual and logical information, along with principles, design decisions, standards and guidelines.

4.7 Combining TOGAF, Prince2 and IAF

Wouldn't that be great, bringing it all together? Combining TOGAF, Prince2 and IAF as best of breed? Using Prince2 as project management method, Using TOGAF as architecture development method and using IAF as architecture content framework?

We can combine TOGAF, Prince2 and IAF to design and deliver a project that works under architecture control:

- At the same time the project brief is created (during Starting up a project), we use TOGAF and IAF to create a 0.1 version of the baseline and target (solution) architecture. The Project Board uses these products for the go/nogo decision regarding the project.
- During Initiating a project, when the Project Initiation Document is created, we use TOGAF and IAF to create the 1.0 version of the target architecture. Reference architectures can be developed beforehand to expedite the creation of the solution architecture.
- The solution architecture is used during Managing Product Delivery to make sure that the right Work Packages are defined and realized in proper order.
- During Controlling a Stage and Managing Stage Boundaries, we use TOGAF and IAF to ensure the solution stays in line with the architecture.

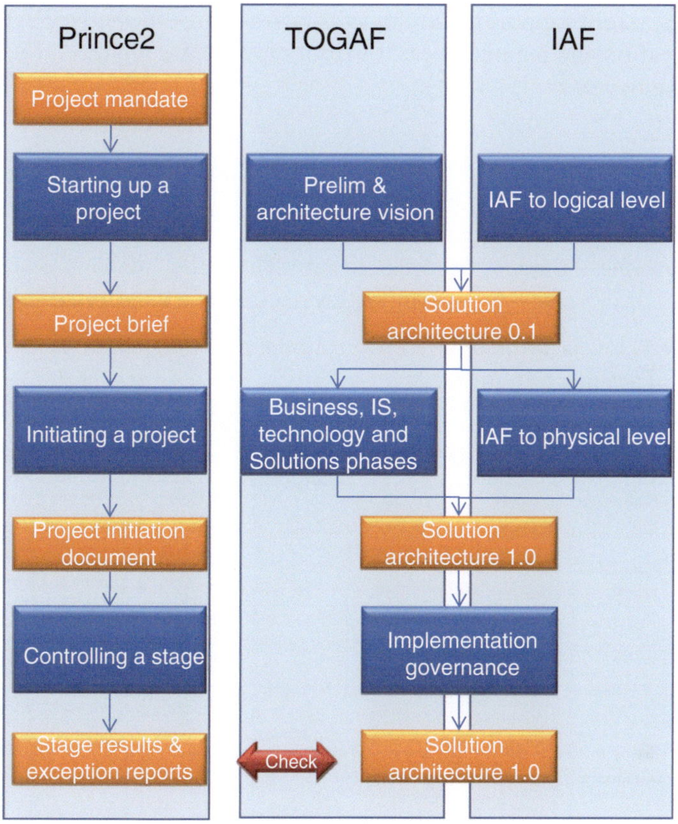

4.8 IAF and Architecture Tooling

4.8.1 Introduction

With the growing complexity of working on architectures, the traditional 'flat' office tools like spreadsheets, graphical design and presentation in many assignments no longer are sufficient. The architect needs to keep track of many dependencies, which requires manipulating a data collection that maintains many relationships. Architecture tooling is the breed of software that supports the work of the architect; it has been around for some years now and the software gains maturity constantly. The intention of this section is to provide an overview of generic services that are required for architecture tooling as well as the specific requirements that have been defined to support IAF in a tool.

Moreover, material from previous architectures is required in the development of the new architecture, but usually not expressed in similar terms; we need a way to align the old descriptions with the new ones.

And lastly, a tool support the architect to work more efficiently: Faster architecture creation and maintenance – the tool supports the architect, for example by generating views.

4.8.2 Generic Services for Architecture Tools

There are dozens of tool sets that support the work of an architect; to keep this section agnostic of the specific tools – which all have their undeniable merits and occasional drawbacks – we approach this issue from a conceptual standpoint.

The figure below is a function reference model that Capgemini has used in the selection of architecture tool sets.

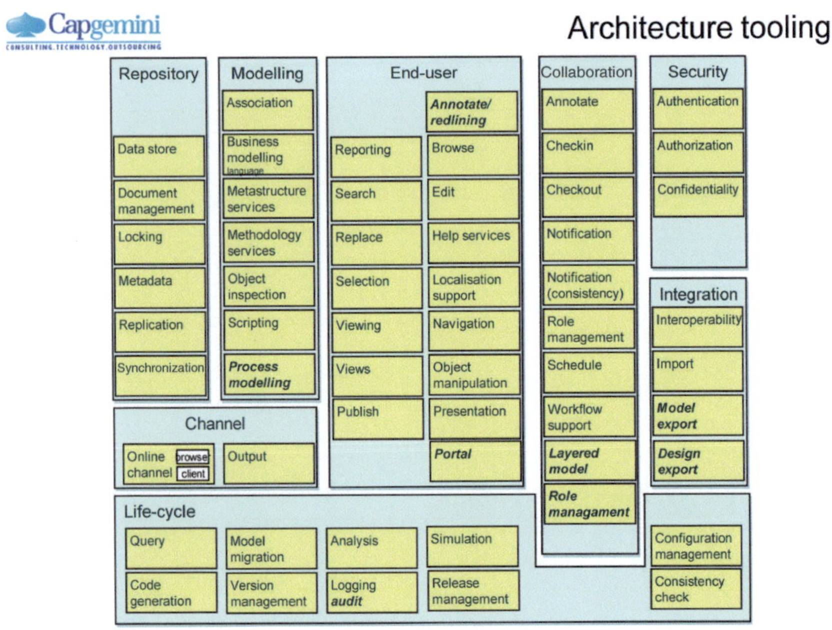

A model as shown above is intended to initiate discussions during tool selection on the emphasis on services, given the scope and objectives of the enterprise architecture, based on architecture functions, processes and actors/roles.

Important service groups are:

- Repository services provide storage and retrieval of elements of the repository, either separate artifacts or documents related to those. Data integrity is ensured through locking relevant parts of the repository for update and controlled extraction of baselines and reloading of updated segments. Traceability of changes to the repository is also part of these services;

- Modeling services provide the base metamodel structure for the repository and – preferably graphically – enable the architect to register new artifacts and relate them to others, as well as executing tasks like what-if analysis studies;
- End-user services are there to serve the entire potential user community, either skilled and trained (architects) or informed users (business representatives);
- Collaborations enable architects and other involved staff to collaborate on building the body of knowledge of the enterprise architecture;
- Security service provide for authorized access to viewing or updating functions of the repository;
- Integration services focus on the program-to-program interactions between the repository and adjacent applications (e.g. MS Excel for uploading, MS Access for extraction or interoperability with an operational configuration management database (CMDB));
- Channels allow for access to the repository;
- Life-cycle services enable the architect to work with current and anticipated version of artifacts, and as such assist in the time-phased aspects of architecture (As-is, To-be, intermediate landscapes).

4.8.3 Specific Requirements for IAF Support

In addition to the generic services required in architecture tools described above, there are some additional requirements specific for IAF support.

In order to support IAF, the architecture tool needs to support the IAF meta-model as discussed in previous chapters of this book. It might be that just a high-level meta-model is supported, as long as the essential elements are the same. Although changes to the meta-model might lead to undesirable results when not carefully thought and executed, it can be an additional quality of the tooling. Just handle changes to the meta-model with care.

In day to day use the tool has to support multiple instances of the same architecture, in order to compare solution alternatives or evolutions of an architecture over time. Surely, views must be supported. Support for different levels of abstraction should be available as well, for example to link enterprise architectures and various related solution architectures at project level.

Features for using and applying the architecture would be of great help too. Guidance for development or support for project portfolio management is desirable. Integration with software and package development teams is essential to re-use the architecture deliverables.

Since architects usually work in teams, the tool needs to support multi-user and multi-location. Of course, version control is an essential element as well as import and export facilities to most common file extensions like Microsoft Word, Excel and Visio or Adobe Acrobat or just plain text.

Anno 2009, multiple tool vendors are in the process of getting their products IAF compliant certified – or have actually achieved that status.

4.9 IAF and Modelling Techniques

4.9.1 IAF and UML

4.9.1.1 Characteristics of UML

Unified Modeling Language (UML) is a standardized general-purpose modeling language in the field of software engineering. UML includes a set of graphical notation techniques to create abstract models of specific systems. It is a graphical language for visualizing, specifying and constructing the artifacts of a software-intensive system.

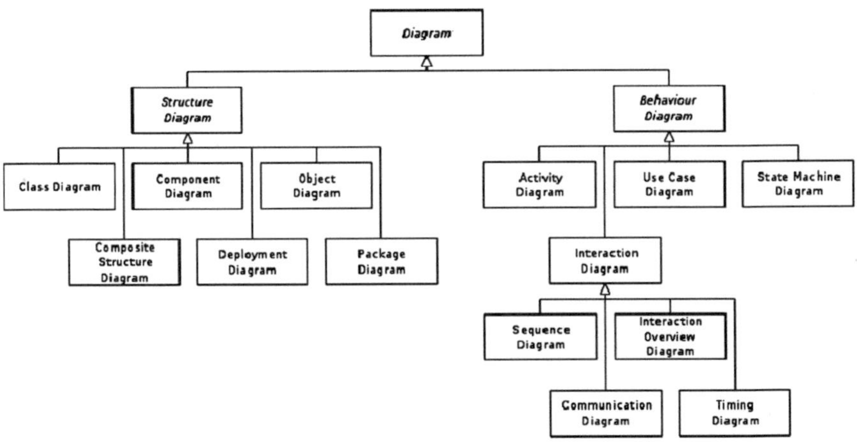

The Unified Modeling Language offers a standard way to write a system's blueprints, including conceptual things such as business processes and system functions as well as concrete things such as programming language statements, database schemas, and reusable software components.

UML combines the best practice from data modeling concepts such as entity relationship diagrams, business modeling (work flow), object modeling and component modeling. It can be used with all processes, throughout the software development life cycle, and across different implementation technologies.

UML is officially defined by the Object Management Group (OMG) as the UML metamodel.

4.9.1.2 Combining IAF and UML

We can use some of the UML graphical notation techniques to visualize architecture. Advantages of doing so primarily are (1) that a wide range of engineers, developers and designers understand UML, (2) standardization mitigates the risk of miscommunication and misinterpretation and (3) it can be supported by tooling. On the downside, you are forced into the UML paradigm, which is aimed at software engineering, not at creating architectures.

The most commonly used are the Interaction diagrams, with the sequence diagram as most commonly encountered in architectures. They resemble IAF Interaction Models.

Interaction diagrams, a subset of behavior diagrams, emphasize the flow of control and data among the things in the system being modeled:

- *Communication diagram*: shows the interactions between objects or parts in terms of sequenced messages. They represent a combination of information taken from Class, Sequence, and Use Case Diagrams describing both the static structure and dynamic behavior of a system.

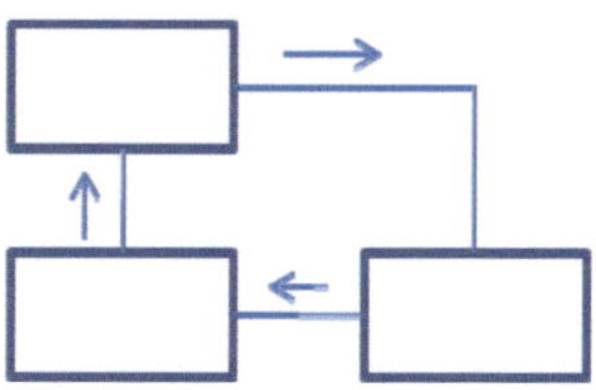

- *Interaction overview diagram*: a type of activity diagram in which the nodes represent interaction diagrams.

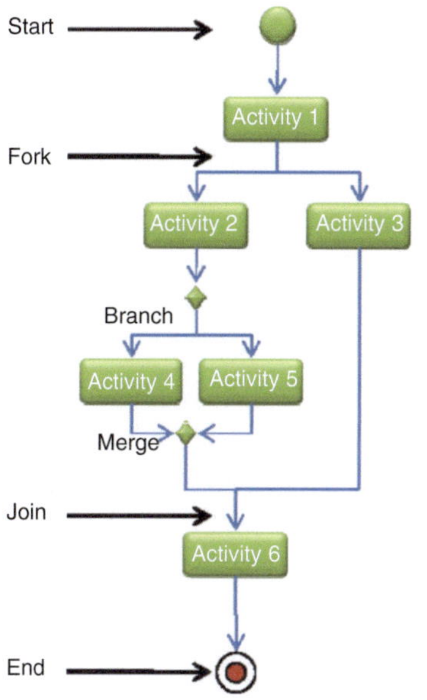

- *Sequence diagram*: shows how objects communicate with each other in terms of a sequence of messages. Also indicates the lifespans of objects relative to those messages.

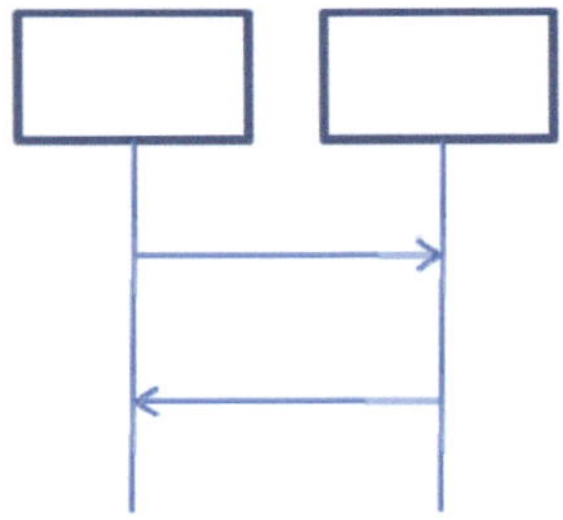

- *Timing diagrams*: are a specific type of interaction diagram, where the focus is on timing constraints.

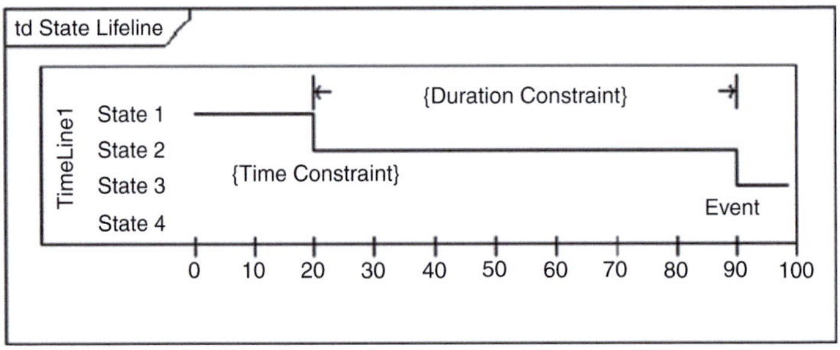

4.9.2 IAF and IDEF

In 1981 the ICAM program, the U.S. Air Force program for Integrated Computer Aided Manufacturing, developed a series of techniques known as the

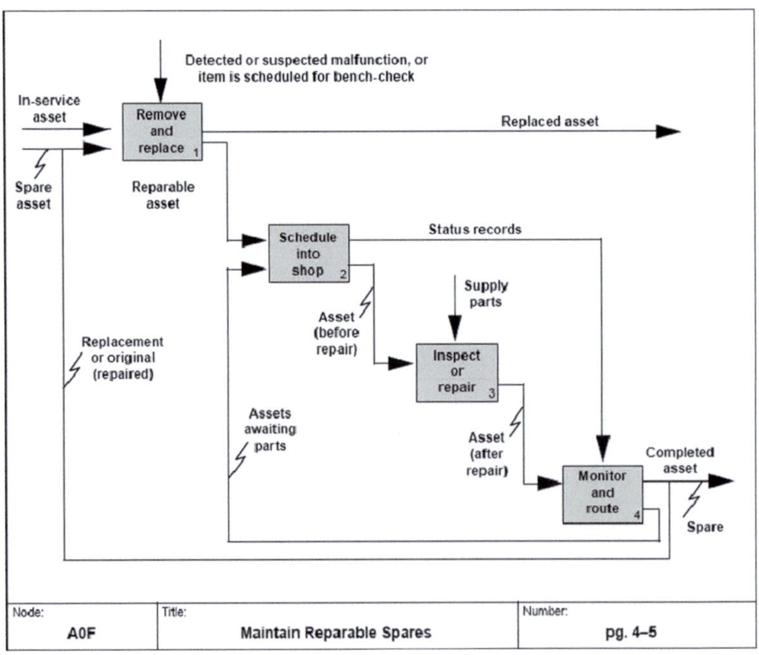

IDEF (Integration DEFinition) techniques. IDEF is a family of modeling languages in the field of software engineering. They cover a range of uses from function modeling to information, simulation, object-oriented analysis and design and knowledge acquisition. These 'definition languages' have become standard modeling techniques.

The most common techniques are:

- IDEF0: Function modeling, used to produce a function model, which is a structured representation of the functions, activities or processes within the modeled system or subject area.
- IDEF1: Information Modeling, used to produce an information model, which represents the structure and semantics of information within the modeled system or subject area.
- IDEF1X: IDEF1 Extended, a semantic Data Modeling technique. Launched in 1983.
- IDEF2: Simulation Model Design, used to produce a dynamics model, which represents the time-varying behavioral characteristics of the modeled system or subject area.
- IDEF3: Process Description Capture, a scenario-driven process flow description capture method intended to capture the knowledge about how a particular system works. It provides modes to represent both Process Flow Descriptions and Object State Transitions.
- IDEF4: Object-Oriented Design, for the design of component-based client/server systems. It specifies design objects with sufficient detail to enable source code generation.

IDEF0 and IDEF1X are widely used in the government, industrial and commercial sectors, supporting modeling efforts for a wide range of enterprises and application domains; both are FIPS standard.

In relation to the use of IAF, IDEF0 function models can be used to visualize IAF Business Interaction models and IDEF3 process models have also been used to visualize processes.

4.10 IAF and TechnoVision

4.10.1 TechnoVision Overview

Since its first edition in 2001, Capgemini's TechnoVision has successfully been used as an approach to help clients to select new technologies that support their goals effectively. In its core, the recent edition of TechnoVision provides a mechanism to our clients to cope with the diversity of technologies that have emerged in the recent past – and will continue to do so in the future. The question which technologies will hold their relevance for their business in particular, and which technologies are more like gadgets or 'one day flies' in that context, has increasingly become an issue for organizations. This is all the more relevant in times where the state of the economy requires a stronger focus on cost efficiency, and expenditures in IT are under constantly high scrutiny from management.

TechnoVision is a framework to group the hundreds of current and new technologies into 'technology areas', which for manageability purposes have been captured into seven theme groups. With TechnoVision, technology is presented in a form that appeals to business and IT representatives alike, and as such helps to bridge the gap that has existed between them.

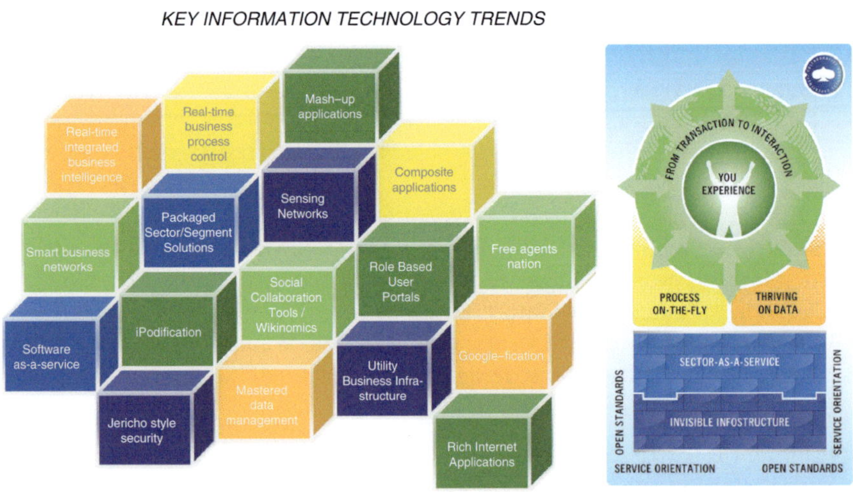

The 'vision' component part of TechnoVision lies in the fact that in Capgemini's expert vision the technology clusters will remain stable, while new technologies will continue to emerge, and that these will fit in the clusters and will be better manageable.

In a technologically volatile environment we must find a way to create a stable business and IT landscape that is flexible enough for changes – we all know that additionally, business will change in its own pace. In Capgemini's opinion, this stability can be achieved through architecture.

The TechnoVision is something every innovation-oriented technology service provider should have: a comprehensive perspective on the evolution of technologies. Capgemini's TechnoVision goes further than most in that it also addresses the impact of technology on our clients' business and our own capabilities.

TechnoVision has three sections:

1. a general view of the expected IT developments, and establishes a high-level inventory of those technologies that appear to be the most relevant to our clients in the future;
2. an examination of how these technologies influence the businesses of our clients; and
3. a look at the consequences of innovation and a presentation of the capabilities that Capgemini will have to develop to satisfy future client needs.

Capgemini identified 17 technology trend areas, which were grouped into 6 technology clusters or ‘manifestations’ of what we will likely see, with one additional ‘meta’ cluster underpinning all of them:

- *The You Experience* cluster introduces a new generation of user interface technologies and Internet-based collaboration platforms that make for a compelling, highly individualized experience. Through it, users connect freely to the outside world to act, interact, collaborate, co-create, learn and share knowledge. (Technology areas: Rich Internet Applications, Role-Based User Portals, iPodification, Mashup Applications)
- *The shift from Transaction to Interaction* involves organizations and individuals in a steady, continual rhythm of learning, experiencing, creating and collaborating. Changing the game and creating new value and growth through business innovation is the challenge here, with markets, players and consumers constantly shifting positions. (Technology areas: Social Collaboration Tools, Smart Business Networks, Free Agents Nations)
- *Processes will be assembled on-the-Fly*, by orchestrating the building blocks of underlying services. Organizations will need to change their processes in near real-time to quickly reflect and accommodate changes in the business ecosystem. The underlying information systems that support and enable these processes must consist of fine grained, configurable services that can be freely composed and orchestrated into new solutions. (Technology areas: Real-Time Business Process Control, Composite Applications)
- Detailed insight into crucial data is a necessity for organizations that want to navigate a constantly changing, information-rich environment. Enterprises that know how to connect the use of data to their strategic objectives are literally *Thriving on Data*. (Technology areas: Real-Time Integrated Business Intelligence, Searching the Semantic Web/‘Googlefication’, ‘Mastered’ Data Management)
- *Sector-as-a-Service* will help organizations focus on differentiation by providing standard and nondifferentiating business services ‘on tap’. This is achieved through little-customized implementations of standard software, through the generation of systems out of reusable industry reference models

and through stabilizing and then ‘service enabling’ the existing legacy systems. (Technology areas: Rationalizing Packaged Sector/Segment Solutions, Software-as-a-Service)

- *Invisible Infostructure* is the end-state of infrastructure as we currently know it, using virtualization, grid and automated management technologies to deliver infrastructural services – including all facilities to securely capture, store, exchange and process (inter)company information – as a commoditized, preferably invisible utility. (Technology areas: Utility Business Infrastructure, De-perimeterized ‘Jericho style’ Security and Identity, Sensing Networks)
- *Open Standards, Service Orientation and Cloud* represent architecture style elements that underpin the other technology clusters, making this a ‘virtual’ or ‘meta’ cluster. As more organizations rely on intelligence from outside the corporate perimeter, open standards for boundaryless information flows are a necessity, both horizontal (infrastructural) and vertical (industry specific).

4.10.2 Using IAF and TechnoVision Together

TechnoVision addresses one of the major driving areas for architecture: new technology. The business needs to decide which technologies to choose from in order to better achieve its goals. TechnoVision supports this process through a tightly facilitated ‘pressure-cooker’ approach. During these sessions, technology options are assessed against selected business drivers, leading to ideas on which changes to initiate.

In order to produce a successful outcome, most change initiatives will as a starting point need a clear picture of the current situation, even maybe in a *green field* situation. Together with the desired situation, this current state must be presented in a way that is comprehensible for all parties involved that have some interest in solving the issue. In other words, it is advisable that the building blocks of the current architecture and those from the target architecture are consistent. When applying to TechnoVision, this implies that the selected building blocks must fit in the overall architecture description.

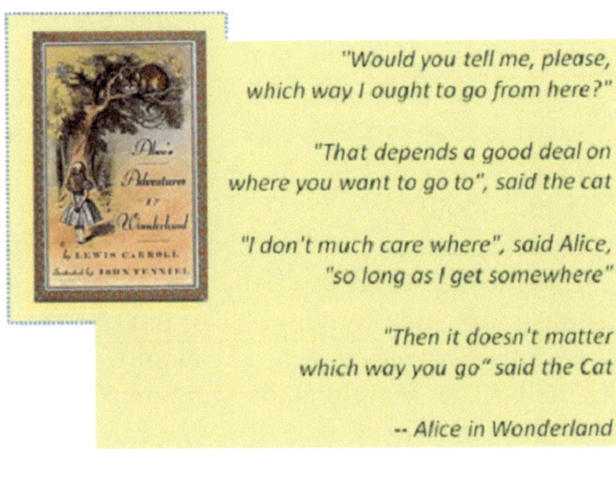

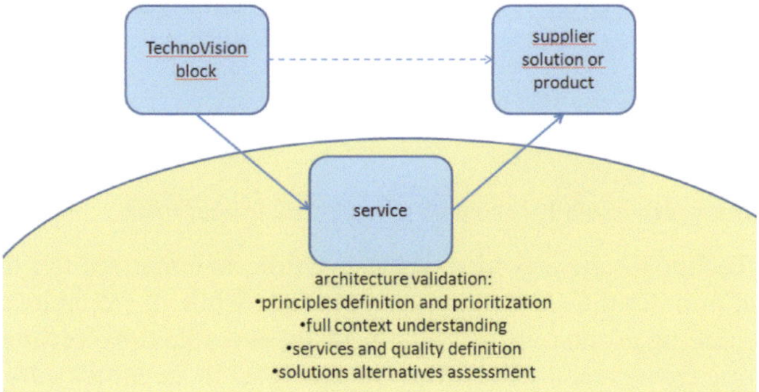

Ideas must be translated into solutions that fulfill them. An architected approach to implement the change initiatives from TechnoVision requires a controlled translation of the selected TechnoVision blocks into solutions and products. Jumping to solutions involves the risks of incompatibilities, difficult integration in the overall landscape, rejection by the end-users, failures to be corrected, and not in the least: higher maintenance effort and costs. To avoid this, IAF provides an elegant approach to deal with the building blocks for a solution. In an early stage of the process, the architect can align business requirements and technology requirements in terms of services and quality. From these service building blocks, the offerings of suppliers can then be matched against the specific quality requirements. This leads to an optimal choice of products and solutions for the selected TechnoVision building blocks in the client's landscape. Alternatives can be transparently assessed with an open eye for the different stakeholders' interests. Products are deployed providing those functions that are needed to fulfill the objectives, while other functions that only just happen to be available in the products can be ignored.

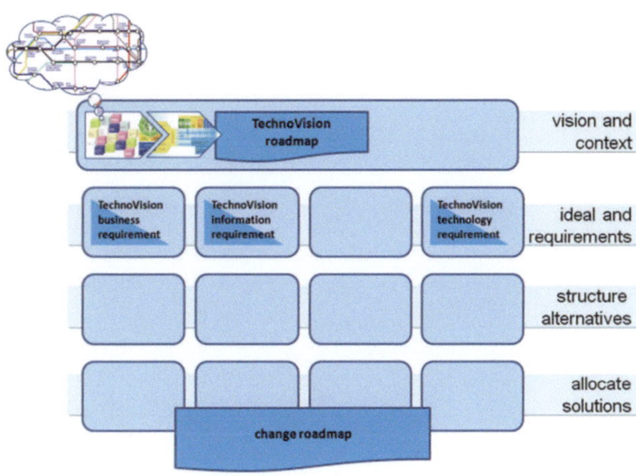

So in effect TechnoVision generates context and requirements for several IAF aspect areas:

- Business: Process on the Fly, Business as a Service, From Transaction to Interaction
- Information: Thriving on data
- Technology: Invisible Infostructure and You Experience

In short, TechnoVision provides the inspiration, summarizes the drivers for change and initiates the ideas to implement them, while IAF enables a safe and successful landing ground for technology changes inspired by TechnoVision in a pre-existing environment. These days, *green fields* in technology are rare, and current investments must be protected; integration of new ideas in the current landscape is a key success factor. This is especially valid for the ideas that new technologies can generate for businesses – sometimes they tend to start small and then grow fast.

Chapter 5
Applying IAF and Using Its Outcomes

Remember the reasons for IAF stated in chapter 1? The IT landscape became more and more complex, and we needed tools to manage that complexity. Architecture was the term that was coined to describe the activities that we were executing to manage the complexity. The ones who actually perform these activities are the architects.

Through time architects gained more visibility and got their own place within the IT organization. It became clear that two architects do not necessarily work the same way or deliver the same products. The call for professionalization of the architecture process and architecture function emerged.

Within Capgemini we experienced that IAF can help to do so. This chapter provides insight in the best ways IAF can be used (implemented) to professionalize the architecture function in an organization.

5.1 Understanding the Context in Which IAF Is to Be Implemented

When implementing IAF it's important to understand the business environment, the context in which IAF is to be implemented. Business environments that produce physical goods (e.g. consumer products, food or beverages) differ a lot from business environments that produce information products (e.g. banking, governmental or public organizations).

Producing information products requires information intensive environments, dealt with in business processes by human workforce. Information systems and computers support these business processes by processing information. At the other end, in business environments that produce physical goods, information systems and computers aim at complete automation of the business. They are the business process.

Another important aspect to consider when implementing IAF is the maturity of the organization. Implementing a mature architecture function within an organization where other departments act at a lower maturity level won't work.

J. van 't Wout et al., *The Integrated Architecture Framework Explained*,
DOI 10.1007/978-3-642-11518-9_5,

Instead of improving the overall benefit for the organization, you might end up with an improved architecture function not aligned with the rest of the organization. The use of architecture maturity models will help in choosing the best way forward to improve the architecture function in line with the maturity of the overall IT organization.

A final aspect to consider is the way IAF and architecture is applied within the organization. Typical applications of IAF implementations in organizations are:

- Support decision making, with focus on shared conceptualization and understanding by stakeholders. Focus is on the aspired future (when doing logical level architecture) and much less on detailed models and guidelines. This is enterprise architecture type of work.
- Guiding realization, with focus on guidelines and standards, entering physical solutions. This is solution architecture type of work.
- Design authority, with focus on getting and being in control regarding the information systems architected and realized.

5.2 IAF for Enterprise Transformation

At the enterprise level, the architecture focus is broad and decisions are much more strategic in nature, concerned with setting direction and policy often as part of the enterprise transformation. Architecture is used to investigate different strategic options or to design a blueprint of the desired future state. In this context, answering 'What' is the priority along with a broad indication of 'How'. We might assess options for implementations (reuse some of the existing parts, whether in business or IT) or assess options for outsourcing, shared service centers or portfolio management or a plateau planning for the enterprise transformation. 'With what' will then produce policies and principles to be followed. In some cases this may extend to products and standards often in the form of architecture constraints, for example, 'We will use our current investment to support all subsequent ERP solutions.'

This is where the architecture scope and objectives are crucial to selecting the correct areas of the framework to use, and even more importantly, the level of detail required to achieve the architecture objectives. For example, is the architecture being used to answer a business transformation objective or an IT Enablement question? In the former case, the focus may be to view the business and information aspects in more detail, whereas the latter will focus more on the IS aspects.

The deliverables from the two examples would often be the same but with different focus and detail:

- Business and technology context aspect focusing on business context and principles for business transformation and on the IT context, and business and IT principles for IT enablement.

- Enterprise architecture covering the requirements and derived logical architecture together with standards and guidelines needed to govern solution architectures:
  - Business transformation will focus on conceptual and logical business and information aspects and the business policies and guidelines;
  - IT enablement will focus on conceptual and logical information, information system/technology infrastructure aspects together with the standards and guidelines for the use and development of information, IS and IT.
- Project portfolio plans or guidance and/or roadmaps to show how the architecture vision is achieved over time, informing either the transformation strategy or the IT strategy.
- Governance model to use the enterprise architecture to guide (and learn from) solutions being delivered.

Overall, using IAF for enterprise transformation is about achieving shared conceptualization and commitment by key stakeholders, about focusing on principles and high level architecture models and views. It provides a sound foundation for detailed solution architectures.

5.3 IAF for Solutions Architecture

The essential message is that the main objective of IAF for solution architecture is to guide development. Our focus is on providing scope, IS and TI standards, rules and guidelines for the developers. Besides that, architecture describes how the solution has to fit into its environment. This paragraph describes some specific aspects to keep in mind. Remember that Sect. 4.7 elaborates on the IAF for solutions architecture approach by combining IAF with TOGAF and Prince2.

The overall principle when working with IAF for solution architecture: less is more. The developers don't want thick documents with an overload of detail. They want just enough, just in time documents and details. IAF can help in that.

When using IAF to develop an IT solution architecture, the overall approach will depend on the availability of appropriate input. Ideally, an existing enterprise architecture will exist, although care should be taken to ensure that the scope and objectives of that are aligned to the scope and objectives of the solution architecture. Using the example from the previous section, it is unlikely that the IT enablement enterprise architecture would be sufficiently complete to support the elaboration of a business solution architecture, although it would provide a lot of valuable information.

This is a very common trap (irrespective of approach, tools and methods used) where the presence of an 'enterprise architecture' leads to assumptions about completeness of information to support solution architectures.

It is also worth remembering that the IAF is a content framework, not a process framework. This means that relationships between artifacts indicate starting points for each aspect area. Completeness of information required from other aspect areas to support a specific aspect comes from all levels. For example, the organizational disposition of business components in reality is not the outcome of logical business levels but part of the physical business specification, i.e. similar specifications exist in the physical information specification for the disposition of master data sources. Whilst the desired logical state of business and information would support a desired IS solution, the absence of this information could significantly affect the physical outcomes of an IS/IT solution architecture.

Deliverables from such an engagement would therefore typically include clear documentation of the:

- Business, technology and architecture context together with the overarching, business and IT principles;
- Conceptual architecture covering the detailed requirements (often with the relevant business architecture);
- Resulting logical architecture including the rationale for any decisions made and relevant solution alternatives;
- The physical architecture, covering specifications, products, standards and guidelines needed to govern the design.

In assessing available architecture documentation, IAF can help in finding out what documents are available and which are not. If you're developing a system, use IAF IS logical and physical architecture artifacts to find out which material is available, what has to be completed or what has still to be done:

- Components and their specification (logical and/or physical);
- Interaction models to learn how components interact with each other (logical and/or physical);
- Contracts to learn the specifications of specific interactions (logical and/or physical)
- Cross references IS/TI to find which IS components rely on which TI components (logical and/or physical);
- Views that provide you insight in specific topics, like integration or distribution aspects (both logical and physical) or storage or product views (physical).

Through time we are able to map multiple project and solutions to the same principles and artifacts, which helps us give guidance to the overall direction of applications available to a company.

Overall, using IAF enables the solution architects to provide developers with consistent deliverables clearly positioned in a common framework. It enables us to discuss solutions in a common vocabulary, despite different level of detail between different projects.

5.3.1 IT Solution Architecture for Package-Based Solutions

Although it is often thought that package-based solutions, for example enterprise resource planning (ERP) packages do not need an IT solution architecture (the package effectively defines it), experience shows that there is just as much a need for the architecture to be developed.

IT solution architecture for a package-based solution is effectively no different from those for new builds, although constraints on the architecture (defined by the package) and their focus will be different. The exact nature of work will depend on whether the package is to be selected as part of the project, or (as is often the case) has already been selected. In both cases, the resulting architecture work will typically focus on:

- ensuring that the business needs are truly delivered by the package, identifying areas where the package may need to be customized and/or extended;
- identifying and designing how the package integrates with existing systems;
- understanding the information aspect (especially for master data management);
- understanding requirements that the package will place on the infrastructure (and any resulting changes);
- ensuring appropriate levels of security and governance for the overall solution.

5.4 Architecture Function and Design Authority

5.4.1 Architecture Function

Developing a design authority or more generally an architecture function (especially at enterprise level) is an important (and growing) objective for organizations. To be credible and successful within an organization, an architecture function needs to be sponsored and supported at the board level. It demands close collaboration between the business and technical functions of the entire organization.

The function also needs a well defined governance structure, clearly defined roles as well as the development of architecture processes and how they integrate into the business change process. The architecture function will also need to develop training and succession plans as well as considering whether to implement some form of certification and accreditation schemes.

Experience shows that there are some fundamental challenges to move enterprise architecture from a good idea to a mature, value-adding professional discipline. A practical and proven approach helps organizations overcome these challenges and accelerates the realization of tangible business benefits of enterprise architecture.

A number of key ingredients must be combined to create an effective internal enterprise architecture function within the organization. Development of an architecture function or a design authority needs to address the following areas:

- Enterprise strategy & vision. Architects translate the strategic objectives and vision of an enterprise into a realizable blueprint for business and IT change. Without such a strategy and vision to steer overall direction and principles, there is little chance of an architecture function or design authority demonstrating tangible value.
- Culture & communication. An effective architecture function will drive a cultural change across the organization, encouraging wider collaboration and alignment between architects across business and IT to deliver on the strategic change agenda. Enrolling the sponsorship, support and commitment of key stakeholders demands a clear and focused communication effort, without which there is little chance of achieving collaboration and alignment.
- Capabilities & competencies. Architecture is complex and requires a strong blend of capabilities, competencies and experiences. A common misconception is that IT people are best suited to this role. Experience shows that it is essential to achieve a balance between technical, business and managerial skills, supported by well-structured skills development and formal training.
- Tools & techniques. Architecture occupies a broad spectrum from strategic planning to project-level solution design. There are tools and techniques that support activities across this, but no single tool or technique provides the whole answer.
- Architecture content. Architecture is expressed through often complex and interdependent content that defines the business and technology landscape of an organization. Whilst it is essential to have knowledge and understanding of the current landscape to plan for and define what the future should look like, it is critical to focus on content that addresses the strategic change agenda and presents a realizable vision of the future.
- Process & governance. Architecture is a knowledge-intensive activity. Experience shows that good governance and a well-defined architecture management process is critical to ensure that knowledge is captured effectively so that it can be applied, managed and maintained at all stages from its initial creation through the key stages of business and IT change projects.

By bringing ingredients together in the right order, at the right time and involving the right people, it is possible to create the basis of a successful and sustainable architecture function.

Setting up an architecture function or design authority is not IAF specific. It's framework independent with one of the activities being selection and customization of the most appropriate framework. However, use of IAF as the framework (or the basis) offers many advantages to organizations building such a capability. It offers a proven, comprehensive and coherent framework complete with supporting material and training.

5.4.2 Design Authority

A key element in an architecture function in an organization is the design authority (DA). Depending on a number of parameters that will be elaborated in following paragraphs, a DA is the authority that ensures that developments stay in line with strategy and vision.

When implementing a DA it is important to know the approach and format of the validation. Not only in shaping the architecture processes, it is also about selecting the right people to act within a DA. Most common formats and approaches to the validation are:

- A peer review, where DA architects provide informal advise aimed at assisting a colleague;
- A formal advice, where DA architects provide a formal advise that is used during decisions making;
- Gatekeeper, where DA architects have veto rights.

A next topic arises: which parts of the solution lifecycle are to be covered by the DA? Do we validate each and every step (this resembles coaching) or do we validate only the end result? There's the balance between minimizing the risk of a negative validation (resulting in extra work) and minimizing the amount of time spent by DA and the responsible architect in the business unit. Regarding this lifecycle scope questions to consider are:

- Will the DA validate the solution portfolio (Portfolio planning)?
- Will the DA validate the solution architecture (Architecture)?
- Will the DA validate the design (Design)?
- Will the DA validate the custom and bespoke software (Build)?
- Will the DA validate the way the solution will be implemented (Implement)?
- Will the DA validate the solution during execution (Run)?
- Will the DA validate changes (Run)?
- Will the DA validate de-commissioning (does not violate standards, rules or guidelines)?

Another aspect of scope is content: which aspect areas will be covered by the DA. Does the DA only address just one or two aspect areas (e.g. only IS and TI) or does the DA address all aspect areas, including security and governance? This topic does not only influence the architecture processes to be implemented, the impact is on needed competences and required standards, rules and guidelines as well:

- If the Business aspect area is included, we need SRG's regarding the way business needs to be structured;
- If the Information aspect area is included, we need SRG's regarding information like naming conventions and usage;
- If the Information Systems aspect area is included, we need SRG's regarding information systems (e.g. custom and bespoke software);

- If the Technology Infrastructure aspect area is included, we need SRG's regarding the way infrastructure is structured;
- If the Security aspect area is included, we need SRG's regarding security (e.g. risk analysis, security policies);
- If the Governance aspect area is included, we need SRG's regarding governance and the overall Quality of Service.

Another factor of influence when implementing a DA is the organizational scope for which the DA operates. The organizational scope might be:

- Business unit, where the DA operates within 1 business unit of an organization;
- Division, where the DA operates within 1 division, across all business units within that division;
- Enterprise, where the DA operates across the enterprise, across all divisions and business units.

Especially when dealing with architecture processes or standards and guidelines it is important to be aware of the organizational scope, especially on how to deal in processes or communication with the organizational parts outside the DA scope.

After dealing with a number of scope topics, there still is the issue about what topics to cover when doing a validation. Do we just validate if the solution is compliant with standards and guidelines? Or do we address other questions relevant to the success of the overall result as well?

- Does the DA validate if the solution adheres to regulatory compliance, industry regulations, etc.?
- Does the DA validate if the solution aligns to standards, rules and guidelines. Since a reference architecture might be part of SRG as well, does the DA validate if the solution aligns with the reference architecture as well?
- Does the DA validate if the solution fits to the functional requirements?
- Does the DA validate organizational readiness: are all involved parties ready to run the solution?
- Does the DA validate economics: is the solution economically viable?
- Does the DA address business continuity: does the solution address business continuity (which is more than just IT or System continuity) at sufficient level?

Implementing a Design Authority might have several objectives. In implementing processes and communication it is important do know the objectives of the organization. Most common are:

- Reduce cost, not only of the architects function but also of the entire (IT) organization in scope. Implement IAF in a way that you can show: How has the DA contributed to cost reduction?

- Reduce complexity of the overall IT landscape, either in business processes, applications, information or infrastructure. Implement IAF in a way that you can show: How has the DA contributed to reduction of complexity?
- Increase flexibility of the IT organization and IT landscape. Implement IAF in a way that you can show: How has the DA contributed to increased flexibility e.g. a shorter time to market?
- Increase Quality of Service. Implement IAF in a way that you can show: How has the DA contributed to increased QoS ?

Then there is the type of validation, which might range from pro-active to reactive.

- The pro-active type is more coaching based. The DA focuses on coaching during work to ensure that the solutions are correct from the beginning and that mandatory validation is more like 'rubber stamping';
- The reactive type by the DA itself is more validation based. The DA coaches less and focuses on a formal validation process;
- The reactive type by an external party is also validation based. The DA guides external EDP-auditors who execute validation.

And what about mandate? Who provides the executive support to the DA? Typical implementations are:

- Support and mandate at CxO level, which covers all levels under that;
- Support and mandate at business unit level, usually Profit & Loss level. The DA is supported by a business unit that has its own profit and loss responsibility. The DA might have to report to a DA at a higher level;
- Support and mandate at project level. The DA is supported by a project or program within their budget. The DA might have to report to a DA at a higher level.

How to organize the Design Authority? Where will it be positioned in the organization?

- A fully centralized Design Authority, all in one central department;
- A fully distributed Design Authority spread over the business units, including enterprise level topics;
- A partly centralized, partly decentralized Design Authority where enterprise level topics are addressed at central level, and where all other topics are addressed decentralized.

Finally, how will the staffing of the DA be?

- Dedicated DA staff for all positions, where all DA staff is directly employed by DA;
- Dedicated DA core team, where the DA has a core team and peak load is managed by allocating staff from other departments;
- Resource pool for DA, where there is an architect's pool from which the DA allocates staff.

5.5 IAF Roadmaps

This chapter elaborates on a number of IAF specific roadmaps. The roadmaps here commonly form the starting point for the identification of the architecture objectives and the roadmap that will achieve the defined objectives.

5.5.1 The Analysis – Synthesis Roadmap

Description	This roadmap uses an analysis – synthesis approach to the creation of the architecture. It ensures completeness and consistency of all elements in scope
Context	The analysis – synthesis roadmap should be considered when it is the intent to execute a fundamental analysis of the business, its information processing structure and the automated support for the business
Architecture areas covered	This roadmap delivers a thorough architecture covering all aspect areas
Design decisions and rationales	• Cover all aspect areas and all abstraction layers to ensure full business – IT alignment • Create a consistent and aligned logical architecture that is the basis for the overall business and IT transformation
Pre and post conditions	Key stakeholders need to support this form of fundamental analysis of their business and IT
Open issues	Unknown
Potential pitfalls	• Ivory tower approach, can seem very theoretical • Taking too long to get the work done
Newly created problems	Unknown

5.5.1.1 Roadmap Details

The analysis – synthesis roadmap starts with contextual. Then it covers business conceptual and logical as completely as desired. It uses the logical business architecture as the basis for the information architecture. Information conceptual and logical are created before the full IS architecture starts. This goes on until all aspect areas have delivered their logical architecture. All logical architecture outcomes are aligned to form the basis for one or more iterations of the physical architecture for all aspect areas. Each iteration of the physical architecture is created to support one step in the overall transformation. These steps are often also called ‘plateaus’ or ‘islands of stability’.

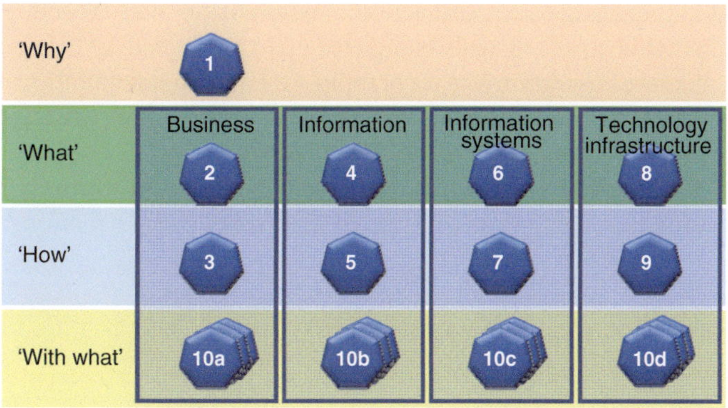

5.5.2 *The Refinery Roadmap*

Description	This roadmap focuses on creating just enough input from the aspect areas business and information to understand the impact on IS and TI, so the IS and TI architectures can be created
Context	If the context is mainly IT driven, i.e. we are focussing on changing the applications and technology landscape, the this roadmap can be considered
Architecture areas covered	Business and information architecture, logical and physical abstraction layers are only touched to the extend needed, mostly only to identify processes in the business architecture
Design decisions & rationales	• Only cover those topics that are required to deliver the IS and TI architecture so the architecture is fit for purpose • This might be the only feasible roadmap if there is a strict separation between business and technology architecture
Pre and post conditions	Pre: Key stakeholders need to understand that this approach is less accurate, but faster Post: Further logical and physical changes to the business and its information processing structure need to be addressed separately
Open issues	Unknown
Potential pitfalls	Making too many business assumptions – especially regarding non functional requirements
Newly created problems	Unknown

5.5.2.1 Roadmap Details

The refinery roadmap starts with contextual. It then addresses business conceptual and only those parts of business logical that are required to understand the full extent of the business requirements that need to be supported by technology. Commonly this means that the business processes are defined. Information conceptual is then created to complete the requirements that IS and TI need to have. The IS architecture is usually completed up to and including IS logical so that the TI architecture has a complete set of input. Of course a first iteration of step 6 – TI conceptual can be started in parallel with the IS architecture. The logical IS and TI architecture are completed to provide a consistent set of input for one or more iterations of the physical architecture. Just like in the analysis – synthesis roadmap, each physical iteration supports one step in the overall transformation.

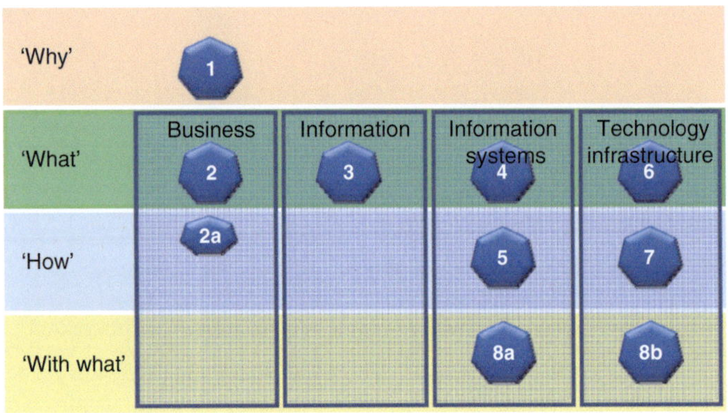

5.5.3 *The Information Ownership Roadmap*

Description	Master data management and information ownership are very current topics, especially in large organizations. This roadmap focuses on the aspects that are required to support decision making in this area
Context	In situations where we need to know who owns information and who does what with which information IAF can provide a structured approach to provide rationales for decisions regarding information ownership and data replication
Architecture areas covered	Business conceptual and logical information architecture to the level required
Design decisions & rationales	Address the topics needed to support information ownership and usage topics
Pre and post conditions	Pre: stakeholder awareness and buy in to the architecture objectives Post: IS and TI architecture might have to be created – for specific parts – based on the outcome
Open issues	Unknown
Potential pitfalls	Ownership and usage discussions can quickly lead to long debates. Take measures to prevent this
Newly created problems	Unknown

5.5.3.1 Roadmap Details

The start with contextual applies here too. After that the conceptual and logical business architecture is defined to the level of detail that we understand who will be doing what in the target architecture. The business information services are created in information conceptual. The LIC and LBIC structure models are created. Views are defined to superimpose ownership on the logical components. The views are used to optimize the logical business and information components from an ownership and data replication perspective. If the logical components might be allocated to multiple physical components then extend the architecture to physical level and redefine and re-analyze the ownership views.

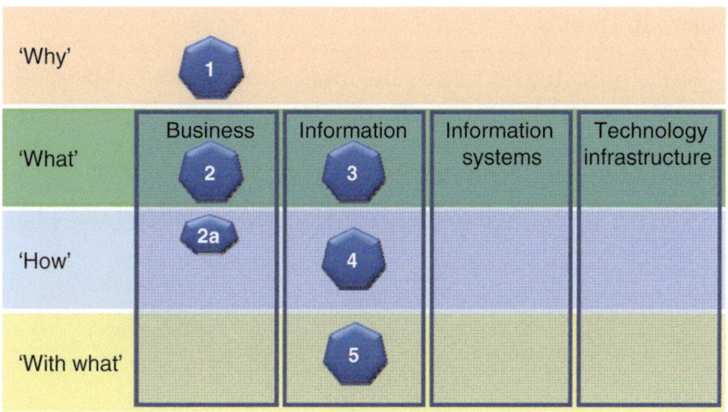

5.5.4 *The Package Focused Roadmap*

Description	This roadmap is aimed at supporting the selection and implementation of packages
Context	The current package paradigm is to fit the organization to the package and not to fit the package to the organization. This roadmap focuses on the architectural aspects such as: • Understanding what the business is so we can determine what will have to change • Understanding which information objects are concerned so we can figure out which master data management guidelines are needed • Understanding which interfaces (collaboration contracts) will be needed • Understanding if the package changes will require infrastructural changes
Architecture areas covered	• Business and information architecture, conceptual and logical to the point desired • Information systems architecture is covered for all 3 levels, with focus on package aspects • Technology Infrastructure is only done if changes to the infrastructure are required

Design decisions & rationales	Focus on package selection and implementation aspects
Pre and post conditions	Pre: Stakeholder buy-in and agreement to the roadmap Post: no special conditions
Open issues	Unknown
Potential pitfalls	Leaving business and information architecture too fast, implicitly increasing the assumptions in that area into high risk levels
Newly created problems	Unknown

5.5.4.1 Roadmap Details

The start with contextual applies. Business services and their collaboration contracts are defined at minimum for the current state. If package selection is part of the engagement, include the future state business services into the roadmap. They will effectively be your package selection criteria. (Current) Business processes are defined to the level required to understand what has to be changed to fit the package.

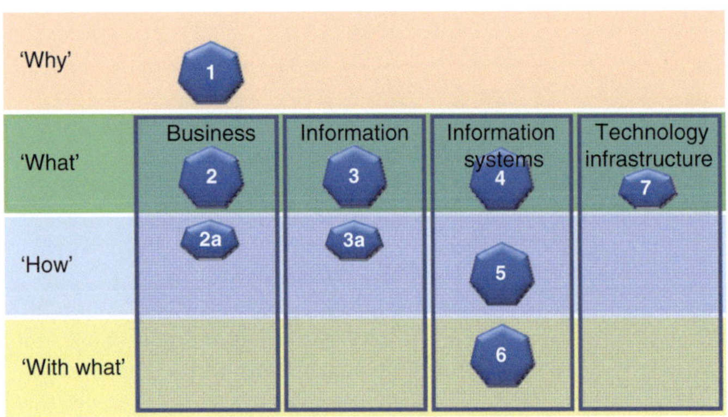

Packages imply data redundancy, because they all need their own sets of customer data etc.. It is often needed to re-engineer the information objects from the package documentation to understand if the package actually meets the information object definitions as described in the conceptual information architecture. Logical information components might be required to resolve information ownership and master data management issues between the products.

The IS architecture focuses on describing the level of support that the packages can provide by either mapping package functions to business services, or describing the package in terms of IS services. It also focuses on describing the interfaces required by deriving interface information from the business service collaboration contracts.

Solution alternatives can be used at logical and physical level to support decision making regarding package selection.

A final check on the infrastructure is done to determine if major changes are needed. A complete TI architecture might be the case, but is a decreasing necessity due to the commoditization of infrastructure.

5.5.5 The Infrastructure Focused Roadmap

Description	This roadmap supports the creation of an architecture that is mainly focused at changing an organization's infrastructure. Optionally it can be expanded to include business, information and IS support that is specific for the infrastructure changes
Context	Technology is evolving. Topics like virtualization and cloud computing are changing the way we approach and architect infrastructure. There are circumstances in which new technology needs to be incorporated into the existing environment, along with organizational and system changes needed to manage the new infrastructure. This roadmap addresses the required topics to do such things
Architecture areas covered	The main focus of this roadmap is technology infrastructure. Business and IS architecture are covered to the level that they provide just enough information to derive TI services
Design decisions & rationales	Focus on the ability to derive TI services and the required collaboration contracts from the input
Pre and post conditions	Pre: Stakeholder buy in and agreement to the roadmap Post: Often a proof of concept is required to ensure the new infrastructure will deliver the desired result
Open issues	Unknown
Potential pitfalls	Leaving Business and information systems architecture too fast, implicitly increasing the assumptions in that area into high risk levels
Newly created problems	Unknown

5.5.5.1 Roadmap Details

The start with contextual applies. Business services and their collaboration contracts are developed to the level that IS and TI services and their collaboration contracts can be defined. Often business services and their collaboration contracts will have to be assumed. Document and validate the assumptions with the key stakeholders. Within this roadmap you are often in a situation that the client and you just don't know. This because the architecture is breaking new ground. In real world architecture people also have to assume things like the number of lanes of a road. They often do not know how many vehicles will be using the road in 15 years time.

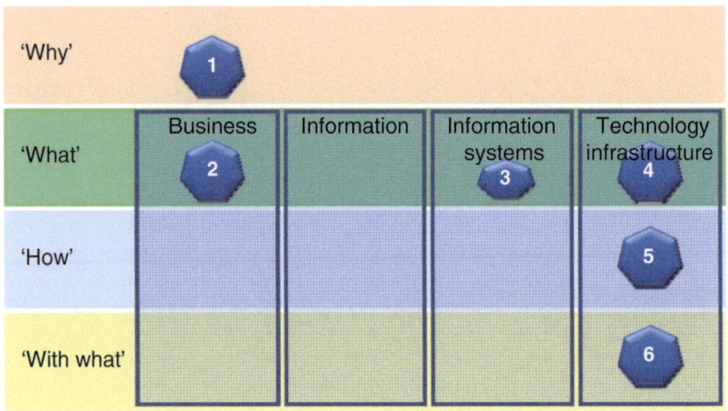

IS service definition[1] is done to the level that you understand what is specific and needs to be part of further IS development and what is generic. The generic parts will form elements of the infrastructure. Finally the TI architecture is developed.

5.5.6 The IAF – TOGAF – Prince2 Roadmap

Description	IAF, TOGAF and Prince2 can be combined to deliver solution architectures as part of large projects or programs. This roadmap provides guidance to do just that. Chapter 4 contains additional information on this roadmap
Context	This roadmap can be applied in situations in which: • IAF is the dominant content framework • The TOGAF ADM process is the dominant process framework • Prince2 is used for project management • Architecture is part of the go/nogo decision making in project management • The end deliverable is aimed at guiding the implementation of a solution (solution architecture)
Architecture areas covered	Commonly all architecture areas are covered except business and information physical

[1] This step can be optional.

Design decisions & rationales	See the context section
Pre and post conditions	Pre: Stakeholder buy in and agreement to the roadmap Post: Execution of further Prince2 stages to build and implement the solution. Architecture control is required between stages to ensure the projects do not deviate from the architecture
Open issues	Unknown
Potential pitfalls	This roadmap commonly requires more investment in time in the early stages of the project. Of course this will lead to much larger benefits later on, but expectations need to be carefully managed regarding this topic
Newly created problems	Unknown

5.5.6.1 Roadmap Details

There are a number of things to take into consideration here.

The first is the Prince2 structure. Prince2 prescribes 3 main deliverables as part of overall project preparation. The project mandate is aimed at ensuring sufficient stakeholder buy in to start the project. The project brief is a first iteration of the project, mainly aimed at ensuring feasibility of the project. The project initiation document is the full blown plan that is the basis for further project execution in one or more stages. Each deliverable implies a go/nogo point.

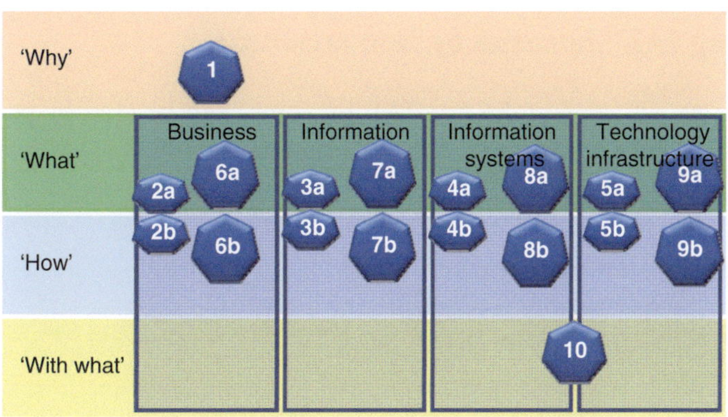

The second thing to take into account is the TOGAF mindset. TOGAF starts off with the creation of a so-called 0.1 version of the architecture, often called an outline of the architecture. After agreement on the 0.1 version, TOGAF proceeds with creating the full 1.0 version.

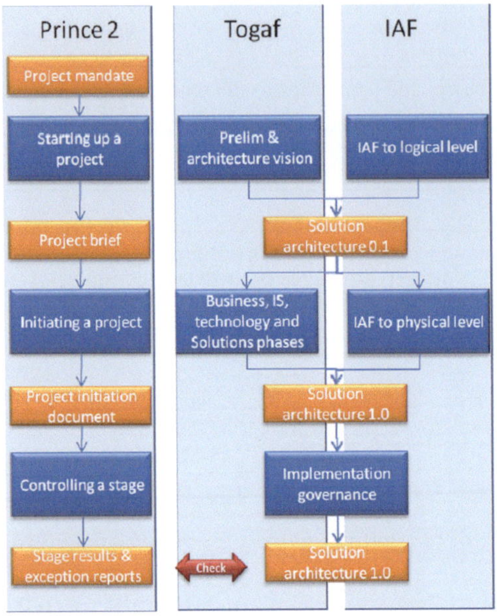

Combining these topics with IAF results in creating a Solution Outline, that consists of a first iteration of all architecture areas, addressing the conceptual and logical levels. This fits, if one allows to make IAF Information architecture synonymous to TOGAF Data architecture.

The solution outline becomes part of the decision making at project brief time in the project.

The 1.0 version of the architecture is created as part of the project initiation document. It contains all the prior aspect areas and levels, and adds IS and TI physical aspects. Combining IAF physical architecture and TOGAF ADM is a bit tricky, but can be done. The main reason behind this is that TOGAF has a separate phase. The so called phase E, Opportunities and solutions, is very similar to the IS and TI physical levels. That is why the two are often combined. TOGAF phases F, G and H are not used in this roadmap, as the solution architecture is used to control further stages in the project.

5.6 Using IAF Outcomes by Non-architects

This chapter will explain the way IAF outcomes can be used by people with other roles in the organization. The roles that will be discussed are:

- Business management;
- Strategist;
- Program/project management;
- Portfolio management;
- Business analyst/engineer;
- Business user.

Before getting into detail about how these roles can use IAF outcomes, first let's have a look at the range of typical architecture products that can be used: models and designs, documentation and specifications, and views.

Models and designs (a big picture, domain models, etc.) are used to communicate with stakeholders. That could be both informally or formally. Informally, to present a solution to a client or to explain options and their consequences to a manager, so that a decision can be made. Formal, to discuss the design of a solution with experts. The major benefit of models and designs is the abstraction from complexity. Remember that one picture tells more than a thousand words. However, sometimes it is difficult to keep it simple.

Documentation and specification (process descriptions, service specifications, etc.) outcomes exist is a wide variety. Assumptions will be documented to determine impact on the architecture. Decisions including their rationale will be documented to enable traceability and improve maintainability. Risks will be documented to determine impact on the architecture. Specifications mainly focus on the artifacts produced: specifications of processes, structures, services, components, etc.. There will be a specification of implementation standards and guidelines to explain to the delivery team how to implement the solution.

Views are non-formal representations that can be used as well, since different stakeholders are interested in different topics. Views can help in satisfying the interests of these stakeholders.

So, how can these architecture products be used by other stakeholders?

5.6.1 How Business Management Can Use IAF Outcomes

Business management needs to understand changes to come and understand the impact of decisions they made. Especially architecture models or specific views can be of great use. Usually pictures will be of great help, although some business managers prefer written text. Don't assume, just ask what they prefer.

To understand what changes are to come the interaction models from conceptual architecture are useful (either Business Interaction Model or IS Service Interaction Model). These models will help in determining or understanding ownership of specific parts of the architecture as well.

To support business management in decision making architecture outcomes are will likely be a key factor. We use logical architecture solution alternatives to rationalize decisions, provide solution alternatives that are traceable to business principles. In providing multiple alternatives we help managers to understand the impact of decisions. As a result, solution alternatives support greatly in rationalizing decisions.

Migration views help business managers to understand or to determine the order of migration. Don't limit the migration view to IS or TI migration view, include Business Architecture Migration view as well to give insight into the consequences on organization, people and processes.

Architecture outcomes to be used by business management requires to use their language, take notice of their culture. Use short presentations and prepare an elevator speech to be used at any convenient moment. Do not communicate technical difficulties or challenges, communicate about business impact.

Example:

Remember the example of enterprise transformation in an insurance company (Section 5.5). Based on the strategy of that company to reduce the number of brands and improve cross-selling, the architects team provided a top-level view. That view showed their customers as group-wide customers instead of product specific customer administrations. As a result business management understood the impact of the transformation and management discussions started, thanks to the top-level view.

5.6.2 How Strategists Can Use IAF Outcomes

At the contextual level, strategists provide supporting inputs like Business Mission and Vision, along with business strategies. IAF outcomes can help these strategists in understanding how the strategy is going to be implemented.

Especially models (Business Interaction Model and IS Service Interaction Model) from the conceptual architecture will show what changes will come. Specific views from business logical architecture, like solution alternatives and distribution view, help to understand how strategy can be realized and what choices have to be made.

If IAF is being used in combination with another framework, it might be useful to use some views that are defined in those frameworks to help communicate how the architecture supports the strategy. A good example is the solution options view as defined in TOGAF.

5.6.3 How Program or Project Managers Can Use IAF Outcomes

At project level, these stakeholders are responsible for running projects and implementing high impact changes into the operational environment. A project manager is responsible for delivering, within time and budget, a solution that fits the business requirements. Project managers working in IS and TI aspect areas manage the projects that develop the software applications and infrastructure components.

Architecture outcomes can provide valuable information when making a business case, if the outcomes are already available at that moment. Solution alternatives and, if available, views on costs and migration provide information regarding planning stages, results, resources, etc.. Scope of a project can be defined in terms of a list of IS services to be covered by the project.

When making a project plan architecture outcomes are very useful as well. Both Business Interaction Model and IS Service Interaction Model provide insight in dependencies and therefore provide input for planning and scoping the project. These models give guidance on what a sensible work breakdown might be.

If available, the Major Interfaces Model (based on IS Service Interaction Model) provides indication of what critical interfaces are, which implies an indication of where the risks are. Migration views help to determine migration planning in timelines, sequence of activities and resources.

Documentation and specification of standards, rules and guidelines to adhere to, provide input for the project plan as well. Documentation on services, components and interactions provide insight in the relative weight and can be used in planning activities, timelines and resources.

We can use architecture outcomes for a review of a project plan as well. Review for completeness and validation of correctness of the project plan is very useful.

During the project the architecture outcomes can be used for validation of solutions, provide guidance in making or preparing decisions or provide help in analyzing impact of changes. This supports project risk mitigation.

5.6.4 How Portfolio Managers Can Use IAF Outcomes

In general, all of the above on how program or project managers can use IAF outcomes is valid for portfolio managers as well. The major difference is that where project managers usually operate at the solution architecture level, portfolio managers usually operate at domain or enterprise level. They coordinate or manage change programs within that domain or organization.

Portfolio managers, just like project managers, use architecture outcomes for scope definition, to find dependencies and define impact analysis. Only, they work at enterprise level so they won't use detailed views if available.

5.6.5 How Business Analysts and Engineers Can Use IAF Outcomes

- Understand scope;
- Understand functional and non-functional requirements;
- Understand principles to be adhered to;
- Understand standards and guidelines to be adhered to.

In order to understand how business analysts and engineers can use IAF outcomes, we have to realize that architecture and design have many similarities on the surface (designing a solution, etc.), but are different and complementary:

- Architecture is focused on defining the scope of the engagement and creating an overall vision for the solution, whereas design is aimed at creating a comprehensive specification for construction;

- Architecture looks to define the desired non-functional characteristics of a solution whereas design looks to meet those non-functional characteristics;
- Architecture looks to scope the functional aspects and define the scope and responsibilities of each major component and/or project, whereas design looks to comprehensively specify those requirements and determine how they will be met within the scope of the major component.

Architecture delivers with the IAF outcomes a key set of inputs and influences into the design process, specifically:

- a documented context;
- the design principles, guidelines, standards and constraints;
- a high level design;
- non-functional requirements.

To enable the correct alignment between architecture and design, architects and engineers must work together on the project from the start. They might work on the same deliverables or engineers might add more details and specification.

IAF outcomes from contextual and conceptual architecture level will mainly provide the context to the engineers, stating *what* has to be achieved. Interaction models are a great way to illustrate this.

From the logical architecture level the solution alternatives, including decisions and the rationale behind these decisions, provide valuable information for engineers, providing reasoning behind the choices made.

In documentation or specification of services there might be Business or IS services that are only identified, not specified yet. This has to be done either by solution architects or by lead engineers.

Engineers can use IAF outcomes to help project management in validation of the project plan, with activities or resource plan and use architecture deliverables to measure progress in realization.

From logical and physical architecture level, engineers can use IAF outcomes to find specific component organization that has to be realized, including the rationale behind this specific organization of components. This enables the engineers to see the overall context, both from a business point of view and from an end-to-end point of view. Besides that, the specific component views are traceable to the business principles as well.

In using these IAF outcomes, the impact of changes, some of which may result from the design stage, can be evaluated in business terms that drive, provide context and constrains design.

From physical architecture level views are useful IAF outcomes as well. Especially integration and distribution view, storage or product view, and migration view are important input.

Specified standards, rules and guidelines are IAF outcomes that have to be adhered to, both in Business, Information, Communication, IS and TI.

5.6.6 How Business Users Can Use IAF Outcomes

Business users can use IAF outcomes as well, mainly to understand what is going to change. Especially interaction models at conceptual or logical architecture level will illustrate changes and will clarify impact on day-to-day work of these business users.

Chapter 6
Real Life Case Studies

6.1 Insurer – Enterprise Transformation

6.1.1 Context

The context of this engagement was an insurer that had grown through a series of mergers and acquisitions. In the past their strategy was to keep the separate brands apart, but that changed. At the time of the engagement the company wanted to reduce the number of brands and to reduce the cost that was caused by duplication of business activities in brands. Alongside with that, cross selling across the remaining brands was to be improved. Costs were to be reduced by using a shared service center approach, combined with outsourcing.

In order to support IT outsourcing the IT department had to reshape itself into a demand organization to coordinate and control services being outsourced. Demand management became a necessity. Besides that, the managers of the organization required support in the way of solution alternatives when considering outsourcing, to justify their decision.

6.1.2 Approach

The company adopted IAF for the improvement of their architecture function and their architects. The common vocabulary and the common framework provided the basis for all architects from all branches and helped them to position and compare current business activities in the framework, thus facilitating to find and eliminate duplications.

To facilitate management discussion the architects team created a top-level view. The top-level view consisted of IAF contextual architecture, enriched with extra material to clarify the impact of strategy and policy on reducing the number of brands and improving cross-selling.

J. van 't Wout et al., *The Integrated Architecture Framework Explained*,
DOI 10.1007/978-3-642-11518-9_6,

Based on their wish to outsource, in the architecture the team anticipated a split between demand and supply side of the organization as well, by structuring the architecture deliverables so that demand and supply were in separate documents. In fulfilling the manager's wish to have solution alternatives to justify decisions, this split was not strictly on the borderline between conceptual and logical, but the architects team included solution alternatives from the logical architecture into the demand side documents as well. This split enabled discussion on positioning shared service centers and finding candidates for outsourcing.

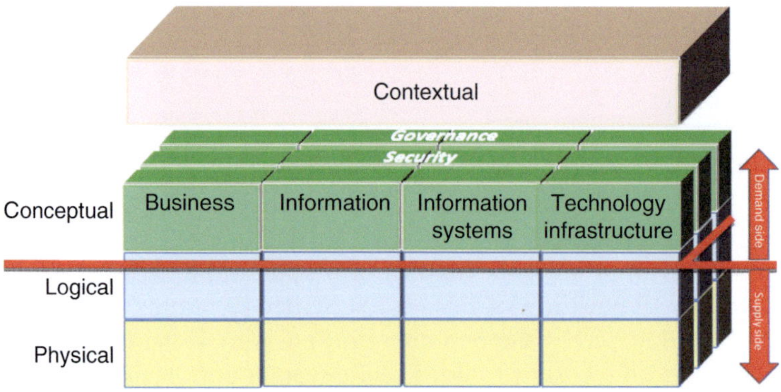

Using IAF this split was made very clear:

- Demand side architecture focuses on what the company want, including the rationale behind this (answering the Why). As a result the architecture deliverables from contextual architecture, conceptual architecture, and solution alternatives were in demand side documents;
- Supply side architecture focuses on how you want to supply the solution and with what realization will be done. As a result the architecture deliverables from logical and physical were part of the supply side architecture.

The architects team made an extension on the lower right part of IAF as well, to facilitate the transition from IAF to RUP.

6.1.3 Challenge

Major challenge for the organization was to deal with the issue of Customer ownership, a topic brought to the table thanks to the top level view made by the architects team. As a consequence of the companies' wish to reduce the number of brands and improve cross-selling, the top-level view positioned Customer as a horizontal layer on top of the vertical brands with their own customer processes and administration.

By doing so, they put the cat amongst the pigeons. Business management of the many business units saw the principle 'a customer is a group level customer' as a threat. The discussion about Customer ownership was brought to table. Of course, the architects' team just initiated this discussion, they didn't play a role in settling this discussion. It took the company years to settle the discussion, thereby hampering implementation speed of the strategy.

Another challenge of the organization was how to deal with business intelligence and risk management, since these topics existed in each and every brand of the organization. Supervisory bodies however require consolidated reports with unambiguous information. This challenge was met by positioning both business intelligence and risk management as a separate column in the top level view, where all brands had to provide information in specified terminology.

6.1.4 Result

The top-level view that was made years ago is still being used as a basis for decision making. Although the customer ownership brought a lot of discussion, this was a major benefit of the top-level view. Without the top-level view the fight would have gone underground and might have caused serious damage to the strategy.

Through the split and use of demand and supply documents, with solution alternatives, the company was able to justify and decide upon which parts to outsource.

6.2 Bank – Design Authority

6.2.1 Context

This case study is about a large bank operating worldwide with headquarters in Western Europe. With over 100,000 employees they provide services in retail banking, wholesale banking as well as insurance products.

The bank struggles with a highly complex IT landscape, characterized by a great diversity in information systems (both package based and bespoke software) and supporting infrastructure (mainframe, midrange as well as web-based platforms). As a result IT costs are high.

Within this context it is increasingly complex to manage and implement change, while on the other hand business requires more and quicker changes to support new financial products to go to market.

The management team of the IT department wants to transform the department in order to reduce costs and meet business demands. They consider architecture and the architects as a cornerstone in achieving such a transformation. Therefore they express their desire to professionalize the architects community.

6.2.2 Approach

The approach chosen to professionalize the architecture community is to create a design authority. Specific tasks of the design authority are creating reference architectures and governing solution architectures.

A project with a joined team of architects of the bank and Capgemini was given the assignment to achieve four main tasks:

- Establish decentralized Design Authorities in business divisions;
- Establish standards, rules and guidelines, as well as reference architectures on a number of business domains;
- Mobilize the large internal architect community by providing communication and training;
- Establish Design Authority processes to ensure and validate that solution architectures adhered to standards, rules and guidelines and worked compliant with DA processes;

This approach was based on own ideas of the bank regarding the areas of work: standards, rules and guidelines, and validation and support. From Capgemini experience the area of communication was added to these.

The bank selected a combination of IAF and TOGAF to work with. TOGAF was in the lead for the architecture process to follow, IAF was in the lead for the architecture content framework. Their choice for TOGAF was driven by their wish to use open standards. At a closer look at TOGAF they found that TOGAF doesn't bring enough content, so that had to be extended. Since IAF knowledge and experience was already available at several places in the organization (thanks to individual trainings and projects) and because IAF aligned very well with their own internal architecture content framework, the choice for IAF was easily made.

6.2.3 Challenges

A major cultural challenge was to cope with the directed approach. The employees of the IT department of the Bank were used to a consensus-based approach. With the introduction of a Design Authority the architects were confronted with a top-down approach directed by management.

The large architecture community was spread throughout the organization in numerous positions, without uniform job descriptions, competences or curriculum. Local autonomy allowed for multiple islands and kingdoms. Communicating with such a large community and later on getting buy-in from all these players in the community proved to be challenging.

Yet another important challenge was to get management agreement on roles and responsibilities throughout the DA and the DA processes.

6.2.4 Result

Within 1 year both central and decentralized DA organizations are in place.

Within 1 year Design Authority processes started to function.

Ongoing professionalization of the architects, with a majority of the architects being certified TOGAF architects and trained in IAF.

Solution architectures feedback into reference architectures, thus establishing a formalized architecture maintenance process.

6.3 Public Transporter – Solution Architecture

6.3.1 Context

The context of this case is a public transporter that needed a unified approach for solution architecture, providing effective and efficient communication. Reason being that architects within the company used their own terminology, causing a lot of confusion with people they were working together with. The architects of this company were already working with the business, where they used terminology and topics that were not a part of IAF: product architecture, process architecture. The company wanted to adopt IAF as unified approach.

6.3.2 Approach

In our approach we had to make some changes to IAF. More or less a cosmetic change was the renaming of business to process architecture, to stay in line with terminology not only used by the architects, but used by business as well.

More than just cosmetic was that we added an architecture area to IAF: Product architecture, left of Business Architecture. At conceptual level this area consisted of products and channels. At logical level we defined how the products would be delivered: which logical products through which channels.

Finally, at physical level we defined the physical products, the real life products available.

To illustrate this:

Conceptual	Products: • Travel information • Travel tickets • Delay information • . . . Channels: o PA systems at the stations o Ticket vending machines o Counter o Internet o Phone o . . .
Logical	Travel tickets through ticket vending machines and over the counter Delay info through counter, internet, phone and PA systems . . .
Physical	National paper tickets with specifications: . . . National electronic tickets using a chip card International paper tickets with specifications: . . .

6.3.3 Challenges

As you might guess from the above, a major challenge was to integrate the existing approach of the architects with IAF. Renaming business architecture to process architecture was relatively easy, adding a new aspect area was a major change that took quite some discussion. Still, it proved very worthwhile e.g. in discussions and alignment with business.

The other challenge was proving the added value to the architects and management. At the start of the project the team encountered a project saboteur, refusing to cooperate because he was of the opinion that the need for a unified approach and an external architect framework was nonsense. The challenge was met by having a close look at the saboteur's way of working, finding the good parts of his work and positioning and embedding these good parts into IAF. The combined result was used in communications to the architects within the company and to the project saboteur as well. As a result the saboteur recognized his own material and found how his own material could be improved as well. He transformed into a supporter of the project.

Yet another example of a common lesson learned: have a close look at the current way of working of the architects, spot the good parts and embed these within the framework. This will help in avoiding the 'not invented here' syndrome.

6.3.4 Result

The approach developed has been used for the last 8 years in the organization, despite many changes in personnel and managers and despite 4 major changes in organization.

Chapter 7
The Making of IAF

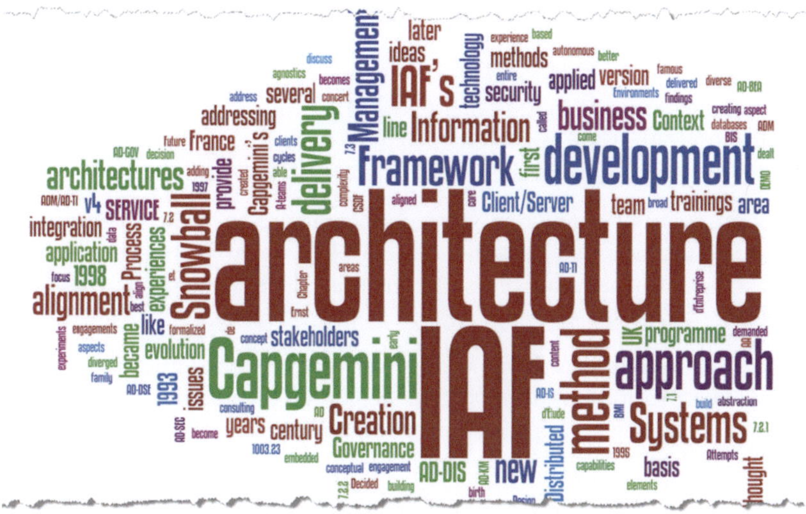

7.1 IAF's Birth

7.1.1 1993

The early nineties of the previous century saw several new technologies maturing and waiting to be applied all in one go: Local networks, relational databases, graphical user interfaces, the object-oriented programming paradigm. The market Capgemini was in demanded that this increased complexity had to be dealt with, in short delivery cycles. Capgemini initiated the 'Snowball' program and staffed it with an international team who put their experiences together, with the initial focus on an iterative development method thought to replace the traditional waterfall delivery models. This lead to Capgemini's rapid

J. van 't Wout et al., *The Integrated Architecture Framework Explained*,
DOI 10.1007/978-3-642-11518-9_7, © Capgemini SA, 2010
Published by Springer-Verlag Berlin Heidelberg 2010 All Rights Reserved.

development method, IAD, embedded in an engagement approach called Client/Server Delivery Framework (CSDF). The Snowball trainings became famous for their new approach, and Capgemini's University became the home ground for the Snowball team doing these trainings. However, in several engagements, experience was that delivery speed was not all: the solutions delivered required better integration in the clients' IT landscape than the 'A-teams'[1] could provide, addressing diverse issues like manageability, security and data integration. The Snowball program was quick to respond and address these broad alignment issues by adding architecture capabilities to these teams, building on the UK and France experiences in application and technology architectures. Their findings have become the basis for IAF, the first version created by a project team existing of: Stefan van der Zijden, Mark Hoogenboom, Petra van Krugten, Herman Hartman and Jack van 't Wout. They conveyed their results with their counterparts in the Snowball program, and started to build IAF.

Conceptual	Business	Data	Application	Technology
Logical				
Physical				

The first version of the IAF

IAF version 1 was not much more than a framework in which we positioned the architecture oriented material we had. This led to an understanding of the gaps and formed the basis for further development of architecture methods.

The material we had was ADM, the acronym for Architecture Development Method. This method was developed in the United Kingdom to support a large infrastructure architecture project for an oil company.

Conceptual	Business	Data	Application	Technology
Logical				ADM
Physical				

ADM positioned in the IAF

7.2 IAF's Evolution

7.2.1 1993–1995

ADM was the only method in the IAF between 1993 and 1995. In 1995 we decided to develop a method to support application architecture in client/server environments. The method was called Architecture Design for Distributed Information Systems (AD-DIS), and was aimed at supporting client/server

[1] A-teams were groups of about six people that delivered IAD projects.

projects in deciding where to position which parts of their applications. At the same time we aligned ADM with terminology we developed in AD-DIS, and re-named the method to Architecture Design for Technology Infrastructure (AD-TI).

IAF in 1995

7.2.2 1995–1997

Security in heterogeneous environments became an important issue in 1997. The IAF team decided to develop AD-DSE, Architecture Design for Distributed Secure Environments. During the development of AD-DSE we came to the conclusion that Security was a topic that spanned all other architecture areas. To visualize that we positioned Security in the third dimension, and determined that governance was a second important topic that needed to be positioned the same way. AD-GOV was also born. This was also the year that we decided to rename the 'Data' area to 'Information', as we intended to do more with that area than just data architecture, we intended to include 'tacit knowledge' as an additional topic in that area.

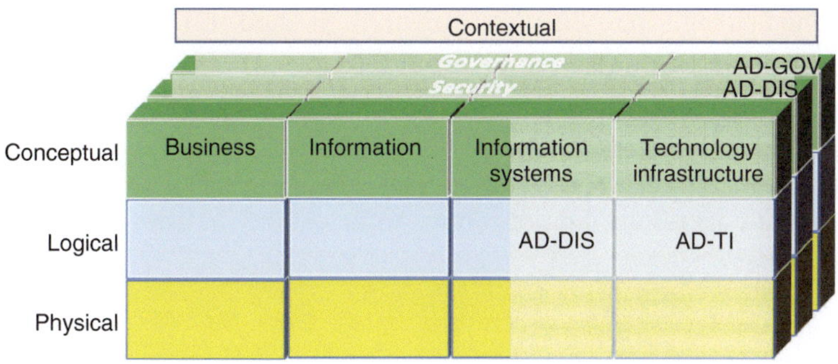

IAF in 1997

1997 was also the year that the standard IEEE 1003.23 was published. That standard was based on ADM, the predecessor of AD-TI.

7.2.3 1998–2000

In 1998 we decided to expand AD-DIS into a method that covered all the topics we needed for Information Systems architecture. AD-IS (Architecture Design for Information Systems) was the result. As this method introduced major new topics, we decided to make this a major release. IAF version 2 was born. As part of the Version 2 work we introduced the contextual layer and again upgraded AD-TI. 'Service' and 'component' were formalized as terms.

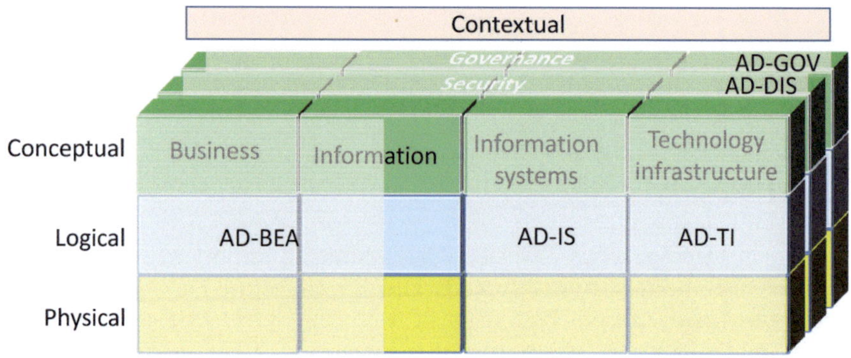

IAF version 2

This was also the period in which we started working on business and information architecture. AD-BEA (Architecture Design for Business and Environment Architecture) was based upon a Dutch method called 'Bedrijfsgerichte Methode voor Informatieplanning' (BMI). The English term for the method would be 'Business oriented method for Information planning'.

A third initiative that was conducted in this period was a study to develop an information architecture method. The working name was AD-KI^2 – Architecture Design for Knowledge, Information and Intelligence. This route was abandoned because its results did not receive sufficient buy-in from the architecture community.

7.2.4 2000–2003

In 2000 the IT consultancy part of Ernst & Young was acquired by Capgemini. As part of the integration of the two companies we developed IAF version 3. The main change was that we decided to split process from content. Roadmaps and the IACF (Integrated Architecture Content Framework) were the two deliverables of the version 3 activities. Besides this the approach for business and information architecture got formalized. A first version of business and information architecture was developed, which was an expansion of AD-BEA.

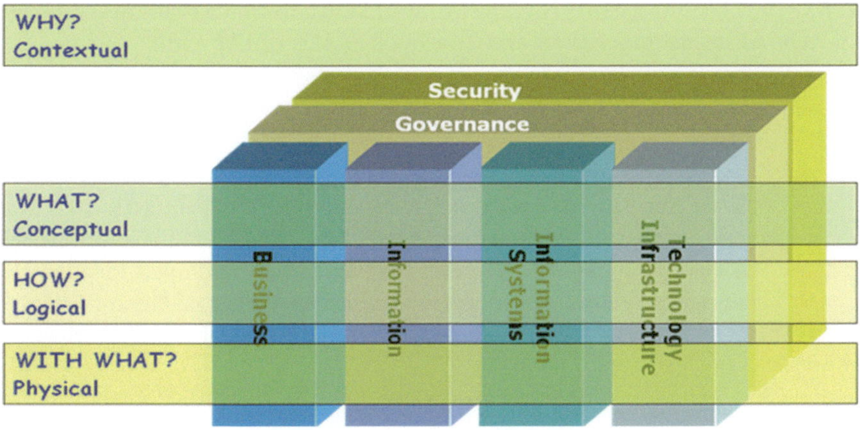

IAF version 3

In this period there were some experiments with the transformational aspects of the architecture, the 'WHEN' level. In the end we decided to leave this topic out of the IAF scope and leave transformation to program management, guided by architecture.

Another initiative that happened as part of IAF v3 was the re-design of the courses. Instead of having a course per architecture area, we merged the courses for Business and Information architecture. We also merged the courses for IS and TI architecture.

7.2.5 2003–2006

This was a relatively stable period for IAF. Version 3 was getting pretty mature, and we did not receive many enhancement requests from the architecture community.

7.2.6 2006–2009

In 2006 we decided to determine if we needed to change anything in IAF due to the growing attention for service oriented architecture. We determined that only Business and Information architecture needed an upgrade. Another decision that was made was to integrate security and governance as topic in the main architecture areas. As this was a major change, we decided to introduce IAF version 4. Finally we created a reference manual to communicate this version of IAF. In this period Capgemini started to participate in The Open Group. In 2008 IAF was accepted by The Open Group as method which qualified for the ITAC

(IT architect certification) program. We started to contribute to the development of TOGAF using material we had developed as part of IAF.

7.2.7 2009

Early 2009 we decided to deliver a minor upgrade for IAF. IAF v4.5 was developed. A number of artifacts were formalized, like domains and business events. We also documented the views that had been developed through the years. The usage of synonyms was described, and business goal hierarchies were made more prominent. We also delivered a new version of the IAF reference manual.

7.3 IAF's Future

Capgemini will continue with IAF development. It is a great incubator for topics we will introduce into the Open Group architecture community. TOGAF version 9 benefited from IAF, and future versions of open standard architectures will too.

The authors know that IAF is a living thing, and intend to keep you up to date with its developments through future versions of this book. We thank you for bearing with us in the digestion of this book. Sometimes it must have been hard for you to stay focused. Trust us, sometimes it was hard for us too. If you have suggestions for improvement, do not hesitate contact us. You can find all of us on LinkedIn.

About the Authors

Jack van 't Wout started in IT in 1978 and joined Capgemini in 1990. He got involved with architecture in 1993, and is generally acknowledged as one of the founding fathers of IAF. Jack has executed over 20 enterprise architecture and governance engagements and has trained more than 500 people in IAF. Jack's focus is on the financial services sector.

Aaldert Hofman started to work with Capgemini in 1990 and worked in the IT industry since 1988. He has developed architectures since 1996 and got involved in IAF development and lecturing in 1998. Aaldert is specialized in security architecture and the broader risk management theme.

Max Stahlecker is the youngest member of the team of authors. He is in the IT industry since 2001. Max did his thesis on enterprise architecture, architectural conformance and the business transformation process. He has been practicing architecture with IAF since he joined Capgemini in 2006 and has been involved with its development since then.

Herman Hartman has worked with Capgemini and its predecessor Volmac since 1976. He became involved in the development of IAF in 1994 when he laid the basis to encapsulate existing architecture best practices in new ways of working. He has conducted architecture work in dozens of projects. Herman focuses on enterprise architecture engagements in the industry sector.

Maarten Waage has worked in the IT industry since 1984 and joined Capgemini's precursor Volmac one year later in the Systems and Networks division. He has been practicing architecture since 1995 and got involved in IAF development and deployment in 1997. Maarten has extensive experience in enterprise architecture and large scale transformations. He focuses on the public sector.

J. van 't Wout et al., *The Integrated Architecture Framework Explained*,

DOI 10.1007/978-3-642-11518-9,

Index

MIX
Papier aus verantwortungsvollen Quellen
Paper from responsible sources
FSC® C105338
FSC
www.fsc.org

If you have any concerns about our products,
you can contact us on
ProductSafety@springernature.com

In case Publisher is established outside the EU,
the EU authorized representative is:
Springer Nature Customer Service Center GmbH
Europaplatz 3, 69115 Heidelberg, Germany

Printed by Libri Plureos GmbH
in Hamburg, Germany